Additional praise for...

Gross Motor Skills in Children with Down Syndrome
A Guide for Parents and Professionals
Patricia C. Winders, P.T.

"This book belongs on the recommended reading list for families of young children with Down syndrome. Pat Winders clearly describes the range of development that parents may see as their child gains motor skills, and suggests activities and strategies that can help to make that development as 'normal' as possible. Lots of questions get answered along the way."

Phil Mattheis, M.D.
Medical Director, Montana Rural Institute on Disabilities
Co-editor of Medical and Surgical Care for
Children with Down Syndrome

"This comprehensive volume demonstrates the author's keen understanding of physical development and how it applies to infants and children with Down syndrome. Detailed guidelines tell parents how to facilitate gross motor development, how to overcome inherent weaknesses, and how to prevent maladaptive postures and movement. Such awareness benefits the child, reassures and encourages the parent."

Valentine Dmitriev, Ph.D.
Founder, model program for children with Down
syndrome at University of Washington
Author of Time to Begin *and* Tears and Triumphs

"When my son was an infant, I can vividly remember the glee his brother and I felt the first time we coaxed him into moving from a sitting position to a crawl, only to be told that it was 'poor positioning.' With this book, parents will be able to access the information they need to encourage skills safely and effectively without worry or having to wait for next month's visit from the physical therapist."

Joan E. Medlen
Editor, Disability Solutions
Parent of an 8-year-old child with Down syndrome

Topics in Down Syndrome

GROSS MOTOR SKILLS in CHILDREN with DOWN SYNDROME

A Guide for Parents and Professionals

Patricia C. Winders, P.T.

All rights reserved under International and Pan-American copyright conventions. Published in the United States of America by Woodbine House, Inc., 6510 Bells Mill Rd., Bethesda, MD 20817. 800-843-7323.

Cover illustration & design: Lili Robins
Photographs: James Winders

Library of Congress Cataloging-in-Publication Data

Winders, Patricia C.
    Gross motor skills in children with Down syndrome : a guide for parents and professionals / Patricia C. Winders.
        p.   cm.—(Topics in Down syndrome)
    Includes index.
    ISBN 0-933149-81-6 (pbk.)
    1. Down syndrome. 2. Motor learning. 3. Motor ability in children. I. Title. II. Series.
RJ506.D68W56 1997
618.92'858842--dc2   97-19243
                                                                                   CIP

Manufactured in the United States of America

10 9 8 7 6 5

dedication

This book is dedicated to further unfolding

the possibility of children with Down syndrome.

We have only begun to tap their potential.

acknowledgements

I wish to acknowledge and sincerely thank the people whose selfless contributions made this book a reality:

- the children and parents that I have worked with who have been my best teachers,
- the Chesapeake Down Syndrome Parent Support Group, who have provided unfailing support and encouragement,
- Sharon Gittelsohn, whose Parent-Infant Group first introduced me to children with Down Syndrome,
- Susan Harryman and Audrey Leviton, who gave me the space to pursue my vision and who encouraged me to go for it,
- George Capone, M.D., who has provided leadership for the Down Syndrome Clinic of the Kennedy Krieger Institute,
- Susan Stokes, whose professional skills and personal experience make her an editor without equal,
- Dr. Daniel Richardson, my nephew, whose statistical wizardry has been invaluable,
- Helen L. Curran, R.N., my mother, who has always been my model for how to truly serve your patients and love your work,
- Elizabeth Winders, my daughter, who has patiently and cheerfully endured two years of: "We can't today, I have to work on the book."
- Jim Winders, my husband, who has been my manager, editor, photographer, statistician, severest critic and greatest fan, and the best partner I could hope for.

Table of Contents

Introduction

Children with Down syndrome have enormous potential, but it is only recently that we have learned to work with them to maximize that potential. Working with them to develop gross motor skills can be particularly rewarding, because this is an area of development where progress is fairly easy to see. Although your child will acquire motor skills more slowly than a child without Down syndrome, he will still master the basic gross motor skills like sitting, walking, running, jumping, and riding a tricycle. He will also learn more complex skills such as dancing, swimming, horseback riding, karate, jogging, and sports. For most children with Down syndrome, gross motor skills eventually become one of their strengths. And like other children, they are able to develop and refine new motor skills all of their lives.

This book will tell you what support your child needs to develop the basic gross motor skills properly, and how you can provide that support in a way that challenges him and gives him confidence in his own physical abilities.

The book will tell you:
1. **what skills are appropriate for each stage of development, from birth through age six;**
2. **how the skills are broken down into their component steps;**
3. **detailed instructions for activities for practicing each step;**
4. **guidelines or tips for doing the activities.**

obstacles to gross motor development

Children with Down syndrome, like other children, develop according to their own timetable—some slower than others, and some faster. In general, though, a number of physical and medical problems can delay your child's development of the various gross motor skills.

physical problems

Hypotonia—Children with Down syndrome have low muscle tone, which is also called *hypotonia*. A precise definition of hypotonia would require a lengthy and complicated explanation, but a working understanding is easy to achieve. Hypotonia is most easily observed in children with Down syndrome when they are infants. When you pick a baby with Down syndrome up, you will notice that he feels "floppy" or somewhat like a ragdoll. If you put him on his back, his head will turn to the side, his arms will fall away from his body and rest on the surface, and his legs will fall open. This floppiness is due to reduced muscle tone. The low muscle tone, along with decreased strength and endurance, makes it more difficult to learn gross motor skills.

Hypotonia affects each child with Down syndrome to a different degree. In some children the effect is mild, and in others it is more pronounced. The low tone improves over time but persists throughout life.

Some areas of the body may be more affected than others. For instance, a child may have lower tone in the arms than in the legs. Or a child may have lower tone on the left side than on the right side. Hypotonia in a particular area will affect the development of skills that require the use of that area. For example, a child with lower tone in his arms will find it more difficult to learn to belly crawl and to pull to stand since he needs to use his arms to perform these activities. A child with lower tone in his stomach will find it more difficult to balance in standing and to learn to creep on his hands and knees, since he needs to use his stomach muscles for these skills.

At first, you may not be able to tell the degree of low muscle tone that your child has or whether some areas are more affected than others. As you work with him, though, you will begin to recognize patterns that give him particular difficulty. For instance, you may notice that he has trouble with and tends to avoid activities that require the use of his arms. He may not like to prop on his stomach or pull himself up. These may be clues that this is an area of weakness for him. As time goes on, you will be able to identify what areas are weaknesses for him and therefore need extra work.

Increased Flexibility in Joints—Children with Down syndrome also have increased flexibility in their joints. This is because the ligaments that hold the bones together have more slack than usual. When your child is a baby, you will notice it particularly in his hips. When lying on his back, his legs will tend to be positioned with his hips and knees bent and his knees wide apart. Later you will notice it in your child's feet. You will notice that when standing, his feet are flat and he does not have an arch.

This increased flexibility will also be present in your child's shoulders. You should avoid lifting your child by his arms because this could cause partial dislocation of the shoulder joint. As your child gets older and gains strength in his arms, the shoulder joint will become more stable.

Decreased Strength—Children with Down syndrome have decreased muscle strength, but strength can be greatly improved through repetition and practice. Increasing muscle strength is important, because otherwise children with Down syndrome tend to compensate for their weakness by using movements that are easier in the near term, but are detrimental in the long term. For example, your child may want to stand, but because of weakness in his trunk and legs, he can only do it if he stiffens his knees. You will be able to help him develop the strength he needs so that he can stand properly without stiffening his knees.

Short Arms and Legs—Children with Down syndrome have short arms and legs relative to the length of their trunks. The shortness of their arms makes it more difficult to learn sitting because they cannot prop on their arms unless they lean forward. When they fall to the side, they have to fall farther before they are able to catch themselves with their arms. The shortness of their legs makes it harder to learn to climb, since the height of the sofa or stairs presents more of an obstacle.

medical problems

Many children with Down syndrome have medical problems that affect their ability to engage in gross motor skills. These include heart problems, stomach or intestinal problems, chronic upper respiratory infections, and ear infections. These may cause a child to fatigue easily and to have poor endurance. Ear problems can also affect balance, particularly when a child is working on standing balance and walking. You will need to make certain that you are not overexerting your child. Once his medical problems have improved, he will be able to do more and can make up for lost time.

For a more detailed and thorough discussion of the physical and medical problems of children with Down syndrome, refer to *Medical and Surgical Care for Children with Down Syndrome* (Woodbine House, 1994).

overcoming the obstacles

Like all children, children with Down syndrome want to move, explore their environment, and interact with people and toys, but their physical problems create obstacles. This book will explain how to provide the support your child needs to overcome those obstacles.

Consider these examples:

A 2- to 3-month-old infant lying on the bed looks at toys and wants to touch them, but cannot hold his head in the center and reach upward because of low muscle tone and inadequate strength. If support is provided under his head and arms and the toy is properly placed, he will be able to touch it.

Once a child has learned to sit, he will want to pull to stand. He will be unable to, however, because he is not strong enough to maintain himself on hands and knees, the position from which children usually learn to pull to stand. If he is provided with an edge to hold onto (like the edge of a laundry basket), he will be able to learn to pull to stand from sitting on a bench.

Providing strategically targeted support gives your child the opportunity to do what he already wants to do, but cannot, due to his physical problems. Once he is successful he will be motivated to do it again. Through repetition of those movements he will begin to develop strength so that he requires less support. Eventually, he will be able to do the skill with no support at all.

guidelines for practicing gross motor skills

Your child will need a motivator to get his attention and to encourage him to move. For example, he might crawl to get to a favorite toy. Motivators can also be special play time with you or family members.

When practicing motor skills, your child's success and enjoyment will be dependent on how you play, what type of toys you use, and where you place them.

For example, when your child is learning to sit, if you give him rattles and he shakes them, he will lose his balance and fall. If, instead, you keep him still and have him watch you play "pat-a-cake" or sing, he will be better able to balance. To motivate your child effectively, you need to know what he is interested in and how to use it skillfully to achieve the motor skills he is practicing.

The quality of the time you spend working on motor skills tends to be much more important than the quantity. A few well-timed moments when your child understands a new skill and succeeds at it will be much more valuable than an hour of struggling that leaves both of you frustrated and upset.

Pick the right time of day to practice motor skills. When he is active and ready to go, challenge him with the next level of skill for him to master. When he is tired, choose easier positions and activities. You need to learn to read his cues and understand what he is saying so that you know whether it is OK to keep going or time to stop.

Proper timing is crucial in teaching your child new skills. You do not want to introduce a new skill until he is ready to accomplish it. If he is not ready, both of you will become frustrated. If he is ready and you can help him practice it, he will learn it and both of you will be successful.

When he is learning a skill, you need to be consistent with how you set it up and practice it. Once he knows the skill, you can use a variety of set-ups.

When practicing motor skills, use your time strategically. Work on skills that require your support rather than skills that he can do by himself.

Alternate hard and easy activities and combine them with play. When he becomes tired, do easier activities or let him play by himself. After he plays by himself for a few minutes, he may be ready to practice again. If not, give him a break until his next active period.

When he is learning a new skill, first motivate him to do it; work on refining it only after he has been successful. For example, first encourage him to take independent steps. After he can do so, teach him to walk with his feet closer together. The key is in motivating him to initiate the skill. Too much intervention or correction will cause him to lose interest.

If he prefers using one side rather than the other, allow him to use that side until he has mastered the skill. For instance, if he prefers to roll to the right side, let him learn to roll this way until he has mastered it. Then he can learn to roll to the left. It will be confusing for him to practice rolling both directions when he is just beginning to learn to roll. Master one direction and then move on to the other.

Practice the motor skills yourself so you really understand the steps involved in doing them. If your child is having difficulty, imitate his movements to see what is keeping him from doing the skill. By imitating his movements and practicing the movements needed to do the skill, you will be better equipped to teach him what he needs to do to master the skill.

temperament

Temperament is defined as a person's characteristic manner of thinking, behaving, and reacting. In this book, temperament will refer to your child's pattern of thinking, behaving, and reacting in his approach to gross motor skills.

In working with children with Down syndrome, I have observed that they fall into two basic categories of temperament: Motor Driven and Observer. You will easily be able to distinguish which temperament your child has by watching whether he stays in one position or moves a lot; whether he is cautious or takes risks; whether he moves slowly or quickly. You can begin to observe these characteristics when your child is 6-12 months old, and you will continue to notice them in more subtle ways throughout his childhood.

Children who are motor driven:	Children who are observers:
1. love to move from one place to another and spend limited time in one position;	1. like to stay in one position and are content to watch, socialize, and play with toys that are available; they need to have a reason to move;
2. tolerate new positions and movements and take risks;	2. are cautious, careful, and easily frightened by new movements and positions;
3. enjoy being held for brief periods and then prefer to be moving and exploring;	3. love to be held and tolerate it for long periods of time;
4. love to move fast;	4. prefer to move at a slower rate so they can feel balanced and in control;
5. like motor skills like rolling, crawling, creeping, moving in and out of positions, climbing, pulling to stand, and walking;	5. love stationary positions like sitting and standing;
6. initially resist stationary positions like sitting and standing.	6. initially resist crawling, creeping, moving in and out of positions and walking.

Once their child has learned to belly crawl or creep, parents tend to think that every child is motor driven. If your child is an observer, however, you will notice the difference once again when your child learns to walk. The motor driven child will take risks to take independent steps, while the observer will be cautious and only take steps when he has become sure of his balance. The motor driven child will be able to tolerate endless falls and continue to try to walk, while the observer will stop trying after a few tumbles.

By understanding your child's "temperament" and what he is motivated to do, you can be more effective in helping him learn gross motor skills. You will know in advance which activities he is likely to enjoy and which he is likely to resist. You can begin with activities he likes and then move to one he resists. If you use a superb motivator he may try to do it. When you know which activities your child will resist, you can prepare by saving the best motivators, doing those activities for shorter lengths of time, and alternating them with activities he likes. Be patient, keep practicing, and he will eventually learn to do all of them.

how the book is organized

Part 1 of the book covers gross motor development from birth to walking, and Part 2 covers post walking skills.

Each of the chapters in Part 1 addresses a particular stage of development from birth through walking. This period of development is divided into five stages. Each stage consists of a cluster of skills that tend to develop at about the same time. Certain skills are prerequisite for the development of other skills.

You should complete most of the skills in one stage before moving on to the next stage. If your child has mastered all of the skills of a particular stage except for one or two, move on to the next stage. But don't push him too fast. Otherwise you may find that your child is missing skills that are necessary for him to succeed at the next level. You should use your own judgement and common sense about when it is time to move ahead and when it is time to keep practicing what he's missing.

There are activities for your child to practice in learning each skill. Practicing these activities will result in mastery of the skills. Each chapter ends with a checklist of the motor skills to accomplish within that stage. You can use the checklist to track the progress your child is making. It will also show you the general sequence of when skills develop and what will develop next.

Part 2 describes skills that develop after a child has begun to walk. Many of these skills can be worked on simultaneously. Chapter 6 offers detailed guidelines for helping your child develop post walking skills.

In both Parts 1 and 2, you will notice that masculine and feminine pronouns are used alternately by chapter when referring to children with Down syndrome. That is, I used "he" and "his" in the even-numbered chapters, and "she" and "her" in the odd-numbered chapters. The only exceptions occur when I am referring to real children with Down syndrome I have known. In these instances, I used their actual names and genders.

An Appendix at the end of the book provides the average age when children with Down syndrome accomplish 45 specific gross motor skills. These averages were arrived at based on data I collected over the past ten years using a sample of 154 children.

Remember that each child develops each motor skill at his own individual time. The ages are provided to give you a guide for when to look for a particular skill. For example, if you know that the average age of walking is 2 years, you will know not to expect your child to begin walking when he is only 1 year old. Conversely, you should not become upset if your child has not walked at 2½ years. The average of two means that some children walked earlier than two and some walked much later. The age at which a child completes a skill depends on many variables, including temperament, physical and medical problems, and the age he decides he is interested in doing it.

PART 1

Infancy through Walking ➤ ➤ ➤ ➤ ➤ ➤ ➤ ➤

CHAPTER 1

Stage 1
Head and Hands in Midline

These first few months are the time for you to get to know your baby. She will spend many hours out of the day eating and sleeping, so your free time together will be limited and therefore precious. In the section on Back-lying, you will learn the best way to support her when you are holding her so that her body is calm and organized. Then she can focus her attention on you and respond to you.

She will learn to look at you when you talk to her and hold her. Her eyes will brighten and she will smile or make faces in response to yours. She will engage with you and then look away. This is her way of saying: "I've had enough for now. I need a break." After a break of a few minutes you can talk to her to get her attention again or she may look at you to get your attention. You will learn to read her messages: "I'm tired, I'm hungry, I'm tuned in and ready to go, I've dropped out." When she is tuned in, talk to her and play with her. When she is tired, hungry, or tuned out, give her what she needs and hold her.

The motor skills to focus on in this first stage of development are:
    **1. head in the center (looking straight ahead, not turned to either side)
        and beginning lifting,**
    2. hands to midline and beginning propping, and
    3. legs together and moving.

Your child will learn these skills using the positions of side-lying, back-lying, supported sitting, and stomach-lying.

This chapter is organized differently than the other chapters in the book. While the other chapters provide instruction proceeding from one skill to the next, this chapter is easier to understand if we proceed from position to position. We will look at how each skill is developed first in side-lying then in back-lying, then in supported sitting, and finally in stomach-lying.

SIDE-LYING

Side-lying is the easiest position for your baby to play in because her head is looking straight ahead, her hands are together and she can see them, and her legs are together. Gravity assists the position of her head, arms, and legs.

Guidelines for **Stage 1**

Use only the positions your baby is ready to use. She will initially tolerate the positions briefly, but her tolerance will improve as she gets stronger in each position. When she is tired and fussy, hold her and calm her down.

Watch her to see when she is comfortable in a position and when she wants to move out of it. When she is finished with one position, move her to another.

Alternate harder positions, such as supported sitting and stomach-lying, with easier positions, such as side-lying and back-lying.

Your baby will have alert and active periods for 20-30 minutes. The time you have to work with her will be limited, so do the activities that are most important. She can either spend all the time in one position or you can use the time to move her through all the positions. After an active period, she may become hungry or sleepy.

When carrying or holding her, support her legs together. Then she will learn to move her legs with her knees in line with her hips rather than wide apart.

For the first couple of months, your baby will be most interested in seeing your face. When she is 3-4 months old, she will become interested in brightly colored toys and toys that make sounds. She will prefer toys that have contrasting colors like black and white.

When she is on her side, you can teach her to move her head to look downward at a toy placed in front of her shoulders. By doing this, she will begin to strengthen the muscles at the front of her neck. With her head in this position, she will also be able to see her hands and watch them move to touch the toy.

She will move her arms so she can bring her hands to her mouth or she will reach forward to touch a toy. It will be easy to move her arms using this position.

She will learn to kick her legs while they are positioned together. By doing this, she will strengthen the muscles that move her legs up and down and those that move her legs together. This position can only be used for a few months. Once your baby is able to roll, she will not use it anymore. It is a good position for her during this stage and should be used as much as possible.

activity guidelines

Motivate your baby by using toys that she can touch or watch. They need to be large and not easily moved. You don't want the toy to roll away when your baby touches it. Use toys that have bright colors and make sounds. Ideal toys include stuffed animals (Big Bird, dalmatian puppy), fabric dolls or clowns with faces, rocking toys that make sounds (Happy Apple, Mickey Mouse), and musical toys.

Discourage her from arching her head and trunk. If this happens, give her more support so her head and trunk are in a straight line. Make sure the toy is placed in front of her shoulders. If a toy is placed above her head, she will automatically arch her neck to look upward at it.

activity #1 **Supported Side-lying** *(see fig. 1.1)*

A. Side-lying on the couch

1. Place your child in side-lying on the couch with her back against the back of the couch. Make sure her head and trunk are in a straight line and her hips and knees are bent.

2. Position yourself on the floor in front of her.
3. Hold her hips to support her in the position and keep her from rolling. If her legs are active, hold them to calm them down. This will enable her to move her arms more easily.
4. Place a toy at shoulder level in front of her hands. Encourage her to touch the toy with one or both hands and play with it. Change the toy as needed to keep her interest.
5. Use the position as long as tolerated. Repeat by placing her on her other side.
6. If she becomes fussy, rock her hips gently and see if this calms her down.

(fig. 1.1)

B. Side-lying on the floor: This can be done the same as above. Provide support behind her head and trunk with a sofa cushion.

BACK-LYING

When your child is lying on her back, she is in the best position for face to face interaction with you. Your face can be close to hers and she can look at you and see you smile and talk to her. She will engage with you by looking at you and may make cooing sounds. She will probably give you her first smile while in this position.

In this position you want her to learn to:

1. **move her head to the center and hold it there**
2. **move her hands to her chest and begin reaching above her chest**
3. **kick her legs up and down**

These movements will take time to develop and you will need to support her fully in the beginning. If she is supported in the right way, she can focus her attention on you and respond to you.

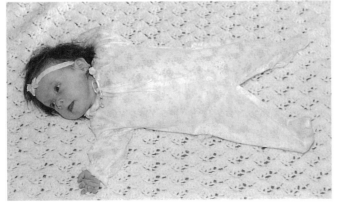

If she is not supported, her head will be turned to one side, her arms and hands will rest on the surface, and her legs will be positioned with her hips and knees bent and her knees wide apart. *(See figure 1.2.)* She will not have the strength to move her head to the center to look at you or a toy. She will also not have the strength to lift her arms so she can bring her hands to her mouth and chest. She may slide her arms on the surface, but she will not be able to lift them. She will move her legs, but they will be wide apart.

(fig. 1.2)

The first position to try is laying the baby in your lap. When she is able to hold her head in the center and move her arms easily while lying in your lap, you can begin placing her on the floor with support. The best way to support her head and arms in the center is to use a "blanket roll." (See Activity #3 for instructions on how to make a blanket roll.)

With practice, your baby's head, arms, and legs will get stronger and support can be taken away. She will learn to hold her head in the center and then you can stop using the blanket roll at her head. When she is able to bring her hands to her chest and touch toys, you can stop using the blanket roll under her arms. When she is able to kick her legs with her knees in line with her hips, you do not need to support her legs together.

activity guidelines

Motivate your baby by using toys that she can interact with. Use brightly colored toys and toys that make sounds. You can hold a lightweight rattle above her hand or suspend it from a play gym and have her hit it. You can use a large toy and place it on her chest and have her touch it.

If your baby's legs are active, hold them to calm them down. She will not be able to kick her legs and reach simultaneously at this stage.

activity #2

Back-lying in Your Lap *(see fig. 1.3)*

(fig. 1.3)

1. Place your baby in your lap as you sit on the couch or other comfortable chair with back support.
2. Place her with her head between your knees, her hips against your stomach, and her legs supported against your chest.
3. Slide your hands along the sides of her body and under her arms until they are under her head. Hold her head in the center and tilt it upward so she sees you easily.
4. With this arm support, she will be able to bring her hands to her chest or mouth.
5. Use your elbows to support her legs so that her knees are in line with her hips and not in a wide position.
6. Lean your head and trunk forward so that you can be close to her and you can see each other. Talk or sing to her and engage with her for as long as tolerated.

activity #3

Back-lying on the Floor *(see fig. 1.4)*

1. Make a blanket roll with a bath towel or a baby blanket. Fold it along its length so that it is 8 inches wide. Now roll each end toward the center until there is just enough space between the two rolled-up ends for your baby to lie in. Turn the blanket roll over so that the ends don't unroll and place it on the floor.
2. Place your baby on her back between the rolled-up ends of the blanket roll so that it is under her head and shoulders. The bottom edge of the blanket roll should be even with your baby's elbows.

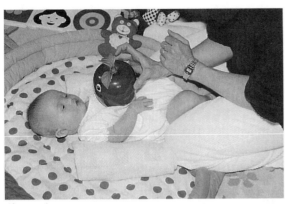

(fig. 1.4)

3. Sit on your heels in front of her and use your knees to support her legs with her knees in line with her hips. Use your legs as a boundary for her legs to move within.
4. With this support, lean your head and trunk forward and talk to her.
5. Place a toy on her chest and encourage her to look downward at the toy and bring her hands up to touch the toy.

activity #4   **Back-lying on the Floor with a Play Gym over Her Chest**

1. Place your child on the floor and place a blanket roll under her head and shoulders. Place her head in the center.
2. Place the play gym above her chest and add rings to the toys on the play gym so they dangle above her elbow or hand.
3. She will move her arms and hit the toys and will learn how to engage with them by hitting them.
4. When she is able to hit the toys repeatedly, eliminate the blanket roll.
5. Watch her leg position and support her legs together if she holds her legs apart.

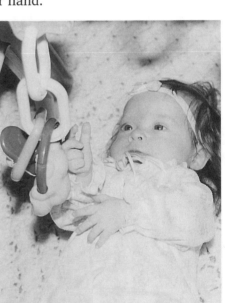

activity #5   **Back-lying and Reaching Upward without Support** (see fig. 1.5)

1. Place your baby on the floor with her head looking straight ahead, not turned to either side.
2. Position yourself sitting on your heels in front of her.
3. Place a large toy on her chest and have her reach and touch it with one or both hands. Or use a play gym.

(fig. 1.5)

4. If her legs are very active, support them to calm them down and then she will be better able to reach.
5. When she is able to consistently reach to her chest to play with the toy, raise it slightly above her chest so she needs to reach higher.
6. Watch her legs and support them if she holds them apart.

SUPPORTED SITTING

When your baby is supported in a sitting position, she is able to look around and see the world from the vertical perspective. In this position, she can be face to face with you or watch people around her. You can begin using this position at 2 to 2½ months of age.

In order for her to be able to lift her head, the rest of her body must be completely supported. With that support, she can focus on lifting her head up against gravity. She will need support behind her head to learn how far to lift her head and to be able to maintain it there once lifted. If she does not have support behind her head, she will lift it too far and it will fall back. As her neck muscles become stronger, she will be able to lift her head without losing control.

To use supported sitting, you can place your baby in your lap, so that she is facing away from you. You can also place her on the couch or on a chair with her head and back supported against the back cushion. In either position, you can talk to her to motivate her to lift her head up and hold it there. When she is tired and is leaning her head forward, it's time to quit.

activity guidelines

Use toys or people to motivate her to lift her head. Use toys that she is interested in watching. You can talk and sing to her to encourage her to look at you. Make sure you or the toy are at eye level or slightly lower. If positioned above eye level, she will tilt her head back rather than lift it.

When using these supported sitting positions, make sure that your baby's head and trunk are up straight and not rounded or slouched. If she is sitting in your lap, sit with your back straight because if you slouch, she will too. If using the couch, you need to hold her hips and chest to make sure they are supported up straight. If her back is rounded, she will not learn to lift her head properly. She will learn to lean her head back on her neck. She can only lift her head properly if her back is supported up straight.

activity #6

Supported Sitting with Maximal Support *(see figs. 1.6, 1.7)*

A. In your lap
  1. Sit in a chair with your back up straight and maintain that position.
  2. Place your baby sitting in your lap so that she is facing away from you. Position her head against your chest, her trunk against your middle trunk, and her hips against your waist and stomach.
  3. Place one of your hands under her buttocks and use your thumb and fingers to hold her legs together.
  4. Place your other hand across her upper chest and under her arms so her arms are free and forward. Support her trunk against you so it is up straight.
  5. With this support, she can lift her head up against your chest.
  6. Use toys or people to motivate her to lift her head. You can sit in front of a mirror or toys that she is interested in watching.
  7. The goal of this position is to have her lift her head and hold it for as long as she can tolerate. As long as

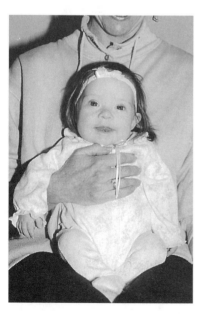
(fig. 1.6)

(fig. 1.7)

her head is against your chest, she is actively lifting it. When her head leans forward, she is resting. This position can be used as long as she works on lifting her head.

8. You can also carry your baby in this position and walk around the house. The motion of walking will further stimulate her to lift her head.

9. When she is able to lift her head up and hold it over time, provide support lower on her chest (around nipple level) and see if she can still lift her head.

B. On the couch

1. Place your baby on the couch with her back up straight and resting against the back cushion.
2. Kneel on the floor in front of her.
3. Place one of your hands at her hips to keep them from sliding forward.
4. Place your other hand at her chest to support her trunk up straight.
5. Lean forward and talk to her with your face at eye level to encourage her to lift her head and hold it up as long as possible.

STOMACH-LYING

Stomach-lying is the most physically challenging position for your baby. She has to move against gravity to lift her head and push up on her arms. This requires her to do two hard motor tasks at the same time. Although it is difficult, it is an important position to use to develop neck and arm strength. It is best to wait to use this position until your baby is ready. She will probably be ready at 2 to 3 months of age.

There are ways to prepare your baby to use stomach-lying. She can begin practicing lifting and controlling her head when you are carrying her on your shoulder or holding her against your chest. She will be able to lift her head for brief periods and then rest it back on your shoulder. Another way to accomplish this is to semi-recline on the couch with her lying on your chest. When she lifts her head, you will be facing each other. When she is tired, her head will rest against your chest.

(fig. 1.8)

After she has practiced lifting her head and does it often, you can begin placing her on her stomach on a firm surface. You will need to support her at her buttocks and arms in order for her to be able to lift her head. If you hold her buttocks down firmly and support her elbows under her shoulders, her body will be supported so that she can focus on lifting her head and pushing up on her arms.

If you do not support her buttocks, her hips will bend and her buttocks will lift up off the surface. This will push her head and upper body downward and make it impossible for her to try to lift her head or prop on her arms. As your baby learns to lift her head and chest higher and prop on her elbows, her buttocks will automatically stay on the surface and she will not need them supported.

Your baby's arms also need to be supported with her elbows placed under her shoulders. If her arms are positioned this way, she will be better able to lift her head and she will learn the best position for propping on her elbows. Without arm support,

port, her elbows will be positioned wide apart and she will not be able to push up to prop. With poor propping, it will be more difficult to lift her head. Arm support will be needed until she can hold her elbows under her shoulders when propping.

activity guidelines

Use motivators that she is interested in watching. *(See figure 1.8.)* You want to encourage her to lift her head to watch you, brightly colored toys, action toys, music boxes, or other people. She will also like to look at a shiny mylar balloon and hear the crinkly sound when it is touched. Change the motivators as needed to keep her interested in watching so she continues to lift her head as long as she can. Place the motivators at eye level to help her lift her head properly.

Your baby will become tired easily in stomach-lying so use the position for short periods. With practice, her strength will improve and she will be able to lift her head higher and stay in the position for longer periods.

activity #7

Lift Head When Placed on Your Shoulder *(see fig. 1.9)*

1. Place your baby against your chest with her head resting on your shoulder.
2. Place one of your hands across her upper back.
3. Place your other hand firmly against her buttocks and gently hold her legs together.
4. Encourage her to lift her head.
5. This position can be done while sitting or when you are carrying her.
6. Watch her head position and support it if she loses control.

(fig. 1.9)

activity #8

Lift Head When Placed on Your Chest

1. Position yourself reclined 45 degrees on the couch or recliner.
2. Place your baby on your chest and support her buttocks firmly.
3. Place her elbows under her shoulders so she can prop on them.
4. Talk to her and encourage her to lift her head to look at you.

activity #9

Stomach-lying with Full Support

A. On floor
1. Sitting on your heels, place your baby on her stomach on the floor in front of you, facing away from you.
2. Use your knees to snugly stabilize her hips on the floor and to hold her legs together.
3. Lean forward and use your hands to support her elbows under her shoulders for propping.
4. Use a mirror, toy, or another person in front of her to motivate her to lift her head.

(fig. 1.10)

B. On elevated surface *(see fig. 1.10)*

1. Place your baby on her stomach, facing away from you. Use an elevated surface like a bed or couch.
2. Place her elbows under her shoulders for propping. Support her elbows if needed.
3. Firmly hold her hips, pressing downward toward the surface.
4. Use a mirror, toy, or another person in front of her to motivate her to lift her head.
5. Have her hold her head up for as long as tolerated.

activity #10 Stomach-lying with Arm Support

1. Place your baby on an elevated surface such as a bed, couch, or table. Place her on her stomach, facing you.
2. Position yourself on the floor at eye level to her.
3. Support her arms with her elbows under her shoulders.
4. Talk to her or use a toy to encourage her to lift her head.
5. When she is able to lift her head up well, let go of her arms and see if she can maintain propping on her elbows and lifting her head.

➤ Motor Milestone Checklist *on next page.* ➤

Motor Milestone Checklist

Side-lying
- ❑ When supported, she brings her hand to her mouth
- ❑ When supported, she looks at a toy
- ❑ When supported, she touches a toy
- ❑ She stays in the side-lying position without support

Back-lying
- ❑ In your lap, she looks at you and focuses on your face
- ❑ In your lap, she brings her hand to her mouth or chest
- ❑ On floor with blanket roll at head and arms, she brings her hand to her mouth
- ❑ On floor with blanket roll at head and arms, she touches a rattle suspended from a play gym
- ❑ On floor with blanket roll at head and arms, she touches a large toy placed on her chest
- ❑ On floor with blanket roll at arms, she turns her head to the center and holds it there
- ❑ On floor with blanket roll at arms, she touches a rattle suspended from a mobile
- ❑ On floor with blanket roll at arms, she touches a large toy placed on her chest
- ❑ On floor without blanket roll, she holds her head in the center and touches a rattle suspended from mobile
- ❑ On floor, she brings one or both hands to her chest to touch a large toy placed on her chest
- ❑ She maintains her legs together and kicks them

Supported Sitting
When fully supported in sitting in your lap or on the couch, she holds her head up for:
- ❑ 10 seconds
- ❑ 30 seconds
- ❑ 2-3 minutes
- ❑ When sitting in your lap or on the couch with support at nipple level, she holds her head up for 5-10 minutes

Stomach-lying
With buttocks supported and propped on her elbows, she holds head up for:
- ❑ 10-20 seconds
- ❑ 1 minute
- ❑ She can hold her head up for 1-2 minutes with support at her elbows
- ❑ She can prop on elbows and hold her head up for 2-5 minutes without support

CHAPTER 2

Stage 2
Head Control, Propping, and Rolling

Now your baby is more alert and wants to move. He notices what is happening around him and wants to participate. He consistently smiles at you and everyone who talks to him. He makes faces and sounds to engage with you. He is motivated to interact with people and toys and initiates the interactions. He is awake for longer periods, and when awake, he loves attention and playing with people and toys.

He has gained strength in his head, arms, stomach, and legs so he is able to use his body more actively. He moves his body to look at what he chooses and plays with what he wants to, as long as it is close to him. He is learning how he can move and repeats the movements.

> **The motor skills to focus on in this second stage of development are:**
> 1. **reaching and hand-to-foot play in back-lying,**
> 2. **propping on elbows and hands and reaching in stomach-lying,**
> 3. **sitting with upper and middle trunk support,**
> 4. **pulling to sit, and**
> 5. **rolling.**

REACHING & HAND-TO-FOOT PLAY IN BACK-LYING

Back-lying is your baby's preferred position early in this stage because he can hold his head in the center and use his hands to reach, touch, and play with toys. He also can look around the room and see the people around him. During this stage, he will learn to reach for toys and engage in hand-to-foot play.

He will begin reaching for toys on his chest and work toward reaching for toys with his arms straight above him. At first, he may hold onto his clothes to keep his hands on his chest. He will let go with one hand to touch a toy while the other hand continues to hold on. By holding his clothes, he keeps his hands in a better position for play.

As your baby develops more strength in his shoulders, he will be able to reach 1 to 2 inches above his chest. *(See figure 2.1.)* He will learn to bring his hands to his

Your baby will be able to use all the positions if you give him the support he needs. He will initially prefer the back-lying position. He will be able to see you and easily play with toys. When he is able to prop well in stomach-lying, he will prefer that position. As his head control improves, it will be easier for him to pull to sit and use the supported sitting position. He will need to practice rolling with support until he is able to do it by himself.

Watch to see which positions he prefers and which ones are harder for him. What he chooses will depend on his tone, strength, and what he is interested in. Alternate the easy positions with the harder ones. Use the activities as long as he tolerates them.

Change the toys often to keep his interest and attention. If he is motivated to see or play with a toy, he will practice the activity longer.

He will be able to be alert and active for 30-40 minutes. When he is tired, he needs a resting break.

chest easily and will reach above his chest to touch a toy. As his control increases, the toy can be raised higher until he is able to reach with his elbows straight and maintain this position while playing with the toy.

After he reaches for the toy, he will be able to hold it and shake it. He will shake it back and forth, to and from his chest. He will bring it to his mouth and may lift it higher toward his head.

The final skill to accomplish in back-lying is hand-to-foot play. You want to focus on this skill because it will strengthen your child's stomach muscles. To engage in hand-to-foot play, your baby will need to be able to reach, kick his legs up and lift his buttocks off the floor, and coordinate the kicking with the reaching so he can grab his feet at the right time. It takes time and practice to achieve this skill.

(fig. 2.1)

When he is able to reach above his chest, he can begin practicing reaching for his feet with his feet supported. You will need to place his feet over his chest so he can see and touch them. You will need to make him aware of his feet and generate interest in his feet. You can rub or pat his feet together, or pat them against your face. By playing with his feet, you will motivate him to touch his feet.

While you are supporting his legs with his feet over his chest, he will feel where his legs need to be so he can touch his feet. *(See figure 2.2.)* He will work on kicking his legs upward until he has the strength to lift his buttocks off the floor. You will need to support his buttocks and legs so he can play with his feet until he is able to do it by himself. He will first be able to reach and touch his knees; later, when he can lift his buttocks off the floor, he will be able to touch his feet.

Your baby will work on the individual skills of reaching and kicking his legs and lifting his buttocks upward. *(See figure 2.3.)* When he is motivated to play with his feet and has developed the strength he needs, he will coordinate these actions to get his feet.

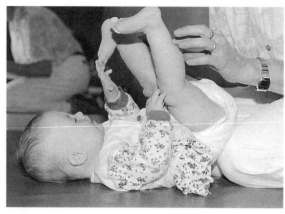

(fig. 2.2)

activity guidelines

When using toys in this position, you need to pick the right toy for the activity you are doing. For **reaching** activities, use colorful, movable lightweight rattles, squeeze/squeak toys, and stuffed animals. The toys need to be big enough to touch and grab. You can suspend them from a mobile or play gym or hold them at the proper level. When he is **holding and shaking** toys, use lightweight toys with the proper size handle to grasp. Make sure the toys are safe and won't hurt him if he hits himself with them. Never use a heavy rattle because it is too hard to move and he will tire too quickly trying to play with it. For **hand-to-foot play,** put foot jingles or lightweight rattles on his feet to motivate him to reach for his feet. When he wants to play with his feet, make sure he is barefoot so he can grab his feet more easily.

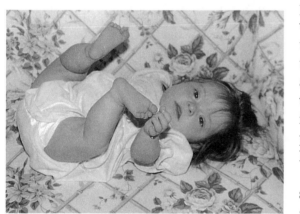

(fig. 2.3)

When he is not kicking his legs up, watch his legs to see what movements he uses. Watch to see if his knees are generally in line with his hips rather than wide apart. During this stage, you want him to learn to move his legs with his knees in line with his hips. You will notice he bends his hips and knees and places his feet on the floor. If he continues to position his legs wide apart, support them together.

It is easier for your baby to engage in hand-to-foot play without his diaper or clothes on. You can let him practice during diaper changes.

activity #1

Back-lying and Reaching above Chest

1. Place your baby on the floor with his head in the center.
2. Sit on your heels in front of him.
3. Place a toy 1-2 inches above his chest and have him reach and touch the toy. Encourage him to reach with each hand by holding the toy to each side in turn.
4. Encourage him to reach and touch the toy as long as tolerated.
5. When he reaches well with the toy 1-2 inches above his chest, raise it to 3-4 inches above his chest. Continue to raise the toy until he is able to reach with his elbows straight.
6. Watch his leg position and support his legs together if he holds them apart.
7. This activity can also be done by positioning a play gym over his chest with the toys placed the proper distance above his chest.

activity #2   **Back-lying and Shaking Toys**

1. Place your baby on a firm surface.
2. Sit on your heels in front of him.
3. Pick out a toy that is easy for him to hold onto.
4. Help him put his fingers around the toy so he can hold it.
5. Hold his hand and shake it while he holds the toy.
6. Let go and see if he will try to shake the toy.
7. Encourage him to hold, shake, and play with the toy as long as tolerated.
8. Use toys that are lightweight, easy to hold, and safe.

activity #3   **Back-lying and Kicking**

1. Take your baby's shirt off and place him on the floor.
2. Tickle his belly or blow on it. Watch to see if he uses his stomach muscles and kicks his legs up. If he uses his stomach muscles, you will see wrinkles across his stomach.
3. If he does not kick his legs up, lift them up and move them for a few seconds and then let go. After you let go, see if he tries to kick them up.
4. Also try this activity when you are changing his diaper. It will be easier for him to kick his legs up when his diaper and clothes are off.
5. When he is able to kick, he may like to kick rattles suspended from a mobile.

activity #4   **Back-lying/Hand-to-Foot Play with Support**

1. Place your baby on the floor.
2. Sit on your heels in front of him.
3. Place his buttocks on your knees and support them so he can see his feet.
4. Play with his feet by patting and rubbing them together and placing them against your face.
5. Watch him and see if he is interested in looking at his feet.
6. Hold one foot close to his hand and see if he will reach for his foot. If he does not try to touch his foot, bring his hand to his foot and pat them together. Help him hold onto his foot.
7. Try putting foot jingles or bells on his feet to entice him to reach for the toy on his foot.
8. Encourage him to reach for one foot while you hold it.
9. When he consistently reaches for his feet with your support at his buttocks and feet, lower his buttocks slightly and see if he can still reach for his feet.
10. Continue to encourage him to reach for his feet as you lessen your support and gradually lower his buttocks to the floor.
11. Continue to practice until he can engage in hand-to-foot play by himself.

PROPPING ON ELBOWS & HANDS & REACHING IN STOMACH-LYING

Stomach-lying is an important position for building strength, particularly in the neck and arm muscles. Your baby is ready to use this position because his neck and arm muscles are stronger. He will need to gain the strength to lift his head and prop on his arms for several minutes while watching or playing with toys.

He will first learn to prop on his elbows. When propping on his elbows, his elbows need to be placed under his shoulders. With his arms properly positioned, he can push up on his arms better and lift his head more easily. If his elbows are placed wider than his shoulders, his chest will sag in between his arms and propping will be more difficult.

When he is able to prop on his elbows, he will choose between two options. He will either learn to reach while propping on his elbows or learn to prop on his hands. You can assist him with both and see what he is interested in doing. To reach, he will need to be motivated to touch toys; to prop on his hands, he will need to have adequate arm strength to push up. He will eventually learn to do both skills.

(fig. 2.4)

If your baby is very motivated to play with toys while on his stomach, he will develop reaching skills. His first method of reaching will be to slide his hand out to touch a toy, keeping his hand on the surface. He will want the toy and will try to hold it and pull it back toward him.

The second method of reaching will be to raise his hand and arm off the surface to reach and play with a toy. *(See figure 2.4.)* In order to lift his hand off the surface, he needs to learn to lean over his other elbow and balance himself so that he can lift his hand to reach. His elbows will need to be positioned under his shoulders to allow him to lean over one side.

Your baby will first learn to reach forward and later will learn to reach to the side. Through reaching, he learns how to lean (shift) his weight from one side to the other and balance on one side. This is essential for the development of future motor skills such as moving in and out of positions, creeping, and walking.

Your baby may prefer propping on his hands to reaching if he enjoys watching toys or people and he has the strength needed to push up on his hands. *(See figure 2.5.)* He may be in his crib and push up to look over the bumper pads or look at a toy. He will be motivated to see something, but not to touch it.

He may not want to prop on his hands because he cannot play while propping. He also may resist propping on his hands if his arms are weak. If he shows no interest in propping on his hands when stomach-lying, don't force him

(fig. 2.5)

to do it. He will learn to do it later in supported sitting. Using supported sitting, he can combine propping and playing.

activity guidelines

When practicing propping on elbows and hands, it is best if you place your baby's arms properly and have him prop as long as he can. I do not recommend using a roll or wedge for propping because your baby will lean and rest on it rather than actively pushing up and propping. He will develop more arm strength by actively propping on his arms rather than by leaning over a roll or wedge.

If he resists propping and puts his arms along the sides of his body, support his arms to help him prop. As he gains strength, he will be able to prop by himself.

Use toys that will encourage the skill you are practicing. For beginning propping, use toys or people your baby is motivated to watch. Place the motivator at eye level or lower. If you place it above his head, he will learn to lean his head back on his neck, which could become a bad habit. When he is reaching forward to touch a toy on the surface, use lightweight rattles that are easy to hold. When he is reaching and lifting his hand off the surface, use toys that rock, make sounds, and have bright colors. Examples include: Mattel Melody Lights Go Round, Happy Apple, squeak toys, and Mickey Mouse. You could also hold a rattle 2-3 inches above the surface. When propping on hands, use toys or play games that he can watch. Examples are: music boxes, play peek-a-boo, talk or sing to him, or use a mirror so he can watch himself.

Watch his leg position and support his legs together if they are wide apart. Children with Down syndrome frequently use a position with the soles of the feet together and the knees bent and wide apart. This leg position should be discouraged because your child needs to learn to move his legs together. This particular position will block the weight shifting necessary for reaching.

activity #5

Maintain Stomach-lying While Propping on His Elbows and Lifting His Head *(see fig. 2.6)*

1. Place your baby on his stomach and place his elbows under his shoulders.
2. Encourage him to lift his head by talking to him or using toys. Place the toys at eye level or slightly lower; do not place them above his head.
3. Encourage him to stay in this position as long as tolerated.
4. Watch the position of his legs and support them together if needed.

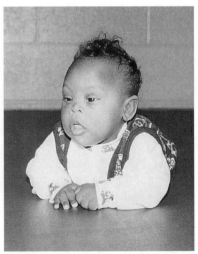

(fig. 2.6)

activity #6

Stomach-lying and Propping on Hands
A. With full support *(see fig. 2.7)*

1. Place your baby on his stomach, facing away from you. Use a firm surface like the floor.
2. Sit on your heels with your knees around his buttocks and legs. Move your legs against his buttocks and legs to hold them firmly.

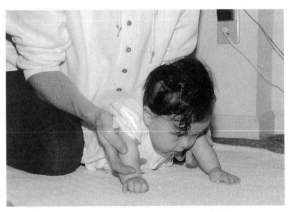

(fig. 2.7)

3. Lean forward and hold his arms with his elbows straight.
4. Pat his hands against the floor and gently bounce him on his hands until his hands are at a 45 degree angle from the shoulders and the width between his hands is wider than his shoulders. (If his hands are placed under his shoulders, it will be too hard for him to push up.)
5. Let go of his arms and see if he will keep his elbows straight for a couple seconds.
6. If his elbows bend immediately and he props on them, use your fingertips to support his elbows until he has the strength to straighten them. If he bends his elbows slightly and keeps them up off the surface, he is beginning to learn to push up.
7. Encourage him to prop on his hands as long as tolerated, working toward 10 seconds.

B. With arm support
1. Kneel on the floor and place your baby on his stomach on a firm surface above you, like a coffee table. Make sure you are facing each other.
2. Hold his elbows so they are straight in front of him.
3. While holding his elbows, bounce him gently on his hands. Gradually move his hands so they are at a 45 degree angle from the shoulders and the width between them is wider than shoulder width.
4. Gradually let go of his elbows and see if he can keep them straight for a few seconds.
5. Use your fingertips to support his elbows as needed until he is able to keep them straight.
6. When he is able to push up and prop on his hands in this position, move his hands so they are 60 degrees from his shoulders.
7. Make sure he bends and straightens his elbows and does not hold them stiff and straight. If he holds his elbows stiff and resists bending them, re-position him with his elbows bent so he does not learn the bad habit of "locking his elbows." If he learns to lock his elbows, he will not develop arm strength properly.
8. As his arms get stronger, he will be able to push up and prop on his hands by himself.

activity #7   **Stomach-lying and Reaching**
1. Kneel on the floor. Place your baby on his stomach on your bed, so you are facing each other.
2. Position him propping on his elbows, with his elbows under his shoulders.
3. Place a lightweight toy such as a rattle in front of his right arm. Hold his left elbow in the propping position and lift his right hand up on top of the toy. As you bring his right hand on top of the toy, you will lean him over the left elbow.
4. Help him maintain this reaching position for 2-5 seconds and then let him return to the propping position.

5. After assisting reaching, place the toy in front of his right hand and see if he can reach by himself.
6. Repeat these steps and help him reach with his left arm while propping on his right elbow.

SUPPORTED SITTING WITH UPPER & MIDDLE TRUNK SUPPORT

Your baby will love to look around when you hold him in supported sitting. Since he is motivated to look, he will lift his head up. During this stage he will be able to hold his head up when supported in sitting and he will learn to sit with upper and middle trunk support.

This will be the critical time for your baby to learn how to lift his head to the center and hold it there. In Stage One, he needed support behind his head and he lifted his head up to the support. Now the support is no longer needed behind his head and he will need to learn how far to lift his head up so that it does not fall back. He also needs to develop the strength and control to lift his head slowly so he can stop lifting it when it is in the right position. If he lifts it quickly, it will probably fall back.

Your baby will need to have his trunk supported up straight so he can learn to lift and hold his head in the proper position. *(See figure 2.8.)* If he is held with his back rounded, he will learn to lean his head back on his neck and rest it there. This is a bad habit to develop because he will not learn how to lift his head

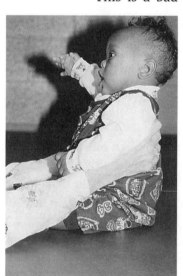

(fig. 2.8)

properly and later, he will sit with his trunk leaning forward and his head tilted back.

At first, he will need support at his upper back and upper chest. With firm support, he will be able to lift his head and he will learn to hold his head up for a few minutes. Refer to Activities 8 and 9 for instructions on how to do this.

When he holds his head up well with upper trunk support, your support can be lowered to his middle trunk, which is the level of his nipples. With this support, he will need to gain the strength to lift his head and upper trunk. Refer to Activities 10-13 for suggestions on how to provide middle trunk support.

When your baby is ready for you to provide middle trunk support, he has developed the head control necessary for sitting and is ready to begin developing the trunk control needed for sitting. To learn to sit, he will need to develop strength in the upper, middle, and lower sections of his trunk. When you provide middle trunk support, he will be strengthening the upper trunk section. During this stage he will develop upper trunk control and in Stage Three he will develop middle and lower trunk control.

As your baby develops head and trunk control in supported sitting, he will further challenge himself by reaching for toys. When he reaches, it will be difficult to keep his head and upper trunk up straight because he will be doing three hard skills at once. You will need to support him more when he is reaching until he develops the strength to do all three activities at once. If he is holding a toy and shaking it, he will be challenging himself even more and will need extra support.

activity guidelines

Place toys or motivators at the level of your baby's eyes or between his mouth and eyes. When he is working on lifting his head and it is hard for him, have him watch people or toys. You can talk or sing to him or have someone entertain him with toys.

When he is able to hold up his head and upper trunk, he will probably enjoy touching toys on a mobile or holding lightweight rattles and shaking them. When he plays with toys, see if his posture changes and give him extra support if he needs it. If he needs a lot of extra support, try to alternate "watching" entertainment and playing with toys.

When practicing the supported sitting position, take your baby's shirt off to see what his head and trunk really look like. With clothes on, you cannot see if his back is rounded or straight. You can also hold his trunk more securely with your hands with the skin-to-skin contact.

activity #8

Supported Sitting on a Table with Upper Trunk Support *(see fig. 2.9)*

1. Place your baby in supported sitting on a firm surface such as a coffee table or kitchen table and position yourself in front of him at eye level.
2. Place your hands at his upper trunk with your thumbs in a vertical position at his shoulders, the palms of your hands under his armpits, and your fingertips horizontally across his back.
3. Use your fingertips to push inward into his back to support his trunk in a fully upright position.

(fig. 2.9)

4. Talk to him and have him watch you and engage with you while you talk to him. Make sure you are both at eye level and encourage him to lift his head for as long as tolerated.
5. If his hips slide forward on the table surface, place a piece of Dycem on the table to prevent sliding. (Dycem is a non-slip vinyl material available through your PT or OT.) You could also use Easy Liner™ or Rubbermaid Grip Liner™, which are available in grocery stores.

activity #9

Supported Sitting Sideways Across Your Lap *(see fig. 2.10)*

1. Sit on a firm chair with your feet on the floor. Place your baby sitting sideways across your lap.
2. Place your hands horizontally with one across his upper chest and the other across his upper back. Place the "back" hand lower than the "chest" hand.

(fig. 2.10)

3. Lift upward with the "chest" hand and press inward with the "back" hand. With this support, hold his trunk up straight.

4. Encourage him to lift his head to watch a toy or look at people in the environment. Have him hold his head up as long as tolerated.

5. When he can hold his head up for 3-5 minutes, lower your hand support. Place your "chest" hand across his nipples and the "back" hand across his back but slightly lower than the "chest" hand. Continue to lift up with the "chest" hand and press in with the "back" hand to support his trunk up straight. With this support, have him lift his head and upper trunk as long as tolerated.

activity #10 **Supported Sitting on a Table with Mid Trunk Support** *(see fig. 2.11)*

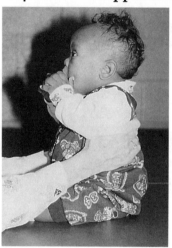

1. Place your baby in supported sitting on a firm surface like a coffee table or kitchen table and position yourself in front of him at eye level.

2. Place your hands at his nipple level with your thumbs horizontally across his nipples, the palms of your hands supporting the sides of his trunk, and your fingertips horizontally across his back.

3. Use your fingertips to press inward into his back to support his trunk in a fully upright position.

4. Talk and play with him, encouraging him to hold his head and upper trunk upright for as long as tolerated.

5. If his hips slide forward on the table surface, place a piece of Dycem, Easy Liner™, or Rubbermaid Grip Liner™ on the table to prevent this.

(fig. 2.11)

activity #11 **Supported Sitting on the Sofa with the Support of Sofa Cushions**

1. Remove one seat cushion from the sofa and place your baby sitting in the corner of the sofa.

2. Place the seat cushion across his lap and snugly hold it against his chest. Prop his elbows on top of the seat cushion.

3. Place a toy on top of the cushion. Pick a toy that is fun to watch and is as high as his shoulders.

4. If he leans to the side that is not supported, use a pillow to support him and prevent falling to the side.

5. Use this position as long as tolerated. This position is useful to help your baby play in the supported sitting position. You can be in front of him to play with him.

6. When he is able to sit well in this position, place him in the middle of the sofa without support on either side and place the seat cushion across his lap and against his chest. Place a toy on top of the cushion and encourage him to stay in the centered position as long as tolerated.

activity #12 **Supported Sitting in between Your Legs** *(see fig. 2.12)*

1. Sit on the floor and place your baby sitting sideways in front of you.

2. Place one of your legs behind him with your knee behind his back.

Place your other leg over his legs with your knee up against his chest. Cross your ankles with the "back" leg crossed on top of the "front" leg.

3. Prop his elbows or hands on your "front" leg to help him sit up straight.
4. Use toys to entertain him and place them at eye level to encourage him to lift his head and upper trunk.

(fig. 2.12)

activity #13

Supported Sitting in front of a Play Gym

1. Sit on the floor and place your baby sitting sideways in front of you.
2. Place a mobile in front of him with the toys at shoulder level.
3. Place your hands horizontally on his trunk with one across his nipples and your other hand on his back, across his shoulder blades.
4. Lift upward with the "front" hand and press inward with the "back" hand to support his trunk up straight.
5. Encourage him to lift his head and upper trunk as long as tolerated while playing with the toys.
6. To help him reach the toys, make sure your "front" hand does not block his arms. Place his arms over your arm and this will help him reach and touch the toys.

PULLING TO SIT

When your child is able to sit with middle trunk support, he will be ready to assist with pulling up to sit from lying on his back. To pull to sit, he will need to hold on with his hands, lift his head forward, and pull up with his arms. During this stage, he will learn to lift his head and pull with his arms. He may or may not be able to maintain holding on with his hands, so you will need to provide the necessary support.

To encourage him to pull to sit, you can clap your hands and say "Come to Mommy (or Daddy)." Then put your thumbs in front of his hands and encourage him to hold your thumbs. Slowly lift your hands upward and wait for him to lift his head and bend his elbows to pull up to sit.

You will use your thumbs because they are larger than your other fingers and that makes them easier to grasp. You can position your fingers over the tops of his hands to help him hold on. With practice, you can lessen your support because his hand strength will improve and he will be able to hold on as he pulls up to sit.

You want him to learn to hold on to your thumbs rather than you holding his wrists. When he holds your thumbs, he will need to work to pull himself up. If you hold his wrists, you will be pulling him.

activity guidelines

If it is too difficult for your baby to pull to sit from the horizontal position, prop him up on a pillow and see if he can pull up from this position. As his strength improves, gradually lower him until he can pull to sit from the horizontal position.

If he is not motivated to pull to sit and his arms are limp, do not pull him up. Only practice pulling to sit if he actively holds on with his hands and pulls with his arms.

Practice pulling to sit when he will naturally be motivated to do it. Do it after diaper changes, when he wants to be picked up, or when he wants to sit up.

activity #14

Pulling to Sit with Two Hand Support *(see fig. 2.13)*
1. Place your child lying on his back in front of you.
2. Place your thumbs horizontally above his chest and encourage him to reach for them and hold them. If he does not, assist him in holding on to

your thumbs. If his grasp is weak or he cannot maintain it, place your fingers over the tops of his hands to give him the support he needs.
3. Lift your thumbs and wait for him to lift his head and pull up with his arms. If this is too hard for him, use a pillow to recline him at 45 degrees and try again. Never pull him up if his head falls back and his arms are limp.
4. Continue to lift your thumbs while he pulls up to the sitting position.

(fig. 2.13)

ROLLING

Rolling gives your baby the freedom to move from one position to another or move from one place to another. He can choose when he wants to be on his back or on his stomach and he can change the position when he wants to. He can also choose to roll across the floor to get a toy. During this stage, he will learn to roll from his stomach to his back and from his back to his stomach. Generally, rolling from stomach to back is easier and develops first.

Rolling from stomach to back can be seen very early and initially is "accidental." *(See figure 2.14.)* If your baby is placed on his stomach with his elbows under his shoulders and he leans his head to one side, he will "fall over" and roll to his back. Sometimes, he will be propping and turn his head to the side and this will lean him to one side and he will "fall over." With practice, he will learn the movements for rolling over and will eventually do it with control.

Later, when he is able to prop on his arms better and maintain his balance while moving his head, he may not

(fig. 2.14)

roll over. Since he is better able to move his arms, he may place his elbows too wide and this will prevent him from rolling. Or, he may place his hands at his sides and rolling will be blocked. If this happens, you need to help him learn where to put his arms in order to roll over. You may need to tuck one elbow in to help him roll over that side. Or, you will need to re-position his arms if he keeps them at his sides. Whenever he is fussy on his stomach and wants to get out of the position, you can help him roll over to show him how he could move to his back. With practice and motivation, he will learn to roll again.

Rolling from back to stomach is harder because it requires two steps. The steps are: 1) rolling from back to side-lying; and 2) rolling from side-lying to

(fig. 2.15)

stomach. Your baby will generally learn to roll from his side to his stomach first. Then when he learns to roll from his back to his side, he will be ready to practice putting both steps together.

Your baby will generally learn to roll from his back to his side when he can kick his legs up vertically or engage in hand to foot play. With his legs in this position, he may turn his head to look at something, or his legs may get off balance and then his body will fall or roll to the side. With practice, he will learn to use his legs to initiate rolling to side-lying.

Some children use a different method to roll from back-lying to side-lying. They lie on their backs and arch their head and trunk and this causes them to roll to the side. This method should be discouraged. It is better for your child to learn to use his stomach muscles to raise his legs to initiate rolling than to use head and trunk arching movements.

You will need to wait for your baby to develop the strength needed to kick his legs up so he can roll from his back to the side. While you are waiting, you can help him learn to roll from his side to his stomach by providing the proper support, as described in Activities 15-18.

When he is able to roll from his back to his side and from his side to his stomach, he will be ready to practice rolling from his back to his stomach. He may need your help to practice or he may practice by himself. He will need to learn to move his body in a coordinated way to roll from his back to his stomach. It will be easier for him if he moves quickly because the momentum will carry him over to his stomach.

Your baby will roll when he is motivated to do it. If he does not roll right away, it could be that he loves being on his back and has no desire to be on his stomach. When he likes being on his stomach, he will be motivated to roll to it.

activity guidelines

Rolling is easier on a soft surface like a bed because it gives. Your baby will do it there before he does it on the floor.

He may roll better over one side and learn to roll over the other side later.

The key in using toys to encourage rolling is to pick toys he really wants and put them in the right place. When he is rolling from his stomach to his back, place the toy to his side and upward to see if

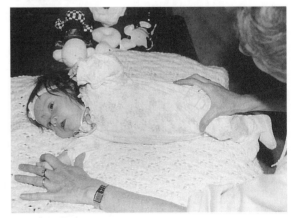

(fig. 2.16)

he will watch it and roll over. You could also position yourself to his side and above him and see if he will roll over to see you.

When encouraging him to roll from his back to his side, place the toy or yourself to his side and just out of reach. Place the motivator at head or shoulder level.

When he is rolling from his side to his stomach, place the toy above his head and diagonally from his shoulder.

How he uses rolling will give you information about whether he is an "observer" or "motor driven." Observers tend to roll to a person or a toy and stop after one or two rolls. Children who are motor driven frequently keep rolling around the room.

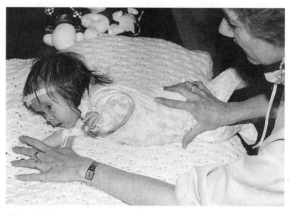

(fig. 2.17)

activity #15

Rolling from Back to Stomach with Full Support *(see figs. 2.16, 2.17)*

1. Place your baby on his back on the floor.
2. Roll him over to side-lying.
3. Place his underneath arm with his elbow above his shoulder and hold it there. If the arm he is rolling over is not supported, it will get caught under his trunk as he rolls to his stomach. With the support, he can easily roll over his arm and will prop on his elbows when he moves to his stomach.
4. Move his buttocks and legs over to the stomach-lying position and hold them firmly.
5. Wait for him to lift his head and move his upper body to roll to his stomach.
6. Repeat rolling over his other arm.

activity #16

Rolling from Back to Stomach

1. Place your baby on his back on the floor.
2. Roll him over to side-lying.
3. Place his underneath arm with his elbow above his shoulder and hold it there.
4. Hold his buttocks and legs halfway between side-lying and stomach-lying.
5. Wait for him to move his body over to his stomach.
6. Repeat rolling over his other arm.

activity #17

Rolling from Back to Stomach

1. Place your baby on his back on the floor.
2. Roll him over to side-lying.
3. Place his underneath arm with his elbow above his shoulder and hold it there.
4. Place your hand behind his buttocks to hold them in side-lying and prevent them from rolling back.
5. Wait for him to move his body over to his stomach.
6. Repeat rolling over his other arm.
7. When he is able to roll well from his side to his stomach, discontinue the arm support and see if he can roll without it.

activity #18 **Rolling from Back to Stomach with Hand Support**
1. Place your baby on his back on the floor.
2. Roll him over to side-lying.
3. Place his underneath arm with his elbow above his shoulder and hold it there.
4. Using his top arm, assist him in holding your thumb with his hand. Pull him gently and rock him.
5. Wait for him to move his legs to initiate rolling to his stomach.
6. Repeat rolling over his other arm.

activity #19 **Rolling from Stomach to Back**
1. Place your baby on his stomach, propping on his elbows with his elbows under his shoulders.
2. Place a toy to the side and upward and encourage him to turn his head to look at it.
3. When he turns his head to look at the toy, he will roll over.
4. Repeat rolling over his other arm.

activity #20 **Rolling from Stomach to Back with Arm Support**
1. Place your baby on his stomach, propping on his elbows with his elbows under his shoulders.
2. Position yourself at his feet, sitting on your heels.
3. Tuck in one of his elbows, and the side of his head will move down to the floor.
4. From this position, wait for him to roll to his back.
5. If he rolls over quickly, assist him so he does not become scared.
6. Repeat rolling over his other arm.

➤ Motor Milestone Checklist *on next page.* ➤

Motor Milestone Checklist

Back-lying
❑ He holds onto his clothes on his chest
❑ He reaches 2-3 inches above his chest to touch a toy
❑ He reaches with elbows straight and holds 10 seconds while playing with toy
❑ He kicks his legs up with his feet above his hips
❑ With his feet supported above his chest, he holds onto his feet
❑ He touches his hands to his knees without support
❑ He plays with his feet without support

Stomach-lying
❑ He lifts his head up and props on his elbows for 30-60 seconds
❑ He lifts his head up and props on his elbows for 5-10 minutes
❑ He props on his hands 5-10 seconds
❑ He props on his hands 20-30 seconds
❑ He reaches forward for a toy with his hand on the surface
❑ He reaches upward and lifts his hand off the surface to touch a toy

Supported Sitting
With upper trunk support, he holds his head up for:
❑ 20-30 seconds
❑ 1-2 minutes
❑ 5 minutes

With mid trunk support, he holds his head and upper trunk up for:
❑ 1-2 minutes
❑ 5 minutes

Pull to Sit
❑ He pulls to sit by lifting his head and pulling with his arms.

Rolling
❑ While on stomach, he leans his head to the side and "accidentally" rolls over
❑ He rolls from stomach to back consistently and often
❑ In side-lying with underneath arm supported and buttocks moved to stomach-lying and held, he lifts his head and rolls his upper body over to stomach-lying
❑ In side-lying with underneath arm supported and buttocks supported half-way between side-lying and stomach-lying, he rolls over to stomach-lying
❑ With buttocks supported in side-lying, he rolls from his side to his stomach
❑ He rolls from his back to his side
❑ He rolls from back to stomach

CHAPTER 3

Stage 3
Pivoting, Sitting, and Preparation for Standing

During this period, your baby will give you lots of surprises. Just as she surprised you with her first roll, she will show you her first pivot, how she can sit by herself, and how she can move to her hands and knees. You will set her up to learn each skill, help her practice the parts, and then she will put them together. You need to wait for the magical moment when she does it by herself. Many of the new positions are off the floor and your baby will have to practice to develop the increased strength and balance necessary to use them.

The motor skills to focus on in this third stage of development are:
1. **pivoting after toys in stomach-lying,**
2. **sitting on the floor,**
3. **moving to sit with support,**
4. **moving out of sitting with support,**
5. **quadruped,**
6. **supported kneeling,**
7. **sitting on a bench, and**
8. **supported standing.**

This is a crucial time in your child's development because it is during this period that children typically develop "bad habits" or abnormal movement patterns. In this chapter you will learn the abnormal movement patterns to avoid (especially standing with legs apart, feet turned out, and knees stiff, and moving in and out of sitting by doing a split) and the movement patterns to encourage in their place.

PIVOTING IN STOMACH-LYING

To pivot, your child will need to move her arms and trunk to the side to slide her body around and reach a toy. She will be ready to practice pivoting when she can reach forward when lying on her stomach. The goal will be to pivot in a full circle. Learning to pivot will prepare her to learn to crawl on her belly.

To teach your child to pivot, first you will place a toy to the side of her shoulder and encourage her to reach for it. She will turn her head to look at the toy and will

Guidelines for **Stage 3**

Your child will show you which skills she likes best. Practice the skills she is ready to learn even if she briefly uses the less preferred ones. The key is to be sensitive to her preferences and continue to help her with the harder positions until they become easier and she likes them. Do not impose the skills she does not like or she will become more resistant to them.

Your child's temperament will become more obvious and you will notice whether she is an observer or motor driven child. Observing and understanding her temperament will give you insight into what she likes to do and why and it will help you plan strategies to practice the skills she does not like. For example, Samantha was motor driven and loved to pivot, pull to sit, move out of sitting, and move up onto her hands and knees. However, she did not like to sit and would scoot to move out of sitting. Therefore, sitting was practiced for short periods, during her "best" times, and with her favorite motivators. She tolerated sitting under these conditions and learned to sit.

There is a sequence of steps for each skill. See what your child is able to do and proceed from there.

The pace and rhythm will change depending on the skills you are practicing. When pivoting, pulling to sit, and moving out of sitting, the pace is faster; when using sitting, supported hands and knees, supported kneeling, and supported standing, the pace is slower.

Vary the way you practice the skills to see what works best for your child. Some children are able to play and practice for 30-45 minute periods if the skills are changed often. Other children do best practicing for short periods, using a different skill for each practice period. Begin with skills your baby likes and briefly intersperse the skills she does not like. Use the best motivators, particularly with the harder activities. If practice time is limited on certain days, focus on what she wants to do and needs your help to do.

These skills require a new level of strength, so your child will fatigue faster until she builds up the strength needed for each skill.

bend her trunk to turn toward the toy. (*See figure 3.1.*) She will then need to shift her weight onto one arm so that she can reach for the toy with the other arm.

Once she has learned to bend her trunk and shift her weight to reach for the toy, you will place it a little further away so that she has to move her body to get it. She will have to grapple with the problem of how to move her body to get to the toy. Be patient and keep encouraging her while she experiments to discover how to do it.

When she first learns to pivot, she will primarily use arm and trunk movements. She will bend her trunk on the side she is moving toward and move her arms, one at a time, to move to the toy. (*See figures 3.2 and 3.3.*) She may move her legs, but they will not assist her in pivoting. When she can pivot well, her legs will assist her. She will bend the hip and knee on the side she is pivoting toward and her other hip and knee will be straight.

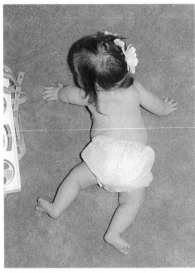

(fig. 3.1)

activity guidelines

The set-up is important when teaching your child to pivot. You need to position yourself at her feet and make sure no toys or other stimuli are in front of her. Make sure you or special toys are the only interesting stimuli for her to watch or engage with. With this set-up, she will turn to look at you and try to move to you.

You will need to be creative to motivate her to keep pivoting. You need to use great motivators, such as crinkled paper, a magazine, the tv remote, the telephone cord, or a brother or sister calling her. You need to generate hoopla and excitement, and wiggle the toy to keep the momentum going so she moves at a fast pace. The key is to move the toy and yourself quickly so she keeps chasing you and the toy.

(fig. 3.2)

(fig. 3.3)

When she can pivot more easily, watch to see if she will pivot spontaneously to move to someone sitting on the floor with her or to something she wants. She may pivot to see where you are if you walk to another room. For example, Samantha loved to be on her stomach and would pivot a couple times to move to a toy. Her mother noticed that Samantha would do her best pivoting when she walked from the family room to the kitchen. When her mother moved out of sight, Samantha would pivot to find out where her mother went.

Encourage her to move toward the right and left sides to see if one direction is easier. If one side is easier, focus on having her move in that direction. When she is able to move in a circle in that direction, begin moving in the other direction.

Your child may try to roll rather than work on pivoting, since rolling is easier and established. If she tries to roll, wiggle or rock her hips playfully to see if she will stay in the stomach-lying position. Or, roll her over a couple times and stop in stomach-lying. Try to get her interested in a toy and see if she will pivot again.

Pivoting is a strenuous activity, especially when your child is just learning it. When she is tired or no longer interested, stop. It is best to practice this skill when your child feels alert and active.

temperament

Children who are motor driven love pivoting and practice it more easily than children who are observers. The *"motor driven"* child keeps going and moves in a circle when she is strong enough to do the skill. The *"observer"* learns to pivot but prefers to do one or two pivots, play for awhile, and then do a couple more pivots. When encouraged to pivot in a circle, she may do it if the motivator is superb or if she has brief breaks to play with the motivator.

activity #1 **Pivoting**

1. Use a firm surface like the floor or rug. Place your child on her stomach, propping on her elbows.
2. Position yourself at your child's feet and remove all toys and stimuli in front of her.
3. Place a toy to the side of her shoulder or between her shoulder and waist. See if she turns her head to look at it and bends her trunk to that side.
4. See if she tries to reach for it or move toward it.
5. If she is unable to reach for it or move to it, hold her elbows and move them so the toy is in front of her and she can reach it.
6. When she has practiced this, pick a superb motivator (like a brother or sister) and see if she will try to move her arms to pivot one time.
7. With further practice, she will learn to pivot two times to move to the toy. Let her play with the toy and then move it again.
8. Work toward pivoting in a full circle. As your child pivots better, you can place the toy at her waist level and later at her feet, and she will move to it. Move yourself to stay positioned at her feet.

SITTING ON THE FLOOR

You may notice that your baby wants to sit up when you are holding her in your lap. She will lift her head up and try to move upward to sitting. Or, when she is in the infant seat, she may lean forward and try to sit up. This is the time to help her sit up and play.

Your child has learned to sit with her middle trunk supported. During this stage, the goal is for her to learn to sit without support. To achieve this goal, she needs to learn to sit with her trunk up straight and learn to balance herself in sitting so she can maintain the position without falling out of it. To do this, she needs to develop strength and control in the middle and lower sections of her trunk and strength in her arms.

To develop trunk control, she first needs to gain the strength in her back muscles to lift her trunk up straight and maintain that position. When she can hold her trunk up straight, then she needs to gain strength in the stomach muscles to balance herself in the middle and prevent falling back. Later, she will learn to use her back and stomach muscles simultaneously to help her balance when she leans in any direction.

As your child is developing the trunk control needed for sitting, she will also learn to use her arms to help her sit. She will learn to prop on her hands or hold

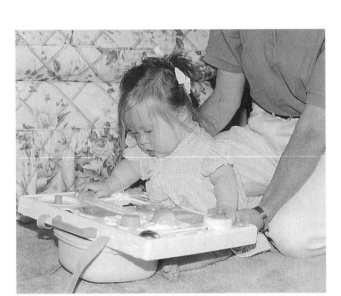

(fig. 3.4)

on to your thumbs to maintain the position. Later, she will learn to "catch" herself with her hands when she begins to fall out of the position.

Children with Down syndrome usually have shorter arms than other children. This makes sitting harder to develop, since propping on arms is necessary in developing the skill. To develop sitting, a typical child props forward on her hands when learning to use the position and then learns to prop to the side to maintain her balance if she falls. When your child is supported properly in sitting, her hands will not touch the floor. If your child learns to sit by propping forward with her hands on the floor, she will learn an abnormal way to sit. Another difficulty is that when your child falls to the side, she has to fall farther before her hand can touch to prop. This makes it harder to develop balance in sitting. You will need to support your child to compensate for her shorter arms. For example, rather than prop her hands on the floor in front of her, you can place an activity center ("Busy Box") across her lap and have her prop on it. *(See figure 3.4.)*

Your child will learn to sit following this sequence:
1. **with middle trunk control with support at her waist,**
2. **with low trunk control with support at her hips,**
3. **with support to balance herself,**
4. **without support.**

sitting with middle trunk support

Your child first needs to develop strength in the middle trunk area. You will notice this area is rounded when you look at her trunk from the side. To help her hold her middle trunk up straight, her trunk needs to be supported just above her waist in the front and back. *(See figure 3.5.)* Her hands can hold onto the low bar of a play gym or prop on a flat surface placed on top of her thighs, like an activity center or tray. Practice using a variety of supported sitting positions. Refer to Activities #2-7.

Do not allow her to prop her hands on the floor in front of her because it teaches her to sit with her trunk leaning forward excessively and her head resting back on her neck. She needs to prop on a flat surface on top of her thighs to hold her middle trunk up straight and compensate for her short arm length.

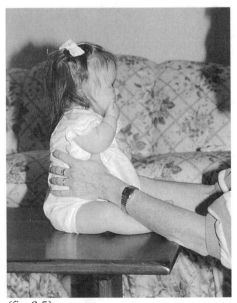

(fig. 3.5)

Propping on an activity center (Activity #3) helps develop arm strength. This is especially useful for children who resisted propping on their hands in stomach-lying. As your child props on the toy and plays with it, her trunk will move up and down. When her trunk is rounded, see if she straightens it in a few seconds by pushing up on her hands. If she leans forward for longer than 10 seconds, reposition her hands so she can prop and hold her trunk up straight. With practice, she will learn to hold her middle trunk up straight while propping and playing with the activity center. It is better to learn to prop on the activity center type surface than on her legs because the activity center is more stable, it provides a flat surface to prop on, and it is entertaining. It is harder for

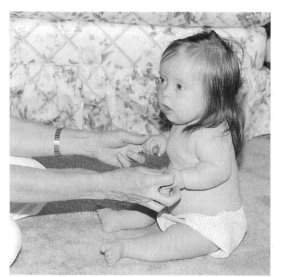

(fig. 3.6)

her to maintain sitting if her hands are propped on her legs because the surface to prop on is small, her thighs are curved rather than flat, and it is not especially motivating for her to stay in the position.

If your child likes to sit, you can have her hold your thumbs to maintain the position (Activity #4). *(See figure 3.6.)* It is best for both of you to be face to face at eye level. For example, you can place her on the kitchen table and you can sit in a chair. This position is not recommended if your child resists sitting and arches back.

If your child likes to reach and play in sitting rather than prop, you can support her trunk and place a play gym in front of her (Activity #6). The toys need to be very close so she can reach them while sitting up tall. If the toys are too far away, she will need to lean her trunk forward to reach them.

Once your child is able to straighten the middle trunk area, she needs to develop the strength to maintain the position over time. To do this, you can either seat her in a high chair or place her on the floor in front of the couch or other piece of furniture with firm, soft support down to the floor (Activities 5 & 7). With this support behind her back, it is easier for her to lift her trunk up straight and hold it there. With practice, she will be able to hold her back up straight for 10-15 minutes. When she is able to hold her back straight consistently, less support can be provided.

sitting with low trunk support

When your child can sit well with support at her waist, you can either support her at the sides of her hips or with one hand below her navel and the other hand across her buttocks. With this support, your child will learn to sit with her entire back straight.

When providing low trunk support, your child's buttocks need to be positioned up straight rather than slouched back. If they lean back, her trunk will be rounded and she will not be able to sit tall. Refer to Activities 8 & 9 for instructions.

sitting with support to balance herself

By this time your child knows the sitting position, how to play in it, and how to hold her trunk up straight with support. She knows the centered or balanced position. She is now ready to work on balancing herself when she leans to the side or backward. She needs to be given strategic support so she can work on moving back to the center. She also will learn she needs to move herself back to the center rather than depending on you to move her.

The support you provide will depend on how far she leans and how quickly she falls. If she leans slowly and in the mild range, you can firmly support her at her hips and see if she will move back to the center. If she falls fast, you need to catch her to stop the fall and then hold her in this position. From here, wait to see if she can move herself back to the center. Refer to Activities 7-10 to learn what support to provide so she can regain her balance. As your child learns how to regain her balance, less support is needed to help her move back to the center.

Since your child has shorter arms, using her hands to catch herself when she falls will be less effective. She will need to learn to use her trunk to balance herself effectively and maintain the centered position. When sitting on a firm surface and playing with toys, she will lose her balance frequently, and this is the best time to work on how she can move to recover her balance.

sitting without support

After your child has practiced these supported sitting positions, you will notice she begins to sit with less support and sometimes briefly without support. She may continue to sit when you slide the sofa cushion away from behind her buttocks. Or, she may prop her hands on her thighs and sit while you entertain her. You will need to watch her cues because she will show you when she is ready to learn to sit without support.

(fig. 3.7)

When she starts sitting by herself, you need to help her gradually increase the time she can sit. The longer she can sit, the more confidence she will have in her ability to sit. To help her sit for longer periods, position yourself at eye level to her and entertain her. If you are above her, she will look up at you and lose her balance. You can sing songs with hand motions (Itsy Bitsy Spider), play pat-a-cake or peek-a-boo, or talk to her. Try to keep the play calm, quiet, and centered in the midline. When she is comfortable and confident with sitting, she can play with toys or hold rings or lightweight rattles. *(See figure 3.7.)*

When she practices sitting by herself, she will be figuring out how to be stable and balance herself. She will experiment to see how far she can lift her trunk before she falls backwards and how much she can play with her hands before she falls over. She probably will learn that if she leans her trunk forward a little, she will not fall backwards. You can use pillows around her so she is safe while practicing on her own. This is the time to let her discover what she needs to do with her body to sit by herself.

All of a sudden, she will consistently sit when you place her in sitting. She will still need supervision, though, until she develops effective balance when leaning in all directions, particularly backwards. For all children, learning to regain balance when they lean backwards is the hardest.

activity guidelines

You need to use the supported sitting positions while she is playing. Then she will become used to sitting, learn what the position is, how to use it, and how to hold it. She will learn the value of the sitting position for playing and will become motivated to sit.

When she is practicing sitting, take her shirt off to check her back. By looking at her trunk from the side, you can see which section she holds up straight and which sections are rounded.

Use a firm surface for sitting—the floor, a table, or high chair. With a firm base, your child will learn to sit up straight and she will know when she is off balance and try to move back to the center. On a soft surface, such as a bed or sofa cushion, she will easily lean and fall to the side because the surface will give as she leans into it. She will have difficulty balancing herself, as the surface will not allow her to move back to the center when she is off balance.

Move at your child's pace and challenge her when she is ready to learn the next step. Sitting takes time to develop properly and you need to complete each step before moving on to the next step. This will help your child avoid common "bad habits," including leaning the trunk forward, holding the legs wide apart, and stiffening the knees.

Use toys appropriate to the level of sitting you are working on. When your child is using her hands to prop or hold on, use toys or entertainment she can watch. If she is reaching for toys, suspend them on a play gym so she can touch and watch them rather than hold them. When she is watching toys, keep them at eye level or lower.

When she is working on holding her trunk up and balancing herself, it is best to do simple, calm hand activities. For example, a good activity is propping and playing with an activity center because it supports her in the centered position and keeps her attention focused in the center. If she played with a rattle, waving her arm and shaking the toy would make it harder for her to hold her trunk up straight and maintain her balance.

temperament

Your child's temperament will influence her desire to sit. If your child is an **observer,** she will love to sit and will sit as long as she can physically tolerate it. Since she is motivated to sit, she will work to maintain her balance in sitting. She will enjoy playing in sitting.

If your child is **motor driven,** she will not like to sit for long. She will prefer to move out of the position. She will need the best motivators to entertain her so she uses the position as long as possible. For example, Samantha was motor driven and sitting had no value to her at first. She felt stuck and confined in the position. She preferred to roll, pivot, or move on her belly. When she did not want to sit, she would arch her back or scoot her buttocks forward to move out of sitting. Later, she worked on balancing herself in sitting when she was motivated to use the position.

activity #2

Supported Sitting, Holding onto the Low Bar of a Play Gym

1. Sit on the floor with your legs crossed in front of you.
2. Place your child in supported sitting in front of your legs with her body sideways to your body.
3. Place the Tyco Sesame Street Baby Play Gym with the cross bar in front of her and help her hold the bar. While she is holding onto the bar, spin the toys to entertain her.
4. Place one of your hands horizontally against her back with the lower edge of your hand at her waist. Place your other hand horizontally against her stomach with the lower edge of your hand at her waist.
5. Encourage her to hold on and hold her head and trunk up tall for as long as tolerated.

activity #3

Supported Sitting, Propping on an Activity Center

1. Sitting on your heels, place your child sitting on the floor in front of you.
2. Place an activity center ("Busy Box") over her legs. Put a large book under the front edge of the activity center to keep it level and at waist height.
3. Place your hands on each side of your child's trunk at waist level and hold the activity center. Pull it so the edge is against the front of her trunk and she is sitting tall. (*See figure 3.4.*)

4. Prop her hands on the activity center with her hands shoulder width apart. Entertain her by playing with the various activities.
5. Encourage her to prop, play, and sit tall for as long as tolerated.
6. When she uses this position well, the activity center can be lowered to rest on her thighs. Use a smaller book to support the front edge. Place your hands on each side of your child's trunk at hip level and pull back and downward. Encourage her to prop, play, and sit tall.

activity #4 **Supported Sitting with Hand Support**
1. Place your child in supported sitting on a firm surface (coffee table or kitchen table) and position yourself in front of her at eye level.
2. Have your child hold your thumbs and help her as needed to hold on.
3. Position her arms with her hands in front of her chest and at the level of her nipples.
4. Entertain her by talking or singing to her. For variety, play pat-a-cake, clap her hands together, play so-big, or move her arms as you sing songs.
5. Encourage her to sit tall and hold on to maintain the sitting position.
6. If her buttocks slide on the table, place dycem, Easy Liner™, or Grip Liner™ under them.

activity #5 **Supported Sitting in the High Chair**
1. Put dycem or a similar material on the seat of the high chair.
2. Place your child's buttocks against the back of the seat. Buckle the hip strap and tighten it.
3. Hold her trunk up straight and place a rolled-up towel on each side of her trunk to fill up the space.
4. Put on the tray and place it close to her chest. If there is space between her trunk and the tray, use a small rolled-up towel to fill the space.
5. Place toys on the tray and play with her.
6. Encourage her to use this sitting position for play as long as tolerated.

activity #6 **Supported Sitting and Reaching for Toys on a Play Gym**
1. Sit on the floor with your legs crossed in front of you.
2. Place your child sitting in front of your legs, with her body sideways to yours.
3. Place a play gym in front of your child, making sure it is close enough that she can reach the toys and keep her trunk up straight.
4. Place one of your hands horizontally against her back with the lower edge of your hand at her waist. Place your other hand horizontally against her stomach with the lower edge of your hand at her waist.
5. Encourage her to straighten her trunk and use her hands to reach and play.
6. When she uses this position well, lower your hands to hip level.

activity #7 **Supported sitting with back support against the couch**
1. Place your child sitting on the floor in front of the couch. Place her buttocks and trunk up straight against the couch.
2. Sit on the floor in front of her with your legs crossed.

3. Place an activity center across her lap with a book under the front edge to keep it level. Hold the activity center on the sides and gently push it against your child's belly and downward. This will stabilize her hips so she can also begin to work on keeping her balance if she leans to the side.

4. Encourage her to sit with her trunk up straight against the couch and prop and play with the activity center. Help her maintain the position as long as tolerated.

5. If she leans to one side slowly, firmly support the opposite hip to see if she will move back to the center. If she leans to one side quickly, use the fingertips of one hand to catch her at her shoulder and use your other hand to firmly support the opposite hip to see if she will move back to the center.

activity #8   Supported Sitting with Hip Support

1. Sit on the floor with your legs in front of you.
2. Place your child sitting in between your legs, facing away from you.
3. Place a play gym or high toy in front of her.
4. Place your hands horizontally on the sides of her hips and hold firmly.
5. Encourage her to sit tall and play with the toys.
6. If she leans back or to the side slowly, see if she will move back to the center.
7. If she leans back quickly, catch her with the palm of one hand and place your other hand below her navel and see if she will move back to the center. If she leans to the side quickly, use the fingertips of one hand to catch her at her shoulder and use your other hand to firmly support the opposite hip to see if she will move back to the center.
8. This activity can also be done with your child sitting sideways in front of you. Place one of your hands horizontally below her navel and your other hand horizontally across her buttocks.

activity #9   Supported Sitting with a Sofa Cushion for Support *(see fig. 3.8)*

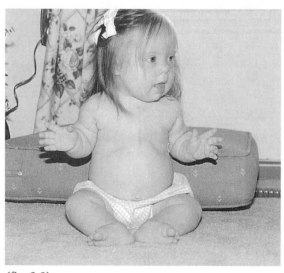

1. Place your child sitting on the floor with a sofa cushion behind her buttocks. Stabilize the cushion against furniture or the wall to prevent sliding.
2. Position yourself in front of her or sitting at her side.
3. Make sure her buttocks are up straight and firmly pressed against the sofa cushion.
4. Place a toy such as an activity center across her lap, or place a high toy between her legs and have her play.
5. See if she can maintain the position without you holding her. If not, place your hands horizontally on her hips. Take the support away periodically to see if she can sit briefly.
6. If she leans back slowly, place your hand below her navel and see if she will move back to the center. If she leans back quickly, catch her with the palm of one hand and place your other hand below her navel and see if she will move back to the center.

(fig. 3.8)

7. If she leans to the side slowly, hold the opposite hip and see if she will move back to the center. If she leans to the side quickly, use the fingertips of one hand to catch her at her shoulder and use your other hand to firmly support the opposite hip to see if she will move back to the center.

8. When she can maintain the position well, give her a rattle and see if she can play with the toy while maintaining her balance.

activity #10 **Sitting with Her Hands Propped on Her Legs** *(see fig. 3.9)*

1. Sit on the floor with your legs crossed.
2. Place your child sitting on the floor, facing you, with her knees bent.
3. Prop her hands on her thighs and see if she can hold the position.

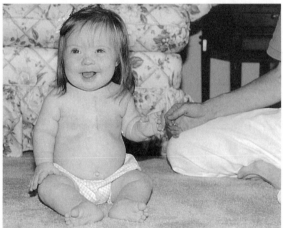

4. Entertain her with toys at eye level or lie on your stomach so you are at eye level. If you have her look up above eye level, she will lose her balance and fall back.
5. Encourage her to hold the position as long as tolerated. Begin with 10 seconds and work toward 2-3 minutes.
6. If she leans back or to the side, follow steps 6 and 7 above.
7. When she can hold the position for 2-3 minutes, see if she can let go with one hand to touch or hold a lightweight toy or bubbles.
8. With practice, she will learn to sit for 5 minutes or longer and will not need to prop her hands on her legs to maintain the position.

(fig. 3.9)

MOVING TO SIT WITH SUPPORT

Your child has learned to pull to sit from back-lying using both hands. The next goal is to pull to sit by pulling with one arm and propping on the other arm as she is moved from back-lying to side-lying and then up to sitting. By teaching her this new method, she will learn to move to sit by moving to the side. This will prepare her to move to sit by herself the proper way.

If she does not learn this method, she may develop her own method of moving to sit by moving her legs wide apart and doing a wide split as she moves from her stomach up to sitting. When she does this, she will hold her knees stiff and straight. Children with Down syndrome can use this method due to hypotonia and increased joint flexibility in the hips. If they only use this method of moving to sitting, however, they will continue to use the wide leg position and stiff knees when standing and walking. They also will not learn how to shift weight from one side to the other, rotate the trunk, and use the arms in moving from one position to another.

Learning to move to sitting the right way is critical for the development of future skills, including moving out of sitting, moving in and out of kneeling, pulling to stand, standing balance, and walking.

When your child can pull to sit with two-hand support, she is ready to begin practicing pulling to sit by moving to the side. You will move her from back-lying to side-lying and then up to sitting. She initially will need to learn to move through these positions as she is moved up to sitting. This will be new for her and she may need extra support until she becomes familiar with the sequence.

In back-lying, she will hold on to your thumb with one hand. With her holding your thumb, you will move her over to her other side and lift her so she can prop on her hand. From this position, you will help her pull up to sitting in the centered position. *(See figures 3.10, 3.11, and 3.12.)* In the beginning, you will move her quickly through the positions so she learns how to move her arms and trunk as

(fig. 3.10)

she is moved up to sitting. When she knows what to do, you can move her slower and she will need to use more control with her arms and trunk. By teaching her to move to sit using this sequence, she will learn to hold onto your thumb and pull to the side, use her other arm to prop and push upward, use her stomach muscles to move up to sit, and pull upward and over to the centered sitting position.

Your child will not learn to move to sitting by herself during this stage. She will learn the sequence of moving to the side when moving from back-lying to side-lying to sitting. This is the time to teach her the preferred way to move to sitting before she figures out the split method.

She will learn to move to sitting by herself in the next stage. When she learns to do it, she probably will not do it from back-lying. Most children with Down syndrome learn to move to sitting from hands and knees (quadruped) and some children move to sit from stomach-lying. Each child learns to sit using her own preferred method. As long as your child learns to move to sitting by moving to the side, it does not matter which method she chooses.

activity guidelines

You can use toys to encourage moving to sitting, but it is difficult because your hands are busy supporting your child. If you practice moving to sitting when changing her diaper, when picking her up, or when she wants to sit up, she is naturally motivated and you do not need toys. You can, however, try placing a toy at her side to encourage her to move to her side, and when she moves there, you can move it to where she can play with it in sitting. When she sits, let her play with it.

Practice moving to sitting often during the day when your child wants to do it. She probably will do it best on the first or second try and will not want to do it over and over.

Practice moving over each side to see if one side is easier. If one arm is weaker, she will generally do better moving over that side and using the stronger hand to hold on and pull. It will be easier for her to use the weaker arm for propping. Practice moving over this side until she can do it well and then you can practice moving to sit over the other side. In the meantime, the weaker hand will become stronger.

(fig. 3.11)

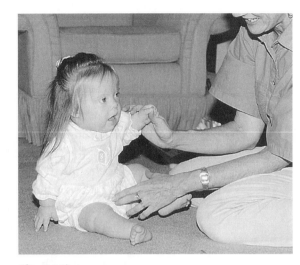

(fig. 3.12)

temperament

If your child is ***motor driven,*** she will like the movement of going from one position to another. Although she may not want to stay in sitting, she will like pulling up, moving over to the side, and then moving over to sitting. She will not be fearful and will go with the flow of movement. If your child is an ***observer,*** she may resist the movement initially or need practice to become familiar with it. She may be fearful with the position changes, but once she is sitting, she will be happy.

activity #11

Moving from Back-lying to Side-lying to Sitting

1. Sit on your heels on the floor.
2. Place your child on the floor on her back, facing you.
3. Moving over her right side:
   a. Place the thumb of your right hand in the palm of her left hand. Gently pull upward on her hand and have her grasp your thumb strongly. If she cannot maintain the grasp, place your fingers on top of her hand to help her hold on.
   b. Place your left hand across her hips to stabilize her buttocks and prevent sliding downward.
   c. Pull upward and to your left with her left hand and move her onto her right side so she is propping on her right elbow or hand. (In the beginning, she may prop on her elbow; later, she will prop on her hand.)
   d. Pull upward and to your right with her left hand to move her to the sitting position.
   e. If it is too hard for her to come to sit from a completely horizontal position, prop her up on a pillow so she can try from a reclined position.
4. Moving over her left side:
   a. Place the thumb of your left hand in the palm of her right hand. Gently pull upward on her hand and have her grasp your thumb strongly.
   b. Place your right hand across her hips to stabilize her buttocks and prevent sliding downward.
   c. Pull upward and to your right with her right hand and move her onto her left side so she is propping on her left elbow or hand.

d. Pull upward and to your left with her right hand to move her to the sitting position.

e. If this is too hard for her, prop her up on a pillow and try again.

MOVING OUT OF SITTING

When your child can sit by herself or close to it, she needs to be taught to move out of sitting. The goal will be to learn to move out of sitting with support by moving to the side. To do this, she will need support to rotate her trunk, prop both hands to one side, and move down to the floor. She will need to be taught this method because she would feel too unstable to initiate it on her own.

Your child needs to have a way to move out of sitting when she wants to or she will figure out her own way, which could lead to bad habits. She might learn to fall backwards, especially if you are behind her. Or, she might move forward and do a wide split with her legs to move down to her stomach. She will prefer to use forward or backward movements rather than moving to the side. The split method tends to be preferred, but should be avoided for the reasons already discussed.

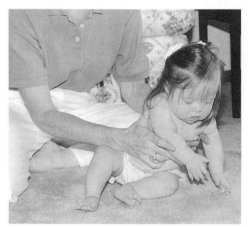 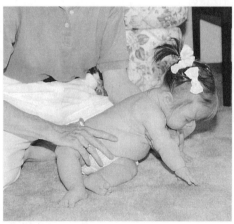 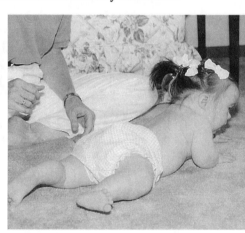

(fig. 3.13) *(fig. 3.14)* *(fig. 3.15)*

At first, your child will need full support and it is best to practice on the bed, since it is a soft, comfortable surface. You will need to move her slowly so she gradually gets used to how each movement feels. Begin by placing both of her hands to one side and propping them on the bed beside her leg. With her arms in this position, she will need to rotate her trunk a lot—probably more than she has ever before rotated it. If she feels stiff or resists the movement, twist her trunk gradually until it becomes easier. After a few practices, she will tolerate it. With her hands propped on the bed, wait and see what she will do. She may fall down and roll over to her stomach *(see figures 3.13, 3.14, and 3.15)* or she may stay in the propped position for a few seconds. She may feel stuck and not know what to do. She might be scared to feel off balance.

Your child will first learn to move from sitting down to the bed by falling. Her elbows will bend and she will fall down to the bed. She probably will move quickly, so you can slow her down by holding her arms. After she falls down over her arms, her buttocks will roll over so she is on her stomach. Her legs will follow her buttocks and generally will not get caught underneath her. When she is familiar with moving down, wait for her to move down rather than helping her. She will learn to lift her head and lower her arms as she is moving down to the bed. When she moves slower and with control, she can practice moving out of sitting on the carpet. Always practice on a padded surface so she is safe.

Your child will learn to move out of sitting by herself during the next stage. She will be able to sit and change positions whenever she wants to. She does not need to do it the perfect way you practiced it. As long as she moves partially to the side and can move over her legs with her knees bent, she has learned an acceptable method of moving out of sitting.

activity guidelines

To help motivate your child to move out of sitting, use her favorite toys. Watch where you put the toy, because she will move to the toy. If you put it in front of her, she will move forward; if you put it to the side, she will move to the side. Place the toy just out of reach. If it is too far away, she will not even try. If it is just out of reach, she will keep reaching for it and will move to get it if she thinks it is worth it. If she quits, try again or get a better toy.

Try to use soft toys so she will not get hurt if she falls on them. If the toy is hard, be ready to move it as she moves out of sitting. She will move farther than you think.

Practice moving out of sitting when she becomes fussy in sitting and wants to change positions. You can also encourage her to move out of sitting if you place a favorite toy to the side of her leg.

Try moving out of sitting over both sides and see if one side is easier. If one arm is stronger, it is usually better to move over that side first because her stronger arm can help lower her down better.

See if your child moves back up to sitting after you prop her hands beside her leg. She might use her hands to push herself back up to sitting. If she does, congratulate her for using her arms so well! However, to help her learn to move down to her stomach, you will need to place her hands further to the side to make it harder to push up to sitting and easier to go down to her stomach.

temperament

If your child is an **observer,** she will not like the feeling of being off balance or falling. She also may not want to move out of sitting because she likes to sit. When you help her move out of sitting, she might get fussy or scared. She might feel stuck when you place both hands to the side of her leg. You will need to support her until she gets used to it. She will do better if you are in front of her face and arms so she can move to you. For example, Katie was scared when moving out of sitting for the first time. She was able to sit with stability and was scared to be positioned off balance. With practice and with her mother in front of her, she learned to tolerate moving out of sitting.

If your child is **motor driven,** she will like falling out of sitting and will enjoy the ride.

activity #12

Moving from Sitting to Stomach-lying
1. Moving over child's right side
   a. Place your child sitting on the bed with a toy on her right side and out of reach.
   b. Position yourself behind your child. Lift both arms and twist her trunk, placing her hands on the bed on her right side, in between her right hip and knee.

  c. See if she tries to move to the toy. If not, place her hands farther to the side and encourage her to move downward to the toy.

  d. If she is scared or does not want to move downward to the toy, position yourself on her right side in front of her arms and face. She will feel better seeing you and moving toward you. Gently hold her elbows and rock them to help her move down to her stomach.

  e. With practice, she will move down by herself after you place her hands. Later, she will move down all by herself.

  f. When she is able to move out of sitting on the bed, you can use a padded surface like the carpet.

2. Moving over child's left side

  a. Place your child sitting on the bed with a toy on her left side and out of reach.

  b. Position yourself behind your child. Lift both arms and twist her trunk, placing her hands on the bed on her left side, in between her left hip and knee.

  c. See if she tries to move to the toy. If not, place her hands farther to the side and encourage her to move downward to the toy.

  d. If she is scared or does not want to move downward to the toy, position yourself on her left side in front of her arms and face. Gently hold her elbows and rock them to help her move down to her stomach.

  e. With practice, she will move down by herself after you place her hands. Later, she will move down all by herself.

  f. When she is able to move out of sitting on the bed, you can use a padded surface like the carpet.

QUADRUPED

When your child is able to prop on her hands in stomach-lying, she is ready to begin practicing the *quadruped* position—getting on hands and knees. The goal will be for your child to maintain the quadruped position when you place her in it. The quadruped position will help her learn to hold her legs together and take weight on them with her hips and knees bent.

Using the quadruped position will be difficult for your child because it will be hard for her to move her legs into the position. When she props on her hands in stomach-lying, her legs will be wide apart, with her knees turned outward and resting on the surface. She will not initially have the leg strength or know how to move her legs into the quadruped position. She will need to learn to bend her hips and knees, move her knees together, and hold this position. Using the supported quadruped position is the best way to learn how to do this.

The best way to practice supported quadruped is to put a sofa cushion on the floor and put your child's hands on the cushion and her knees on the floor. *(See figure 3.16.)* With her hands on the cushion, her shoulders are positioned higher than her buttocks. This puts more weight on the legs and helps to keep the knees bent. There is also less weight on the arms so she can more easily use her hands to play.

When you first use the position, you need to hold your child's knees together, position them under her belly, and lean her buttocks on her heels. With

(fig. 3.16)

this support, her hips and knees will bend and she can work on holding her knees together. Without support, her knees may slide apart until her buttocks are on the floor. Begin with consistent support and then decrease the support as she learns to hold her knees together and bent by herself.

Over time, the height of the cushion can be lowered until your child can be placed in quadruped with her hands and knees on the floor. To maintain this position, she will need to develop arm and leg strength and use her stomach muscles to balance herself. Once she has become familiar with the position, she will rock back and forth and will try to move into the position by herself.

To move into quadruped, she will need to be able to push up on her hands and hold that position. She also will need to bend her hips and knees and move her knees together. She probably will develop the arm position first. To test to see if she can move her legs into position, wait for her to prop on her hands and then lift her belly. With this support, see if she will move her legs into position. If she can, she has the arm and leg movements needed to move into quadruped and just needs to learn to put them together. This usually happens in the next stage.

activity guidelines

Use the supported quadruped position as an alternative position for play. Choose toys depending on what your child is practicing. When supported in quadruped on the cushion, you can use any entertaining toy, such as a pop-up box, because she will easily be able to use her hands. When you put her in a position with her trunk more horizontal, it will be harder to use her hands. To help her maintain the position, use toys that she can watch. You can also have her prop on a busy box/activity center if she wants to play with her hands.

Encourage your child to use the position as long as tolerated. When she is no longer interested in playing in the position, help her move to sitting. For example, when Junior first started using supported quadruped, he would only tolerate the position for brief periods. He would arch his back and keep looking at me when he wanted to get out of the position. He did not care what motivator I used at that point. He was ready to change positions and he was persistent with giving me the sign.

Take steps to prevent your child from stiffening her hips and knees, causing her to fall out of the position. To avoid these leg movements, prepare her before you put her in the quadruped position. Pick her up and hold her across your lap. Place one arm under her chest and with your other hand, bend her hips and knees and hold her knees together. When she is relaxed with her legs in this position, place her in supported quadruped on the sofa cushion. Then hold her buttocks down firmly over her feet to maintain her hips and knees in the bent position.

temperament

If your child is *motor driven,* she will probably develop quadruped sooner because she will experiment with moving her legs and be playful with the movement of rocking. If your child is an *observer,* she may wait to use it until it serves a purpose such as in moving to sit or pulling to stand.

activity #13 **Supported Quadruped on a Cushion**

1. Place a sofa cushion on the floor or rug. Position your child with her elbows or hands propped on the cushion and her knees on the floor. Support her knees together and under her belly.
2. Sit on your heels behind her. Move your knees around her legs to hold her knees together.
3. Place a toy on top of the cushion and entertain her while she maintains the position.
4. If her legs stiffen and straighten, reposition her knees under her belly and hold her buttocks over her feet firmly.
5. When she is able to hold the position, you can sit on the floor beside her and give intermittent support to hold her knees together as needed.
6. When she is tired of being in this position, move her to sitting by holding her buttocks and lowering them to the side and down to the floor.

activity #14 **Supported Quadruped on the Floor**

1. Place your child on the floor on her stomach, then sit in front of her.
2. Wait for her to push up on her hands.
3. Put your hand on her belly and press your fingertips into her belly and lift it up.
4. As you lift her belly, see if she bends her hips and knees and moves her knees together to move into the quadruped position.
5. If she does not move her legs, help her.
6. When she is positioned on hands and knees, hold her buttocks and rock them back toward her feet. Gently rock her forward and back, keeping her buttocks over her legs. If her buttocks are moved forward of her knees, she will fall forward.

SUPPORTED KNEELING

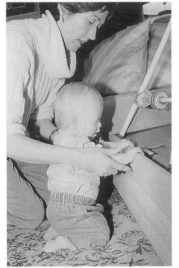

(fig. 3.17)

Supported kneeling is resting on your knees and maintaining the position by leaning against or holding onto a surface such as a sofa or a footstool. Your child will be ready to use this position after she has used the quadruped position. Or if she resisted supported quadruped and stiffened her knees, you can try this position and she may like it better. The goal will be to teach your child to use the supported kneeling position when you place her in it. By kneeling, she will strengthen her legs as she learns to hold them together and take weight on them with her knees bent. This will help prepare her to stand properly.

This position is most easily done using your sofa with the seat cushion removed. The chair should be at nipple or armpit level. Place your child against the sofa with her knees on the floor and her arms on the seat of the sofa. At first, you will need to support her legs to keep her knees together or they will slide apart.

Once she is able to hold her knees together, she will be ready to learn how to hold on with her arms and hands. (See figure 3.17.) The sofa bed type of sofa works best because the frame of the sofa has an edge to hold onto. A regular sofa is flat and is harder to hold.

When your child can maintain supported kneeling, she will learn to move her buttocks up and down. She will begin kneeling with her buttocks resting on her heels. She will experiment with moving her buttocks up until she is able to kneel up straight with her trunk, buttocks, and thighs in a straight line. Then she will play with moving her buttocks up and down. The up and down movements will strengthen her stomach, buttocks, and hip muscles. When she is tired of supported kneeling, you can help her move to sitting by moving to the side. She will learn to do it by herself in the next stage.

activity guidelines

Let your child play with any type of toy she wants using supported kneeling. At first, she will use one or both hands to support herself, so offer toys based on how much arm support she needs. She can look at a book, play with a pop-up box or activity center, touch a baby doll or stuffed animal, listen to music or a See N' Say, or play with a xylophone. With practice, she will hold on with one hand and use her other hand to play.

Use a carpeted floor so your child will be more comfortable. If she resists the position, try using extra padding on the carpet, like a blanket or comforter.

temperament

If your child is an **observer**, she will like kneeling because she can stay in one place and play with toys. If your child is **motor driven**, she may like it because she can move up and down. If she is really active, she may pop up to standing.

activity #15

Supported Kneeling *(see figs. 3.18, 3.19, 3.20)*
1. Use the sofa with the seat cushion removed. Place your child on her knees in front of the sofa and place her arms on top of the seat of the sofa.
2. Sit on the floor behind your child.
3. Make sure her knees are together. Support them if she cannot maintain this position.
4. Put toys on the sofa and encourage her to play in supported kneeling. Have her hold on with her hands to maintain herself in the position. She can hold on to the edge of the seat or place her hands on top of the seat.

(fig. 3.18)   *(fig. 3.19)*   *(fig. 3.20)*

5. She will move her buttocks up and down, moving from resting her buttocks on her heels to kneeling up straight.

6. When she is ready to move out of kneeling, help her move from kneeling to sitting.

7. Moving over her right side *(see figs. 3.18, 3.19, 3.20)*:

    a. Place your hands on her hips and move them to the right side and down to the floor. Make sure her knees stay together.

    b. As you are moving her down to the floor, move her left hip toward you until she is sitting sideways in front of you.

8. Moving over her left side:

    a. Place your hands on her hips and move them to the left side and down to the floor. Make sure her knees stay together.

    b. As you are moving her down to the floor, move her right hip toward you until she is sitting sideways in front of you.

SITTING ON A BENCH

When your child is able to sit well on the floor, the next challenge is for her to sit on a bench with her hips and knees bent 90 degrees. *(See figure 3.21.)* This is called 90/90 sitting. You can build a bench the appropriate height or you can improvise and find something around the house that is the right height. Using 90/90 sitting, your child will learn to sit with her trunk up straight, hold her legs together, balance with her legs in this position, and take weight on her legs with her knees bent. Her feet will be flat on the floor and she will need to actively use her feet to help her maintain her balance when she leans forward. Later, 90/90 sitting will be used to teach her to pull to stand and lower herself back down to sitting.

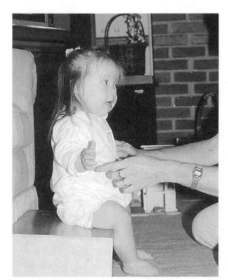

(fig. 3.21)

Your child can continue to sit on the floor to play but when you are with her, you can use 90/90 sitting to further refine her sitting skills. When sitting on the floor, your child will continue to sit with a wide base and even if you narrow the base by straightening her knees, she will move them back into the original position. When she uses 90/90 sitting, her legs will be positioned closer together and she will learn to balance with a smaller base. The base is smaller because bringing the legs together makes the width smaller and sitting on the bench makes the front-to-back length (buttocks-to-knees) shorter.

In 90/90 sitting, she will also learn to hold her trunk up straight because, if she leans her trunk forward, she will fall forward off the bench. When she sits on the floor, it is easy to lean forward and she may do it to feel more secure. By practicing sitting tall in 90/90 sitting, she will strengthen her back muscles and learn to maintain her trunk up straight. This will carry over to sitting on the floor.

When you begin using 90/90 sitting, supervise your child closely. She will easily fall forward or backward until she learns how to lift her trunk to the balanced position. You need to keep your eyes on her at all times because she could fall in a split second and become scared. If you help her learn to use the position properly, she will be comfortable with using it and learn what she needs to do to maintain it.

It is best to start slowly with a 2-3 inch bench or a thick book or phone book. Your child's knees will be bent about 45 degrees so her base will be longer (buttocks to feet) and the position will be easier to get used to. She may want to prop her hands on her thighs for support. Have toys or yourself at eye level to her for entertainment. If your child is scared, hold her hands to help her adjust to the position. Focus on building her control and confidence in using the position.

When she can sit well using the 2-3 inch bench, progress to a bench whose height best supports 90/90 sitting (usually 4-6 inches). For 90/90 sitting, the correct height of the bench is determined by the leg measurement from the back of the knee to the heel of the foot. This is best measured with your child sitting on a bench with her knee bent 90 degrees and her foot flat on the floor. If the bench is too high, she will be on her toes, which will make her insecure and unstable. Her feet need to be flat on the floor so she can work on her balance using a stable position. It is best if she is barefoot so her feet do not slide forward. Socks with non skid soles are another option, but regular socks will cause her feet to slide and she will not be able to use her feet effectively to balance herself.

The sitting surface of the bench should be at least 12 inches from side to side and 10 inches from front to back. Your child will feel less stable if the surface is smaller. Do not use a chair with back and side supports, because she will learn to lean against the supports rather than sit tall and learn to balance.

Place the bench on a firm surface. If you place it on the rug, make sure it does not rock. If it rocks, your child will not feel secure enough to try this activity. Place dycem, Easy Liner™, or Rubbermaid Grip Liner™ on the top of the bench to prevent her buttocks from sliding. Since her thigh length is short, place her thighs on the bench with her knees at the front edge to give her the longest base possible on which to balance.

activity #16 — Sitting on a 2-3 Inch Bench

1. Place your child sitting on the floor in front of you, facing you. Place her on a phone book or little bench that is approximately 2-3 inches high. Place dycem or a similar material under her buttocks to prevent sliding.
2. Place her knees at the front edge of the bench and her heels on the floor in front of her.
3. Position yourself or place a toy at eye level to her.
4. Place your fingertips on her chest to help her lift her trunk to the right position and then let go. See if she can hold her trunk up in this position. She will tend to lean her trunk forward but will learn that she will fall forward if she leans too far forward.
5. See how she adjusts to this position. Hold her hips or her hands to help her get used to the position. Let go when she is ready. Entertain her with toys or songs so she can watch while maintaining the position. Use quiet, calm toys. Blow bubbles and catch one bubble with the wand and place it in front of her hand to pop it. Or sing songs with hand movements she can watch.
6. Closely supervise her in this position until she learns to maintain the sitting position.
7. When she can hold the position, encourage her to play with lightweight toys, such as blocks, rattles, and rings, and see if she can continue to maintain her balance.

activity #17 **Sitting on a Bench with Her Feet on the Floor (90/90 Sitting):**

1. Follow steps 1-7 above, but this time seat your child on a 4-6 inch bench. See above for instructions on determining the proper height of the bench. Position her knees bent 90 degress with her heels under her knees and her feet flat on the floor.

8. When your child can maintain this position well, encourage her to reach forward, to each side, and behind to grasp a toy or pop a bubble. She will need to work on maintaining her balance while reaching. It will be easier for her to pop bubbles when reaching; when she is stable reaching for bubbles, she can reach for lightweight toys.

SUPPORTED STANDING

During this stage supported standing is defined as standing with the legs properly positioned and holding on with both hands. Your child will be ready to practice supported standing skills when she can maintain 90/90 sitting on a bench. The goal will be to learn to stand properly and maintain the position with hand support.

The best way to begin supported standing is to help your child pull to stand from 90/90 sitting and then lower herself back to 90/90 sitting. *(See figure 3.22.)* In this activity, she uses supported standing and the focus is on bending and straightening her knees as she moves up and down. It will be easier for her to straighten her knees and harder for her to bend her knees. By moving up and down, she will learn to bend her knees more easily. This is a critical movement to work on at this stage.

To stand properly, your child needs to learn:
1. **to hold on to a support,**
2. **to keep her knees and feet positioned under her hips with her feet pointing straight ahead, and**
3. **to be able to bend her knees slightly rather than hold them stiff.**

 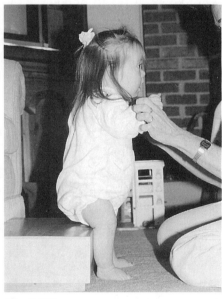

If a child begins standing before her legs are strong enough or does not learn to stand properly, she will develop bad habits. She will stand with her feet wide apart and turned outward, her knees will be stiff, and she will lean her belly against a support.

It is important to help your child learn to use her stomach muscles to balance rather than leaning against a support. The best way to do this is to have your child hold on to your thumbs instead of you holding her hands or wrists. *(See figure 3.23.)* When holding on, her hands need to be in front of

(fig. 3.22)   *(fig. 3.23)*

her chest, and no higher than her shoulders. With this hand support, she will be responsible for moving herself back to the center if she leans sideways or backwards.

Later, when she knows how to hold on in standing, she can hold on to a surface with an edge. An edge gives her better gripping and holding power because she can put her fingers around the edge. Examples of surfaces with an edge include: a laundry basket, an open drawer, a crate, a toy box, or a plastic storage box.

When she is in supported standing, look at her from the front and side to see how her hips, knees, and feet line up. Her knees and feet should be in a straight line under her hips. If she stands with her buttocks leaning back and her knees stiff, support her buttocks over her knees and feet to help her stand properly.

Her knees should be a little bent or easily able to bend rather than stiff and rigid. If you place a bench behind her knees, she will feel more stable and bend her knees more easily. Make sure the bench is secure and does not move or slide on the floor. If she feels it move, she will feel insecure and stiffen her knees. Using the bench also allows her to sit down when she is ready to move out of standing.

Watch your child's feet closely and reposition them if she moves them. You need to begin teaching her early to stand with this narrow base. With her feet in this position, she will learn to move her hips, knees, and feet properly to develop the strength and balance needed for supported standing.

activity guidelines

Be prepared to be the primary motivator, since your child will be standing holding your thumbs and moving from sitting to standing. You can entertain her by singing, talking, saying "up" and "down," or listening to music. You can also help her touch your nose, hair, and parts of your face. You can kiss her hands or belly and play peek-a-boo.

When your child is learning to stand, do not allow her to stand and lean her belly against the sofa. Also avoid supporting her under her arms or at her hips. If she is supported in any of these ways, she will lean into the support rather than learning to use her stomach muscles to balance herself.

For similar reasons, I generally do not recommend using walkers and Jolly Jumpers. They have no therapeutic benefit and will not accelerate the rate at which your child learns to walk. If you choose to use one, adjust the seat so that your child's hips and knees are bent about 90 degrees. Avoid a seat height that encourages her to stand with knees locked and feet wide apart.

When she is learning to stand with support, have your child go barefoot. Then you can observe her feet and see how they are positioned. She will also be able to move them more easily and begin to develop strength and balance. If it is cold, she can wear socks with non skid bottoms. Do not use regular socks because they are slippery. Shoes are not recommended because you cannot see how her feet are positioned inside the shoes. In addition, the firmness of shoes around her ankles would prevent her from moving her ankles, which would make her stiffen her knees and feet.

temperament

If your child is *motor driven,* she will like moving to stand, rocking in standing, and bouncing. She probably will be bored with stationary standing and use it for brief periods. If your child is an *observer,* she will like to stand and will stand for longer periods. She will stand up and sit down if you are playing something fun. She probably will not initiate bouncing but she will dance if you put music on.

activity #18   **Moving from 90/90 Sitting up to Standing and from Standing to Sitting**

1. Sit on the floor with your legs in front of you.
2. Place your child sitting on the floor in front of you, facing you. Place her on a bench with her feet flat on the floor and her knees bent 90 degrees. Secure the bench against furniture or the wall to prevent sliding.
3. Encourage her to hold your thumbs and pull up to stand. Use your fingers to support the tops of her hands if she needs help holding on or maintaining her grasp.
4. She will pull up to stand with her arms and hands and push off with her legs to move into the standing position.
5. When she is standing, move her feet so the back of her legs touches the bench. Place her feet under her hips and pointing straight ahead.
6. Support her hands in front of her chest below shoulder level.
7. After she has been standing for a few seconds, encourage her to sit down on the bench holding your thumbs. Place a toy on the bench and have her move to it. Say "down."
8. If she holds her knees stiff and will not bend them, help her. Hold both of her hands in one of your hands and place your other hand across her hips. Push in at her hips and move her hands down to her waist and pull downward. Wait for her to bend her knees to sit.
9. She needs to learn to pull up to stand and lower herself to sitting. You can say "up" and "down" to cue her. You can repeat this as long as your child wants to do it.

activity #19   **Holding onto Your Thumbs in Supported Standing**

1. Sit on the floor with your legs in front of you.
2. Place your child sitting on the floor in front of you, facing you. Place her on a bench with her feet flat on the floor and her knees bent 90 degrees. Secure the bench against furniture or the wall to prevent sliding.
3. Encourage her to hold your thumbs and pull up to stand. Use your fingers to support the tops of her hands if she needs help holding on or maintaining her grasp.
4. She will pull up to stand with her arms and hands and push off with her legs to move into the standing position.
5. When she is standing, move her feet so the back of her legs touches the bench. Place her feet under her hips and pointing straight ahead.
6. Support her hands in front of her chest below shoulder level.
7. Encourage her to hold on and maintain standing as you sing; play pat-a-cake, peek-a-boo, and so-big; listen to music; or bounce or rock. Make sure you are at eye level to her so she is balanced with her head in the proper position.
8. When she is ready to sit down, encourage her to hold on to your thumbs, bend her knees, and lower herself to sitting on the bench.

➤ Motor Milestone Checklist *on next page.* ➤

Motor Milestone Checklist

Pivoting
- ❏ She reaches to her side at shoulder level
- ❏ She pivots one time
- ❏ She pivots 180 degrees
- ❏ She pivots 360 degrees

Sitting
With support above waist level:
- ❏ She holds bar of play gym
- ❏ She props on activity center across lap
- ❏ She holds your thumbs
- ❏ She reaches for toys on play gym
- ❏ She maintains supported sitting in high chair

With support at hips/buttocks level:
- ❏ She props on activity center across lap
- ❏ She reaches for toys on play gym
- ❏ She sits against couch and holds trunk up with hands propped on activity center
- ❏ She moves back to center if she leans to the side with hips supported
- ❏ She moves back to center if she leans backwards with hips supported

- ❏ She sits for 10 to 15 seconds with both hands propped on her thighs
- ❏ She maintains sitting for 2 to 3 minutes with both hands propped on her thighs
- ❏ She sits without propping 3 to 5 minutes

Moving to sitting
- ❏ She pulls to sit with one hand when moved from back-lying to side-lying to sitting

Moving out of sitting
- ❏ After her hands are placed to one side, she moves down to her stomach

Quadruped
- ❏ She holds supported quadruped on cushion for 20 to 30 seconds
- ❏ She maintains the quadruped position for 20 to 30 seconds

Supported kneeling
- ❏ She holds knees together in supported kneeling
- ❏ She holds on in supported kneeling
- ❏ She moves her buttocks up and down
- ❏ She assists with moving from kneeling to sitting

(continued on next page)

Motor Milestone Checklist *(continued)*

90/90 sitting
❑ She sits on 2 to 3 inch bench for 30 to 60 seconds
❑ She maintains 90/90 sitting for 1 to 2 minutes
❑ She maintains 90/90 sitting with trunk up straight for 5 minutes without propping

Supported standing
❑ She pulls to stand from 90/90 sitting
❑ She bends her knees to lower herself from standing to 90/90 sitting
❑ She holds onto your thumbs in supported standing for 1 to 5 minutes

CHAPTER 4

Stage 4
Crawling, Quadruped, Climbing, Moving in and out of Sitting, Pulling to Stand, and Standing

During this stage, there will be an explosion of skills that your child can do by himself. These skills will make him independent and capable of exploring on his own. You will have many firsts to celebrate. You will experience the first time he crawls, the first time he sits up by himself, and the first time he pulls to stand.

What skill he chooses to do next will be influenced by his temperament, by what he is motivated to do, and by his strength. If he is very motivated to sit, he will find a way to move into sitting. If he is an observer, he will love to sit and play for a long time. If he is motor driven, he may love to crawl. If his arms and legs are strong, he may move into the quadruped position and learn to creep on hands and knees. If he wants to stand, he will learn to pull to stand.

The motor skills to focus on in this fourth stage of development are:
1. crawling,
2. moving into quadruped,
3. creeping,
4. climbing,
5. moving to sit,
6. moving out of sitting,
7. pulling to kneel,
8. pulling to stand,
9. moving from standing to sitting on the floor, and
10. standing holding on.

Your child built the foundation needed to learn these skills in the last stage by learning proper movement patterns for moving in and out of sitting with sup-

Guidelines for **Stage 4**

Do not expect your child to develop the skills of this stage in a particular order. The order will be determined primarily by what he is interested in doing. Casey made this point very clear. She had learned to sit on the floor so I started her practicing belly crawling. Every time we practiced, she looked very sleepy and tired. Then, one day, after practicing 90/90 sitting, I encouraged her to pull up to stand from sitting on the bench. She was ecstatic! She would pull up to stand, stand holding on to the edge of the toy bin, sit down, and then repeat the sequence again for many repetitions. She was showing me what *she* wanted to do and she was energetic again!

Try concentrating first on the easier skills to learn: moving out of sitting, pulling to stand from 90/90 sitting, crawling, pulling to kneel from sitting, standing with support, and moving from standing to 90/90 sitting.

Work on the more difficult skills later: moving into quadruped, moving to sitting, creeping on hands and knees, pulling to kneel from quadruped, and pulling to stand from quadruped. These skills are harder because they require use of the quadruped position. Your child will learn to climb after he is able to crawl or creep.

Practice when your child is interested and giving you his best performance rather than when he has lost interest and is only partially participating. He will generally like to practice each skill briefly or for 2-3 repetitions. Change the position or activity when he is no longer interested.

Practice for 5-10 minute periods and then give him a break for independent play. Planning an hour-long practice session is not recommended. At this stage, you may be considered an interruption in his plan of exploration or playtime. So, you need to be subtle and try to weave your agenda into his.

If he dislikes a position, try to do it briefly with his best motivator. If he still does not cooperate, stop working on it for a couple of days and try again later. Never force a skill. This will make him grow to hate it if done often enough. There are plenty of other skills to work on, so focus on them until he is ready to try the skill he is resisting.

Vary the pace of the skills you choose to practice. Alternate slow-moving skills such as kneeling and standing with faster skills such as moving in and out of positions, crawling, and climbing.

port, supported quadruped, supported kneeling, and supported standing. Unlike in the past, your child will now be the one taking the lead. Before, you initiated new activities; now he is going to decide what he wants to do. If he is motivated to do a new skill, you need to let him try it on his own. Once he has shown that he wants to do the new skill, then you can help him learn to use the proper movement patterns.

CRAWLING

In order to understand this section, you need to know the definitions of crawling and creeping. The technical definitions we will use in this book are somewhat different than those in popular usage.

> *Crawling* refers to your child moving forward with his belly on the floor, pulling with his arms and pushing with his legs.
>
> *Creeping* refers to your child moving forward on hands and knees, stomach up, in quadruped.

Most children with Down syndrome crawl before they creep. Some children spend so little time crawling that you hardly notice that they crawled at all before they learn to creep. Creeping then becomes their usual method of getting around.

Your child will be ready to learn crawling when he can pivot 360 degrees. The goal will be to crawl approximately 10 feet (across a room).

Children with Down syndrome often have trouble learning to crawl because their arms are not strong enough to pull their body weight forward across the floor. Their legs may be strong enough to help push, but if the arms are too weak to pull, they cannot move forward. If your child is having a hard time moving forward, it could be due to weak arms. Give him time to strengthen his arms using other activities and he will pull forward when he is ready and motivated. In the meantime, he may use a combination of rolling and pivoting to move after toys.

To learn to crawl, he will need to figure out his own way to move forward. He will choose the way that works best for his body size and arm strength. Your main role in helping him learn to crawl is to place the "ultimate" toy in front of him, just out of reach. If it is too far, he will just quit. If it is close enough, he will try to do something to get to it. You will also be amazed how far he can reach without moving forward! Wait and see if he tries to move forward. If he does, reward him with the toy. If he is excited but does not use any arm movements, help him by having him hold your thumbs and pull him forward to the toy. With practice, he will initiate arm movements to move himself forward.

There are things you can do to help him (like pulling him forward with your thumbs or blocking his foot so that he can push himself forward), but they will result in him becoming dependent on you. They will not help him develop the strength needed to crawl on his own. You may provide this support in the beginning to keep him from getting too frustrated, but ultimately he will need to learn to do it himself.

Your child will not begin with a coordinated crawling pattern. He will begin with one of four basic methods. They will not look like what you might think of as crawling, but over time, they will develop into normal crawling. You need to be aware of them so you recognize them as early attempts to crawl and you can encourage them.

The methods are:
1. **"reach and roll,"**
2. **pull forward with both elbows at the same time,**
3. **pull forward with one elbow at a time,**
4. **move onto hands and knees and fall forward.**

The "reach and roll" method is done by reaching with one arm, then rolling over that arm, and reaching with the other arm and rolling to that side. With these

(fig. 4.1)

(fig. 4.2)

movements, he can move forward enough to touch the toy. When reaching, his hand is stretched as far forward as it will go; when that hand cannot touch the toy, he reaches with his other hand. *(See figures 4.1 and 4.2.)*

If your child chooses to use the method of pulling forward on his elbows, he needs to have his elbows in front of his shoulders and will either pull forward with both elbows at the same time or pull with one elbow at a time. When he pulls with both elbows at the same time, he pulls his body forward like a log or as one unit and does not use his legs.

If he pulls with one elbow at a time, he leans to one side and pulls forward with that elbow and then leans to the other side and pulls forward with that elbow. *(See figure 4.3.)* With this method, he shifts his weight from side to side and his legs can participate when they are ready.

If your child has strong arms and is beginning to move onto hands and knees, he may choose the method of moving onto hands and knees and falling forward to get the toy. *(See figures 4.4 and 4.5.)* When he is really motivated to get the toy, he will get on hands and knees to try to reach it, find that he cannot move his arms and legs to move forward, so instead will just thrust himself forward on his belly.

As your child continues to practice moving forward, he will begin using his legs. In the beginning, his legs may be positioned with his knees pointing out-

(fig. 4.3)

ward and wide apart and his feet close together. You will probably see this position if he uses the method of pulling forward on both elbows at the same time. If he uses the "reach and roll" method or pulling forward with one elbow at a time, he will shift his weight from one side to the other and one leg will bend and the other leg will straighten. With these leg movements, he will learn to push off with the foot of the bent leg.

The most difficult part of learning to crawl is moving forward the first 1-2 feet. Once your child figures out a method, he will practice it and be able to crawl longer distances. When you see the method he uses in the beginning, you will agree it is his method and probably is not how you would have taught him. That is why it is so important for him to figure out how he wants to do it; then, he can do it by himself.

After he has a crawling method and consistently moves forward 3-5 times in a row, you can gradually work on increasing the distance. Place the toy about 12 inches in front of him and see if he will move himself forward to touch the toy. When he does this easily, place the toy 2 feet in front of him. Continue to increase the distance up to 5-10 feet. When he can crawl 10 feet, he will be able to crawl around a room and begin crawling around the house.

activity guidelines

To stimulate beginning crawling, use the "ultimate" motivators. Some examples are: a shiny watch, pompon, tv remote, Slinky, brother or sister, paper, magazine with baby photos, a book, tower of blocks to knock down, "push button" book or radio, V-Tech smart driver toy with push buttons for music or talking, or maybe a new toy he has never seen before. The best motivators are needed so he works on moving forward to the toy no matter what he has to do with his body. He just thinks

(fig. 4.4)

(fig. 4.5)

about getting the toy and tries whatever movements he can to move forward. Through experimenting with different movements, he will develop a method of crawling. Mendy was a ten-month-old observer who would only crawl if he was highly motivated. His mother discovered that if she took the parakeet out of the cage and placed it on the floor in front of him, he would do whatever was necessary to pull himself forward to try to get the parakeet.

Remember that your child's size will affect his ability to crawl. If he is small, it will be easier for his arms to pull his body across the floor; if he is large, he needs more arm strength to succeed in crawling.

When he is first figuring out how to crawl, experiment to see which surface works best for the method of crawling he chooses. Try vinyl flooring, tile, hardwood floors, and different types of carpet. The vinyl and hardwood floors will provide a slippery surface which may make it easier to move forward. If you have a deep pile carpet, your child may grip the carpet to help pull himself forward. If you use a shorter pile or berber carpet, he may prefer this because it is easier to move across than a deep pile carpet.

Cover areas of his body that need to slide across the surface and expose the bare skin on areas of his body that need to pull or push. For example, a short sleeve shirt will help him use his elbows to pull himself, and long pants will help his legs slide more easily over the floor.

Practice only for brief periods, when he is most alert and active, and with the best motivators. At the beginning crawling stage, he may only tolerate practicing for 2-3 repetitions and then be tired or lose his motivation. It will take time for him to develop the arm strength required for crawling. If he rolls over, it is probably a sign that he is finished. You can try again later when he is motivated and ready.

temperament

If your child is ***motor driven,*** he will love to crawl and will be motivated to move as far as he can. If your child is an ***observer,*** he will learn to crawl when he thinks it is useful for him. After he learns to crawl, you may change your mind and think he is motor driven because his activity level will increase. However, you will see some observer characteristics, such as being cautious, return when he is learning to walk.

activity #1

Crawling on Belly

1. Place your child on his stomach on the floor and put a toy in front of him, slightly out of reach. Place the toy close enough so he is motivated to try to get it, but not so close that he can reach it.
2. Watch and see if he tries to move forward to touch the toy.
3. Do this activity periodically to see when he is ready to move himself forward. When he is ready, he will move his arms and body to move forward slightly.
4. If he is not able to move forward but is excited and wants to move, have him hold your thumbs and pull him forward.
5. Try a variety of surfaces—vinyl flooring or different types of carpets. Try clothes on or off. See what makes it easier for him.
6. He will begin with one move forward. Continue to practice this until he knows he can do it and has a method. Then move the toy so he needs to do two moves to get it. Gradually increase the distance to 3 feet, 5 feet, and 10 feet. When he is able to do 10 feet, he will move within a room or from one room to another.

MOVING INTO QUADRUPED

Your child practiced supported quadruped during the last stage and learned to prop on his hands and hold his knees together and bent. After learning this, he may have spontaneously moved into quadruped by himself. If not, continue to encourage the position for brief periods until he is able to move into it by himself. The goal will be for him to move into quadruped.

Moving into quadruped is hard for children with Down syndrome to develop due to weak arms, wide leg posture, and weak stomach muscles. It occurs at a unique time for each child depending on his temperament, and the strength in his arms, legs, and stomach muscles. Some children like being on their stomachs, develop belly crawling, and wait to use quadruped until later. Other children may move into quadruped and then rock forward and back to play in the position.

When your child is able to use quadruped, he will be able to learn many new skills. Quadruped is a key position from which a child learns to move to sit, creep, pull to kneel, and pull to stand. If he does not develop quadruped until later he will need to learn other ways to move into these positions.

Using quadruped gives your child a more efficient way to move from one position to another and from one place to another. If he is able to use quadruped, he will move from sitting to quadruped, creep to the sofa or table, pull to kneel, and then pull to stand. If he is not able to use quadruped, he will move from sitting to stomach-lying, belly crawl to the sofa, move from stomach-lying to sitting, pull to kneel from sitting on the floor, and then pull to stand.

activity
guidelines

Use a wide variety of toys to motivate your child to use the quadruped position. Let his interests guide you in selecting toys. It is most important to think about where you place the toy. If it is placed on a low stool or bottom stair, he will be motivated to stay in quadruped to play with it.

Do not force your child to use quadruped or to maintain it when he is resisting it. If he does not like quadruped, try supported kneeling (Activity #15, Chapter 3). If he tolerates using supported quadruped for play, use it (Activity #13, Chapter 3) until he is ready to move into quadruped with your help (Activity #14, Chapter 3). If his arms are too weak to hold the quadruped position, work on strengthening them through activities like supported quadruped, supported kneeling, pulling to sit, moving from sitting to stomach-lying, belly crawling, pulling to stand, and "holding on" in supported standing. If he is able to belly crawl and does not use quadruped, begin climbing activities, which are discussed later in this chapter.

temperament

If your child is ***motor driven,*** he will like to experiment with pushing up on his arms and legs when on his stomach. He may push up on his hands and feet and then bend his knees or he may move onto his knees and then push up on his hands. Once he finds quadruped, he will like to rock forward and back. If your child is an ***observer,*** he will use quadruped when it is helpful. He may learn to use it to move to sit or to position himself close enough to the sofa to pull to kneel and stand. Whether he is an observer or motor driven, he needs to have enough strength in his arms, legs, and stomach muscles to use the quadruped position.

CREEPING

Creeping is moving on hands and knees from one place to another. The goal will be for your child to creep at least 10 feet. It is important for your child to learn to creep because it teaches him to balance using his stomach muscles and bend his knees and move them within a narrow base. Learning these movements will help prepare him for walking. Creeping will particularly help him bend his knees when walking with hand support. Until he is able to creep, he will probably walk with support with his knees stiff.

When he is able to move into quadruped and rock, he is not necessarily ready to move forward and creep. By moving into quadruped and rocking, he is developing the strength and balance needed to hold the position and move forward and backward over the stable base. More complex, coordinated movements are needed for creeping. When he is first learning to creep, he needs to be able to shift his weight and maintain his balance while he moves his arm or leg forward.

Children develop creeping at different times, depending on when they are strong enough and motivated to use it. If a child's arms and legs are strong, he will generally creep earlier. If he learns to creep before he belly crawls, creeping will be the main method he uses to move in his environment. If his arms are weak, he may develop belly crawling first and build up arm strength to prepare him for creeping later. He will be motivated to learn to creep when he figures out it is easier to pull to stand if he can creep close enough to the surface and pull to stand from quadruped.

When you see your child trying to move forward on hands and knees, his first movements will be slow and uncoordinated. He will experiment with moving one arm or leg at a time for a short distance in order to keep his balance. *(See figure 4.6.)* His first creeping pattern will be with his knees wider than his hips. He will become fast and efficient in creeping and will move his right arm and left leg at the same time and then his left arm and right leg at the same time. You will be surprised how fast he can creep and will find yourself chasing him a lot!

Some children initially learn to creep on one foot and one knee, but later progress to creeping on both knees. If your child persists in this pattern, you and your physical therapist should check his legs in standing to see if his knee and foot are turned outward on the side where he uses his foot. Generally, this is not the case, but if it is, the problem should be addressed when practicing standing. Your child will not like it if you try to change his creeping pattern and it will only frustrate him.

(fig. 4.6)

Some children develop even more creative ways to move around their environment. For instance, Sam moved around in sitting by using his arms to scoot himself backwards. Melissa moved around in sitting by using her feet to pull herself forward. Jordan was able to scoot himself along the floor by moving himself from sitting to hands and knees and back to sitting again until he had moved himself sideways across the floor to where he wanted to be. However your child learns to move around is all right. He will learn to creep when he is ready, and he will not tolerate you interfering anyway.

activity guidelines

Place the toy close enough that your child will be motivated to creep to it, and place it at eye level so he needs to be on hands and knees to see it. If the toy is too far away or it is placed on the floor, he will automatically belly crawl to it.

Do not try to rush your child into creeping. If he does not creep during this stage, he will do it during the next stage. If he is an excellent belly crawler or if he has created a scooting pattern he likes, he may not want to change his method to creeping yet.

Binding your child's legs together to create a narrower base is not necessary. Your child will learn to keep his legs together if you practice supported quadruped, supported kneeling, 90/90 sitting, moving in and out of sitting, and supported standing.

temperament

Whether your child is *motor driven* or an **observer,** he will learn to creep. He will develop this skill when he is ready, motivated, and strong enough to do it. All of a sudden, he will begin practicing it and that will be your cue to help him learn to do it. When he is able to creep, you will begin saying how active he is. Even if you said he was an observer before, you will probably think he is motor driven now. If he is truly an observer, however, you will notice the observer traits return when he is learning to walk.

activity #2   **Creeping on Hands and Knees**
1. Place your child on his stomach on the floor. Place him 2 feet away from the surface you will put the toy on. The surface can be a low stool or the seat of the sofa with the cushion removed.
2. See if he will move onto his hands and knees to look at the toy. Encourage him to creep to it. If he does not move onto hands and knees, help him. If he does not try to creep to the toy, move him closer and see if he will.
3. When he will creep a distance of 2 feet to the toy and does it well, gradually increase the distance to 3 feet. Continue to increase the distance as tolerated.
4. If he resists creeping farther than 2 feet, place the toy 2 feet away and have him creep to it. Let him play with it briefly and then move it 2 feet away again.
5. Work toward creeping within a room and around the house.

CLIMBING

Climbing skills begin to develop during this stage. Climbing up develops before climbing down. The goals will be to climb up on the sofa, climb up 2-3 stairs, and climb off the sofa with support. To succeed in climbing up, your child will need to use his whole body. He will need to pull or prop with his arms, push off with his legs, and use his stomach muscles to move his body forward. He will be ready to learn to climb after he learns to crawl or creep, whichever he does first. If he crawls but does not move into quadruped or creep, climbing will teach him the movements needed to learn to use quadruped and creep.

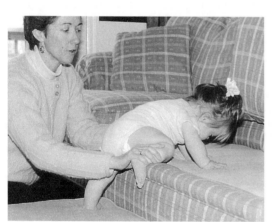

It will be difficult for your child to climb up on the sofa because of his short legs. You can lower the height of the sofa by removing the seat cushion. With the seat cushion removed, the top of the seat will be even with his hips, and he can manage to climb up on a surface at this height. In the beginning you can help him learn to climb up, by putting the seat cushion on the floor in front of the sofa and having him stand on the cushion. *(See figure 4.7.)* Once he learns to climb on the sofa with this support, you can stand him on the floor in front of the sofa and help him climb up from this position.

(fig. 4.7)

At the same time your child is learning to climb on the sofa, he can also start learning to climb up stairs.

When he first learns to climb on the sofa or up stairs, his legs will be positioned with his knees wide apart and pointing outward and he will push off with his feet. Later he will position his knees under his hips and he will use a narrower base. This leg pattern will also be practiced in creeping and climbing up stairs.

After your child has learned to climb up, you can begin to practice climbing off the sofa with support. *(See figure 4.8.)* In the beginning, you will need to move him through the steps until he is familiar with them. He will want to climb down head first because he will see something he wants and he will move toward it. He will do it this way because he is used to moving directly to what he sees or wants to do. He will need to be taught to roll over to his stomach and then slide down until his feet touch the floor. This will be confusing to him because he will not be able to see what he wants or where he wants to go. He will need to learn to plan how to climb down from the sofa safely rather than spontaneously moving after what he wants. You will need to repeat the steps until he learns them and he can do them by himself.

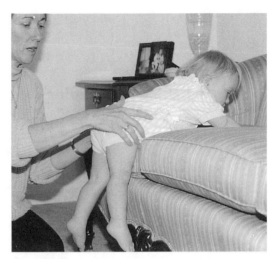

(fig. 4.8)

activity guidelines

When you are helping your child learn to climb up stairs, move his arms and legs when needed and supervise him so he is safe. When he no longer wants to climb or wants to take a break, he will try to sit on the stair and will not know how to do it safely. He will move his buttocks back to try to sit and would fall down the stairs if you were not there.

It is best to teach climbing up stairs beginning at the top. When climbing to the landing, he has a safe place to play once he gets to the toy. If climbing was begun at the bottom of the stairs, he would climb up 2-3 stairs and then would want to sit and play. He would not know how to sit safely by himself.

When possible, use carpeted stairs. They are more comfortable and less slippery than wooden stairs. They are also safer when your child bumps his head. If carpeted stairs are not available, supervise your child closely so he does not bump his head on the edge of the stair above him.

activity #3

Climbing on the Sofa without the Cushion *(see fig. 4.9)*

1. Remove the seat cushion of the sofa so the top of the seat is even with his hips or between his waist and hips.
2. Place the seat cushion on the floor in front of the sofa and hold it there.
3. Place your child standing on the cushion, facing the sofa. Put a toy on the seat and encourage him to climb up on the seat to get it.
4. If he is motivated to move after the toy but cannot figure out how to do it, help him by bending one knee and placing it up on the seat. Hold his knee and wait for him to use his arms and other leg to climb up on the seat.
5. After he climbs up, encourage him to sit and play with the toy. Help him move to sit if needed.
6. When he is able to climb up while standing on the cushion, remove the cushion and place him standing on the floor, facing the sofa. Place the toy on the seat and out of reach and see if he can climb up to get it. If needed, help him by supporting his knee. Continue with the knee support until he can do it by himself. After he climbs up, encourage him to sit and play.

(fig. 4.9)

activity #4   **Climbing Up the Top 1-2 Stairs to the Landing** *(see figs. 4.10, 4.11, 4.12)*

1. Place your child on his feet on the stair below the landing and place his hands on the landing.
2. Place a toy on the landing, out of reach.
3. See if he will try to move after the toy. If not, bend one knee and place it on the landing. Hold his knee and wait for him to move his body forward.
4. Continue to practice this activity until he can move up by himself without your help.

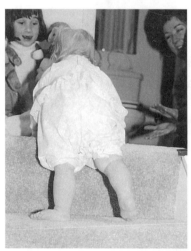
(fig. 4.10)

(fig. 4.11)

(fig. 4.12)

5. When he climbs up on the landing from the first stair, place his feet on the second stair from the top. Place his hands and a toy on the landing.
6. See if he tries to climb up. Climbing up will require:
   a. moving each knee up to the first step
   b. sliding his hands forward on the landing
   c. moving onto his feet
   d. moving each knee onto the landing
7. Supervise him so he is safe and help him as needed. Position yourself behind him and help him learn the movements required. If his feet slide, block them from sliding.

activity #5   **Climbing Off the Sofa with Support**

1. Place him on the sofa in sitting without the seat cushion so he is closer to the floor.
2. When he is ready to climb off, move him to his stomach and slide him down off the sofa until his feet touch the floor.
3. He will need to practice this many times to learn the steps to climb off safely.
4. When he is familiar with the steps, let him practice climbing off the sofa without removing the seat cushion.

MOVING TO SIT

During this stage, the goal will be for your child to learn to move to sit by himself. The first time he does it, he will move to sit from either his stomach or his hands and knees. You will also teach him to move to sit from kneeling.

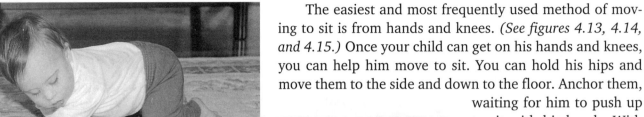

(fig. 4.13)

(fig. 4.14)

(fig. 4.15)

The easiest and most frequently used method of moving to sit is from hands and knees. *(See figures 4.13, 4.14, and 4.15.)* Once your child can get on his hands and knees, you can help him move to sit. You can hold his hips and move them to the side and down to the floor. Anchor them, waiting for him to push up to sit with his hands. With practice, he will begin leaning his hips from side to side when in the quadruped position as a way of practicing weight shifting through his hips. Eventually, he will move his hips to the floor without your support. When he does this, you only need to anchor his hips so he can push up to sit. In time, he will do all the steps by himself. This is the easiest way to move to sit because his buttocks can fall to the floor and then he is in the perfect position to push up to sit with his arms. This will happen easily if he holds his knees together when in quadruped. You will always need to watch the position of his knees. If they are wide apart or wider than his hips, he will be blocked from moving from quadruped to sit.

Your child may try to move to sit from stomach-lying. *(See figures 4.16, 4.17, and 4.18.)* From stomach-lying, he will roll onto his side so he is propping on his elbow. From this position, you can help him pull to sit by having him hold your thumb with his free arm (top arm) and then pull upward to sitting. Later, he will learn to push up with both arms from the side-lying position. He will move to side-lying on his elbow and then use both arms to push up to sitting. When he is in side-lying, you can help him by anchoring his hips; this will make it easier for him to push up with his arms.

When your child plays in kneeling, have him practice moving from kneeling to sitting (Activity #7). This will prepare him for moving from quadruped to sit.

Some children with Down syndrome learn to move from stomach-lying to sitting by spreading their legs wide apart and doing a split as they push up to sitting with their hands. *(See figure 4.19.)* Some children figure out this method even though you have practiced the methods of moving to the side. If your child develops this method, let him use it during his free play because it enables him to move to sit independently. When you are on the floor playing with him, continue to practice the methods of moving to sit by moving to the side. When he can get into the quadruped position, he will learn to move to sit by moving to the side.

activity guidelines

Place the toy to his side so that he moves to his side. Once he has moved to his side, move the toy in front of his feet so that he moves to sitting.

Do not worry if he figures out his own unique method of moving to sit. As long as he moves to sit by moving to the side, his variation is acceptable.

(fig. 4.16)

(fig. 4.17)

temperament

If your child is *motor driven,* he will like to experiment with moving from one position to another. He will try to move to sit as he is moving around. He may not want to sit for long but he will enjoy moving to sitting. If your child is an *observer,* he will want to sit. Since he loves to sit, he will be motivated to figure out how to move to a sitting position.

(fig. 4.18)

activity #6

Moving from Quadruped to Sitting

1. Sit on your heels on the floor.
2. Place your child in quadruped in front of you, facing away from you, with his feet close to you. Position his knees together.
3. Moving over his right side:
   a. Place a toy to his left side at the level of his stomach.
   b. Hold his hips and move them over to the right side and down to the floor.
   c. Move the toy in front of his feet, where he will be when sitting.
   d. Hold both hips and move his left hip down to the floor and toward you. Anchor his hips and wait for him to push himself up to sitting with his arms.
4. Moving over his left side: repeat the steps in #3 but help him move over his left side.
5. When he is familiar with these movements, continue to move the toy and decrease your support until he can move from quadruped to sitting by himself.

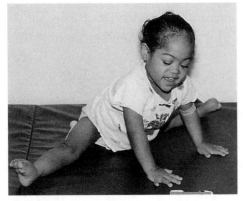

(fig. 4.19)

activity #7   **Moving from Kneeling to Sitting** *(see figs. 4.20, 4.21, 4.22)*

1. Place your child kneeling against the sofa with the seat cushion removed. Place his arms on top of the seat and position his knees together.
2. Position yourself behind him sitting on your heels.
3. Moving over his right side:
   a. Place a toy on the floor on his left side.
   b. Hold his hips and move them to the right side and down to the floor.
   c. As you are moving him down to the floor, move his left hip toward you until he is sitting sideways in front of you.
4. Moving over his left side: repeat the steps in #3 but help him move over his left side.
5. When he is familiar with these movements, continue to move the toy and decrease your support until he can move from kneeling to sitting by himself.

(fig. 4.20)

(fig. 4.21)

(fig. 4.22)

activity #8   **Moving from Stomach-lying to Side-lying to Sitting[1]**

1. Position yourself on the floor sitting on your heels.
2. Position your child on his stomach in front of you, facing away from you, with his feet close to your knees.
3. Moving over his right side:
   a. Place a toy on his left side at waist level to encourage him to look at the toy and move to his right side, propping on his elbow.
   b. Move the toy in front of his feet, where he will be when sitting.
   c. Have him hold your right thumb with his left hand and then pull himself up to sit. He will pull with his left hand and push up with his right hand.
   d. If his buttocks slide, place your left hand across his abdomen to stabilize him.
4. Moving over his left side: repeat the steps in #3 but assist him in moving over his left side.

---

[1] Only use this activity if your child moves to side-lying on his elbow and has not assumed quadruped yet.

5. When he can pull up to sit using this method, it is time to support his hips and have him push up on both arms. When he is in side-lying on his elbow, hold his top hip and press it downward toward the floor. Anchor his hip and wait for him to move his arms to push up to sitting. When he is familiar with these movements, decrease your hip support.
6. With practice, he will move from stomach-lying to side-lying to sitting by himself.

MOVING OUT OF SITTING

During this stage, your child will learn to move out of sitting by himself. He will figure out a method and will use it consistently and spontaneously, whenever he wants to move out of sitting. The ultimate goal will be to move out of sitting by moving to the side. As long as he moves to the side and moves over his legs with his knees bent, he will have accomplished the goal.

He will first learn to move from sitting to his stomach by moving to the side. *(See figures 4.23, 4.24, and 4.25.)* This is the easiest method since he can begin by falling down. He may initially need you to prop his hands to the side and then he will move down to his stomach. As he practices moving down to his stomach, he will learn to lift his head so he does not bump it on the floor and he will learn to lower himself down slowly, using his arms. When he is first propped with his hands to the side, his elbows will be straight. He will learn to slowly bend his elbows to lower himself with control rather than falling fast. Later, he will learn to place his hands to the side by himself. If you place a toy to his side, he will place his hands to the side and move down to his stomach with control.

When he can use the quadruped position and is able to creep on hands and knees, he will learn to move from sitting to quadruped. From sitting, he will prop both hands to one side and then lift his buttocks up to move onto hands and knees. You can help him practice this using Activity #10.

If he does not like using the quadruped position, you can help him learn to move from sitting to kneeling. He can learn to pull up to kneeling from sitting by moving to the side. This gives him an alternative method to pull to kneeling rather than from quadruped. The movements required to move from sitting to kneeling are similar to the movements used in moving from sitting to quadruped. Therefore, when he uses the quadruped position, he will easily move from sitting to quadruped.

Your child may learn to move from sitting to his stomach by spreading his legs with his knees straight and doing a wide split. He will use this method until he feels comfortable using another method. Continue to encourage moving out of sitting by moving to the side.

(fig. 4.23)

(fig. 4.24)

(fig. 4.25)

activity
guidelines

Place the toy so that it will motivate your child to move to the position you are practicing. To motivate him to move from sitting to stomach-lying, place the toy to the side to encourage him to move to the side. If you place the toy in front of him and out of reach, he will move forward over his legs. To encourage moving from sitting to kneeling, place the toys on the surface he will kneel against, like the sofa without the cushion. To encourage him to move from sitting to quadruped, place the toy about a foot away on top of a stool. With the toy on this surface, he may move to quadruped to be at eye level to the toy. He will spontaneously move from sitting to quadruped if he wants to creep.

Allow your child's preference to determine whether you can help him practice moving from sitting to his stomach, quadruped, or kneeling. He may choose to move from sitting to his stomach and then pivot or crawl to a toy. He may choose to move from sitting to quadruped and creep to someone he wants. He may choose to move from sitting to kneeling at the sofa to play with a toy. With practice, he will develop the strength needed in his arms, legs, and stomach muscles to move out of sitting with control.

temperament

If your child is **motor driven,** he will love moving out of sitting. He may not want to sit for long and will move to other positions to be active. If he is an **observer,** he may want to sit for a long time and not want to move out of the position. If the choice is between sitting or stomach-lying, he may prefer to sit. When he is able to crawl, creep, kneel, or stand, he will be more motivated to move out of sitting.

activity #9

Moving from Sitting to Stomach-lying

1. Moving over your child's right side:
    a. Place him sitting on the carpet with a toy on his right side and out of reach. Place the toy at knee level.
    b. See if he tries to move to the toy. If not, place both hands on his right side, in between his right hip and knee.
    c. Wait for him to move down to the floor and provide support for safety if needed. You may need to move the toy so he does not bump into it.
    d. With practice, he will lift his head effectively and lower himself slowly with control.
    e. You can position yourself sitting behind him or on your stomach behind the toy. Use the position that provides the support and motivation he needs.
2. Repeat the steps above but help your child move over his left side.

activity #10

Moving from Sitting to Quadruped

1. Sit on your heels on the floor.
2. Place your child sitting on the floor in front of you, facing away from you.
3. Moving over his right side:
    a. Place both hands to his right side and have him prop on them. Place your right hand under his chest.
    b. Use your left hand to bend his knees and move them together.

c. Move him onto his hands and knees by lifting his chest with your right hand to prop him on his hands and lifting his buttocks with your left hand to prop him on his knees.
4. Moving over his left side: repeat the steps in #3 but assist moving over his left side.
5. When he is familiar with these movements, decrease your support until he can move from sitting to quadruped by himself.

activity #11 **Moving from Sitting to Kneeling**
1. Moving over your child's right side:
    a. Place him sitting sideways in front of the sofa facing to your left. Remove the seat cushion.
    b. Position yourself sitting on your heels, behind him.
    c. Place the toy on top of the seat of the sofa.
    d. Place both of his arms on top of the sofa and support them with your right hand.
    e. Use your left hand to bend his knees and move them together.
    f. Move him to kneeling by lifting his chest with your right hand at his right armpit and lifting his buttocks with your left hand.
    g. Position his knees together.
2. Moving over his left side: Repeat the above steps but help him move over his left side.
3. When he is familiar with these movements, decrease your support until he can move from sitting to kneeling by himself.

PULLING TO KNEEL

Since your child now knows the kneeling position, he is ready to learn how to pull to kneel. He knows he can play in the position and will be motivated to pull to kneel to play with toys. He will learn to pull to kneel from stomach-lying, sitting, and quadruped. Pulling to kneel is a building block for pulling to stand.

Pulling to kneel from sitting is generally the best method to begin with. First, you need to familiarize your child with the movements required to move to kneeling from sitting. You can place him in front of the sofa, sitting sideways. Remove the seat cushion so it is the right height. Put both of his arms on top of the seat and support them. Use your other hand to bend his knees and move them together. Then hold and turn his chest and lift his buttocks to move him to kneeling. When he is used to these movements, you can encourage him to pull up with his arms and gradually decrease your support until he is able to do it by himself.

The best way to motivate your child to pull to kneel from stomach-lying is usually to let him climb up on to your stomach when you are lying on the floor nearby. First, while your child is lying on his stomach, get him to hold on to your clothes and pull up with his arms. Second, he needs to bend his hips and knees to move up on to his knees. Third, he needs to move his knees forward, one at a time, to move to the kneeling position. You can help him with each step until he is able to do it by himself.

Pulling to kneel from quadruped can only be done after your child can move into quadruped. Place him in quadruped facing the surface and close enough so he can put

(fig. 4.26)

(fig. 4.27)

(fig. 4.28)

his hands on top of the surface. *(See figures 4.26, 4.27, and 4.28.)* You will initially need to help him place one hand on top and then he will place the other hand. Next, he will need to move his knees forward, one at a time, to move to the kneeling position. When he knows the steps, you can place him in front of the surface, put a toy on it, and then wait for him to pull to kneel by himself.

Pulling to kneel is often difficult for children with Down syndrome because it requires arm strength. Since your child's arms may be weak, it will take time and practice to develop. If your child is having difficulty you can make it easier by using a surface with an "edge" he can hold onto. Some examples are: an open drawer, a laundry basket, a toy box, a plastic storage box, a plastic vegetable bin, a toy stacking bin, and crib rails. The edge needs to be narrow enough for him to hold easily with his small hands. If he does not use a surface with an edge, his hands will be on top of a surface, like the sofa or table, and they may slide off as he tries to pull up. Using an "edge" will enable him to access the arm power he does have since he will be able to hold on and pull. You will need to stabilize some of these surfaces to keep them from moving when he is pulling up on them.

activity guidelines

Use motivating toys that your child will want to move after. Place them on top of the couch or hold them at the edge to get his attention and interest. He will know he needs to pull up to play with them. Once he pulls up, encourage him to stay in the kneeling position to play.

Begin with a surface that is lower than the height of his shoulder when in quadruped or sitting (about 9 inches). Some examples are a bottom stair that is carpeted or a foot stool. Reaching up to hold on to surfaces at this height requires less balance than surfaces that are above shoulder height. When he has mastered pulling to kneel on these surfaces, he can begin pulling up on surfaces higher than his shoulder; for instance pulling to kneel on the sofa with the cushion removed. The ultimate goal is for him to pull to kneel on surfaces of any height.

temperament

If your child is *motor driven,* he will like to move from one position to another. He will be challenged with pulling up and moving his legs. If he is an *observer,* he will pull to kneel if the toy is worthwhile and he is motivated to get it.

activity #12   **Pulling to Kneel from Sitting**

1. Begin with moving from sitting to kneeling (Activity #11) until he is familiar with the sequence of movements.
2. When he is ready to begin pulling to kneel, use a surface with an edge so he can actively and effectively pull up. Begin with a low surface (9-12 inches). You can also use the sofa with the cushion removed and have him hold your fingers to pull up.
3. Moving over his right side:
   a. Place him sitting sideways in front of the surface facing to your left.
   b. Sit on your heels behind him.
   c. Place the toy on top of the surface or at the edge to motivate him to move after it.
   d. See if he will place his hands on the edge of the surface and try to pull up. If not, place his hands on the edge and wait for him to pull up. (In the beginning, he may need you to put your hand over his hands to help him hold onto the edge.)
   e. As he pulls up, assist his legs by bending his knees and holding them together.
4. Moving over his left side: Repeat the steps in #3 but help him move over his left side.
5. When he is ready, decrease your support and have him pull up to kneel by himself. Make sure that the knee of the leg he is moving over is fully bent. This will make it easier for him to move over the leg to kneeling.
   (See figures 4.29, 4.30, and 4.31.)
6. When he can pull to kneel on low surfaces, gradually increase the height until he can pull to kneel on all surfaces.

activity #13   **Pull to Kneel from Stomach-lying**

1. Place your child on his stomach on the floor.
2. Lie on your back on the floor beside him.
3. Encourage him to pull to kneel on your stomach.
4. Help him by having him hold your fingers or your clothes.
5. Once he has pulled up to kneeling, encourage him to play in this position.

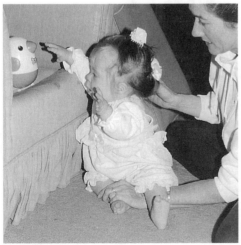  

(fig. 4.29)   *(fig. 4.30)*   *(fig. 4.31)*

activity #14   **Pulling to Kneel from Hands and Knees**

1. Place your child on hands and knees in front of a low surface with an edge.
2. Position yourself beside him and next to the surface.
3. Place a toy on the surface.
4. See if he will place his hands on the edge of the surface, one at a time. If not, you place one hand on the edge and hold it there, waiting for him to place his other hand.
5. After both hands are holding the edge, he will need to move his knees forward, one at a time, to move to kneeling. Help him if needed.
6. When he is ready, decrease your support and have him pull to kneel by himself.
7. When he can pull to kneel on low surfaces, gradually increase the height so he can pull to kneel on all surfaces.

PULLING TO STAND

During this stage, your child will learn to pull to stand. He will first learn to pull to stand from 90/90 sitting. By learning a way to pull to stand, he will increase his motivation and desire to pull to stand. Later, when he is ready, he will learn to pull to stand from kneeling.

During the previous stage, he learned to pull to stand from 90/90 sitting holding your thumbs. Now you will set him up sitting on the bench in front of a surface with an edge. You can place a toy on the surface and encourage him to reach out, hold the edge, and pull up to stand. *(See figures 4.32 and 4.33.)* Then, when he is ready to move out of standing, he can lower himself to sitting on the bench.

He can use the method of pulling to stand from 90/90 sitting until he is ready to pull to stand from quadruped or sitting on the floor. To pull to stand from quadruped or sitting on the floor, he first needs to be able to pull to kneel from either position (Activity #12 or 14). When he is able to pull to kneel, he is ready to learn the next step of pulling to stand from kneeling. When he can pull to stand from kneeling, he will be able to pull to stand from sitting on the floor or quadruped.

From kneeling, he will first pull to stand by pushing up on both legs at the same time. If he is kneeling at a low surface, like the sofa without the cushion, he will lean his trunk over the seat and push up on his feet to move to stand. If a higher surface is used, like a toy box with an edge, he will pull up with his arms and push up on both legs to move to stand.

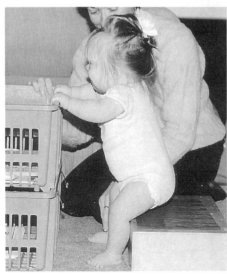

(fig. 4.32)

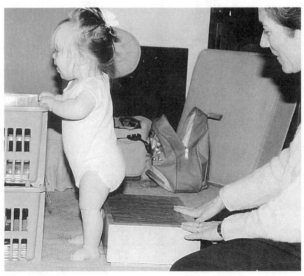

(fig. 4.33)

 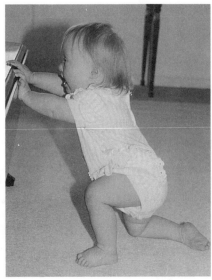 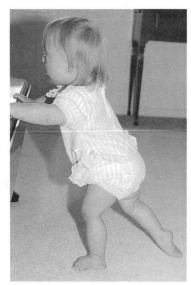

(fig. 4.34)   *(fig. 4.35)*   *(fig. 4.36)*

With practice and if his knees are under his hips (no wider), he will learn to move into the half kneel position. The half kneel position is the kneeling position with one knee on the floor and the other foot on the floor. To move into the half kneel position from kneeling, he will lean his hips to one side, hold that position, and lift his other foot up on the floor. To move from the half kneel position to stand, he will lean his hips over his foot and push up to stand. *(See figures 4.34, 4.35, and 4.36.)* He will automatically learn to use the half kneel position when pulling to stand if his knees are in the proper position when kneeling and he has learned to lean his hips from side to side.

activity guidelines

Use all kinds of toys to encourage pulling to stand. Your child will initially pull to stand because he wants to get the toy you put in front of him. You need to place the toy on top of the surface so he can see it but not reach it until he is standing.

Provide a surface with an edge to help him learn to pull to stand. In the beginning stages of pulling to stand, his arms will do the majority of the work to pull his body weight up to standing. He will need to hold the edge to use his arms most effectively. When he is an expert in pulling to stand and moves his legs into the half kneel position, his arms and legs will share the work of moving his body up to standing. At that time, he can begin to place his hands on top of a surface, like a sofa or coffee table, and pull to stand. When he moves up to stand very easily, he will be able to prop his hands against a surface, such as the wall or refrigerator, and use his legs primarily to move his body up to standing. He will prop on his arms to help him maintain his balance but they will not be needed to pull up.

Adjust the height of the surface depending on what activity he is practicing. When pulling to stand from 90/90 sitting, he needs to be able to reach the top edge of the surface from sitting. The height of the surface should be at chest level once he is standing. When beginning to pull to stand from kneeling, he can begin practicing at a low surface until he is familiar with moving to stand. When he is familiar with pulling to stand and wants to stand, he needs to use a higher surface so he learns to pull with his arms, move into the half kneel position, and push off with his legs.

You can use an open storage box as a surface with an edge. You can stabilize the storage box by putting a 25 lb. bag of sand in the bottom. That way you will not need to hold it and your child can pull up on it without needing your assistance.

temperament

If your child is **motor driven,** he will be interested in moving up so he will pull up to stand. He may not want to stand for long but he will like the action of pulling to stand. If he is an **observer,** he will initially stand up only to get the toy. Later, he will like to stand so he will pull up purely to move to the standing position.

activity #15

Pulling to Stand from 90/90 Sitting[2]

1. Place your child in 90/90 sitting on a bench in front of a surface with an edge.
2. Put a toy on the surface so he can see it but not reach it.
3. Encourage him to reach out and hold the edge of the surface. Wait for him to pull up to stand. Help him if needed with these two steps.

4. Place the bench against his legs and firmly hold it to prevent sliding.
5. Encourage him to hold on and maintain standing while being entertained with the toy. Check his legs and adjust them if needed so he is in the proper standing position.
6. When he wants to move out of standing, wait for him to bend his knees and sit while holding the edge. Hold the bench to keep it stable. Help him lower himself to sitting if needed. (*See figure 4.37.*)
7. Allow him to sit on the bench and then encourage him to stand up again when he is ready.
8. Continue this activity as long as he likes it.
9. This can also be done in the playpen or crib and he can hold onto the top bar.

(fig. 4.37)

activity #16

Pulling to Stand from Kneeling

1. Place your child on his knees, facing the surface he will use to pull to stand. Use a low surface with an edge. (You can place him in kneeling or he can move from sitting or quadruped to kneeling.)
2. Position yourself at his side and next to the surface.
3. Place a toy on top of the surface, just out of reach, and encourage him to hold on to the edge and pull up to stand to play with the toy.
4. In the beginning, he will pull up with his arms and push off with his legs to move up to stand.
5. When he can pull to stand from a low surface, practice pulling to stand on higher surfaces.
6. When he is familiar with pulling to stand from kneeling, you will notice he will begin using the half kneel position. He will move from kneeling to half kneel and then up to standing.
7. If he continues to push off with both legs and does not use the half kneel position, try using a higher surface such as a toy box.

---

[2] The height of the bench is determined by the leg measurement from the back of the knee to the heel of the foot. This is best measured with your child sitting on a bench with his knees bent 90 degrees and his feet flat on the floor.

MOVING FROM STANDING TO SITTING ON THE FLOOR

Now that your child is able to stand up, he needs to learn to move from standing to sitting on the floor. He is excited and motivated to stand but will become tired and needs to know how to sit down. Moving from standing to sitting requires two skills: 1) "holding on" to the surface, and 2) bending his knees as he lowers himself down to the floor. He needs to learn these two steps rather than "letting go" and having you catch him. The goal is to move from standing to sitting on the floor by bending his knees. *(See figure 4.38.)*

(fig. 4.38)

Your child has already practiced moving from standing to 90/90 sitting (Activity #15), so he is familiar with holding on and bending his knees to sit. However, it is a longer distance to move down to the floor and he will need to practice this until he feels comfortable with doing it by himself. He may allow himself to fall down fast and "plop" his buttocks on the floor, or he may hold on and lower himself very slowly. You can assist him until he feels comfortable and does it safely.

activity guidelines

To encourage your child to move from standing to sitting on the floor, practice this activity when he wants to move out of standing. If he likes to stand a lot, you can place favorite toys on the floor to motivate him to move down to the floor. It is best if you take all the toys off the surface he is standing in front of and move them to the floor. If he has toys to play with in standing, he will prefer to keep standing.

Continue to encourage knee bending as much as possible. When he is comfortable with moving from standing to sitting on the floor, he may prefer to keep his knees straight and "plop" on his buttocks to move quickly. You can encourage knee bending by having him bend down to pick up toys on the floor and move from standing to 90/90 sitting. Knee bending movements will be needed in developing standing balance, moving to stand from hands and feet, and walking.

temperament

If your child is *motor driven,* he will probably move fast and "plop" his buttocks on the floor to move to sit. When he is first learning, he will be a little slower until he knows what to do. Once he is familiar with how to do it, he will go fast and will enjoy the feeling of falling. If he is an *observer,* he will lower himself slowly and carefully. He may stop halfway down and move back up to standing. Once he understands how far he needs to go and feels confident lowering himself, he will lower himself faster.

activity #17

Moving from Standing to Sitting on the Floor
1. Place your child in standing, holding onto a surface with an edge.
2. Position yourself to the side of him and next to the surface he is holding onto.
3. Place a toy on the floor and encourage him to move down to the floor to get it.

4. Encourage him to hold on to the edge and bend his knees until his buttocks touch the floor. Assist him as needed. (If he "lets go" and falls to you, discourage this.)

5. If he is fearful, place a sofa cushion behind his legs and he can learn to move down to sit on it. Gradually decrease the height of the pillow until he learns to move to sitting on the floor.

STANDING HOLDING ON

During the last stage your child learned to stand with your support. During this stage, he will learn to stand while holding onto a surface with one- or two-hand support. He will need to learn to be responsible for maintaining his balance.

He will begin holding onto a surface with an edge with two-hand support. *(See figure 4.39.)* By holding on with his hands, he will learn to maintain his balance using his hands and his stomach muscles. If he leans back or to either side, he will learn to move back to the center. To make it easier for himself, he may try to lean his belly against the surface and move his feet wide apart. This will delay him learning the movements necessary to balance himself properly in standing and the development of standing balance and stepping. If he does this, reposition his hands on the edge of the surface and his feet under his hips.

When he can stand with two-hand support using the proper posture, he will be ready to add knee bending and ankle movements. He may bend his knees to bounce in standing or dance to music. With his feet under his hips, he will begin to move his ankles to help him balance when he leans backwards or to either side. These foot movements will only happen if he is barefoot and his feet are under his hips and pointing straight ahead. If his feet are wider than his hips or turning outward, that positioning will hinder ankle movements and using his feet for balance.

(fig. 4.39)

When he stands well with two-hand support, he will begin letting go with one hand to play with toys. Initially, he will be wobbly when he stands with one-hand support and may need to hold on temporarily with his other hand to regain his balance. With practice, he will develop better strength and balance. He will hold the stick for the xylophone and play a song or he will turn pages in a book.

activity guidelines

When your child is first standing with two-hand support, use toys he can watch so he can use both hands for balance. Some examples of toys are: spinning toys, music box, tv, and a tape recorder with music. You can also sing songs, whistle, or encourage him to dance.

When he can stand with one-hand support, use lightweight toys to play with. Some examples are: xylophone, books, push button sound books, soap bubbles to pop, rings, blocks, toys that fit into a container, interesting rattles or bells, and push button toys. Place the toys in front of him initially. As he gains strength and balance, he will be able to reach to the side.

The height of the surface needs to be between nipple level to 3 inches below his nipples. If the height is too short he will lean over. When the height is correct, his trunk will be up straight when he is holding on with his hands.

Have him go barefoot when he is practicing standing. If he wears shoes, his ankles will be held stiffly and he will not learn to move his ankles to assist with balance. With his ankles stiff, he will automatically hold his knees stiff. If he is barefoot, he has access to developing strength, balance, and controlled movements in his feet and knees.

temperament

If your child is *motor driven,* he will stand as long as the toys are motivating enough to play with. Since he prefers to move, he will stand to play but then will get down to the floor to move around. When he can cruise, he will enjoy standing and cruising to move around. If he is an *observer,* he will love to stand as long as he can. He will love to play with toys in standing and will stand to look out a window. He will get down from standing when he is tired or if he decides to do something else.

activity #18

"Holding On" with Two Hands in Supported Standing

1. Place your child in standing and have him hold on to a surface with an edge.
2. Position his legs with his feet under his hips and pointing straight ahead.
3. Place a bench behind his legs and stabilize it. He will use the support of the bench to bend his knees slightly and to sit down when he is ready.
4. Entertain him while he is standing and encourage him to maintain his balance.
5. When he feels comfortable maintaining his balance with two-hand support, encourage knee bending by turning on music and having him dance.
6. If he leans to either side or backwards, see if he can move himself back to the centered standing position. If not, help him until he can.
7. When he stands well with two-hand support holding a surface with an edge, begin using a surface without an edge. He can place his hands on top of the surface. Watch him and if he gets into the habit of leaning his belly against the surface, reposition him.

activity #19

"Holding On" with One Hand in Supported Standing

1. Place your child in standing and have him hold onto a surface with an edge.
2. Position his legs with his feet under his hips and pointing straight ahead.
3. Place a bench behind his legs and stabilize it. He will use the support of the bench to bend his knees slightly and to sit down when he is ready.
4. Entertain him or encourage him to play with lightweight toys with one hand. See the "Guidelines" for examples.
5. Encourage him to maintain his balance as long as tolerated.
6. When he consistently maintains his balance, encourage him to reach for toys to his side and behind him.
7. When he stands well with one-hand support holding a surface with an edge, begin using a surface without an edge. He can place his hand on top of a surface such as the sofa or a table.

► Motor Milestone Checklist *on next page.* ►

Motor Milestone Checklist

Crawling
- ❏ He moves on his belly for 1-2 pulls forward
- ❏ He moves 5 feet
- ❏ He moves 10 feet

Moving into Quadruped
- ❏ He moves onto hands and knees by himself

Creeping
- ❏ He moves forward 2-4 steps
- ❏ He creeps 5 feet
- ❏ He creeps 10 feet

Scooting
- ❏ He scoots using his own method for 5-10 feet (optional)

Climbing on the Sofa
- ❏ He climbs onto sofa (with cushion removed) from standing on sofa cushion placed on the floor
- ❏ He climbs onto sofa (with cushion removed) from standing on floor with his knee supported on the sofa
- ❏ He climbs onto sofa (with cushion removed) by himself

Climbing off the Sofa
- ❏ He tolerates being moved to his stomach and sliding down until his feet touch the floor

Climbing Up Stairs
- ❏ He climbs onto the landing from the top stair when you place his knee on the landing and support it there
- ❏ He climbs from the top stair to the landing by himself
- ❏ He climbs up the top two stairs to the landing with your help
- ❏ He climbs up the top two stairs to the landing by himself

Moving to Sit
- ❏ He moves to sit from hands and knees
- ❏ He moves to sit from stomach-lying
- ❏ He moves to sit from kneeling
- ❏ He moves to sit using his own method (optional)

(continued on next page)

Motor Milestone Checklist *(continued)*

Moving Out of Sitting
- ❑ He moves from sitting to stomach-lying with control
- ❑ He moves from sitting to quadruped
- ❑ He moves from sitting to kneeling

Pulling to Kneel
- ❑ He pulls to kneel from sitting using a low surface with an edge
- ❑ He pulls to kneel from sitting using a high surface with an edge
- ❑ He pulls to kneel from stomach-lying by climbing onto your stomach as you lie on the floor
- ❑ He pulls to kneel from quadruped using a low surface with an edge
- ❑ He pulls to kneel from quadruped using a high surface with an edge
- ❑ He pulls to kneel from sitting or quadruped using a flat surface

Pulling to Stand
- ❑ He pulls to stand from 90/90 sitting using a surface with an edge
- ❑ He pushes up on both legs at the same time when he pulls to stand from kneeling using a surface with an edge
- ❑ He moves into the half kneel position when pulling to stand from kneeling using a surface with an edge
- ❑ He pulls to stand using any surface

Moving from Standing to Sitting on the Floor
- ❑ He moves from standing to 90/90 sitting by himself using a surface with an edge
- ❑ He holds the edge and bends his knees to lower himself to sitting on the floor
- ❑ He moves from standing to sitting using any surface

Standing Holding On
- ❑ He stands holding on with both hands to a surface with an edge
- ❑ He bounces or dances in standing holding on with both hands to a surface with an edge
- ❑ He stands holding on with one hand to a surface with an edge

CHAPTER 5

Stage 5
Standing, Cruising, Climbing, and Walking

Your child is now independent in her environment. She can move from one place to another by crawling or creeping, move from one position to another, use the positions of sitting, quadruped, kneeling and standing, and has begun climbing. During this stage, she will make the transition from mainly being on the floor to mainly standing up. She will want to play in standing and will learn to balance, and finally will learn to walk. During this time your child is going to master many different skills. Life will be very active for both of you. You will need to spend more time chasing, managing, and supervising her.

Because there are so many complex skills to master during this stage, the chapter will be divided into five sections so that each skill can be considered individually. Although these skills will be discussed separately, remember that you will be working on them concurrently as your child develops.

> **The motor skills she will develop during this stage are:**
> 1. **standing balance,**
> 2. **cruising,**
> 3. **plantigrade and moving from plantigrade to stand,**
> 4. **climbing off the sofa and up and down stairs, and**
> 5. **walking with and without support.**

You will need to look and see when your child is interested in practicing the skills of this stage. She will automatically want to stand and then you can practice standing balance and cruising. After standing, you can help her take steps with whatever support she needs. When she likes standing and walking, you can help her learn to move to stand from plantigrade. To give her a break from standing and walking, you can practice climbing. She will have her own menu of motor skills she is motivated to do. Look for it and practice the skills she is interested in learning.

Section 1: STANDING

During this stage your child will learn to balance herself in standing without holding onto a support. The goal will be to stand 5-10 seconds without support. Until she is ready to stand alone, standing with one-hand support will be the main position she will use to practice standing balance. By using this position, she will help her stomach muscles become more effective in maintaining her balance, improve her leg strength, and learn to move her feet to assist with balance. She will learn to rely less on her hands for balance as she uses her stomach muscles, legs, and feet more. As she spends more time playing in standing, she will learn to stand tall and no longer lean over the surface she is standing against. When she is ready, she will let go with her propping hand and stand alone.

Steps in: Learning to Stand

She will learn to stand:
1. with support behind her back;
2. propping her hands on top of a surface;
3. propping her hands against a surface;
4. reaching with one hand while propping with another; and
5. without support.

When she learns to do Steps 2 and 3, she will begin by using both hands for support. She will learn to maintain standing with two-hand support and then progress to standing with one-hand support.

standing with support behind her back

When you place your child in standing with her back against the wall or sofa, you will encourage her to stand tall without using her hands for support. You can use this position as long as tolerated, beginning with brief periods of up to ten seconds. Experiment with different surfaces to stand her against. The wall is a good surface to start with because it provides full support from head to feet. However, you need to watch her head so she does not bump it against the wall. If she does bump her head against the wall, place her against the back of the sofa. It also provides head to foot support and is softer. When your child is familiar with the position, use the front of the sofa or a toy box. These surfaces only provide support from the middle of her trunk to her feet.

propping hands on top of a surface

After your child has practiced holding on to a surface with an edge, she will be able to use her legs and trunk more effectively to maintain standing. When she no longer needs to hold onto a surface to maintain her balance, she can prop her hands on top of a surface. With her hands propped on top of the surface, her arms will be in a horizontal position and she can lean her trunk over the surface if needed to help maintain her balance. (*See figure 5.1.*)

(fig. 5.1)

propping hands against a surface

When she props her hands against a surface, her hands will be in a vertical position and she will need to stand tall and use her stomach muscles and feet to maintain her balance. Her hands will only prop and will provide little support if she leans to either side or backwards. *(See figure 5.2.)*

(fig. 5.2)

reaching with one hand while propping with the other

Your child will be motivated to use one hand to play while propping with her other hand. She will want to play with the toys and, when she is ready, will spontaneously let go with one hand so she can play. Where you place the toy can further challenge her balance.

It will be easiest for her to reach for lightweight toys on the surface in front of her. If she plays with a lightweight toy or plays calmly, it will be easy to maintain her balance. If she tries to lift a heavy toy or wildly shakes a toy, however, she will probably lose her balance.

When a toy is placed to the side of her trunk, it will be harder because she will need to twist her trunk to look at it and position her hand to reach it. She will need to balance herself in this position as she lets go with her hand to get the toy. This activity will help her develop the standing balance required for cruising from one piece of furniture to another, placed side by side. She will need to maintain her balance in standing as she reaches out to the next piece of furniture.

The biggest challenge will be reaching for a toy behind her trunk. *(See figure 5.3.)* She will need to twist her trunk significantly, which will cause her to let go. Then she will need to maintain her balance in this position while reaching for the toy. This activity will prepare her for cruising between two parallel surfaces, for example, from the sofa to the coffee table.

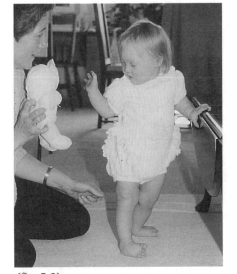

(fig. 5.3)

standing without support

All the standing positions described so far will help your child develop the proper posture, strength, and balance to stand by herself. She probably will first do it accidentally for 1-2 seconds when she lets go briefly to play with a toy. Once she realizes she is not holding on, she will hold on or sit down. If you praise her and clap for her, she will learn you like it and may become motivated to do it more.

When your child is able to stand easily with one-hand support, she will be ready to learn to stand alone. Help her stand up and then to hold on to your thumb with one hand only. Entertain her until you feel that she is balanced. Then, slide your thumb out of her hand quickly and see if she will stay standing while you entertain her. She may

(fig. 5.4)

reach for you or she may stand alone. Continue to practice until she can stand by herself. *(See figure 5.4.)*

With practice, she will learn to stand alone for 10 seconds or more. If your child likes to stand alone, she may stand for more than 10 seconds. Your child may become bored in standing and may stand only 5-10 seconds. As long as she has the balance to stand alone for 5-10 seconds, she has accomplished the goal.

activity guidelines

Make sure your child uses the proper standing position when practicing each position. To stand properly, her feet must be under her hips and pointing straight ahead, her trunk must be up straight and not leaning against the surface, and her hands must be holding on or propping against the surface.

With her legs and feet in the proper position, she will learn how to balance herself properly. If she leans her hips behind her feet, her toes will lift off the floor; if she leans her hips to the side over one foot, the inside edge of the foot will lift up; and if she leans her hips forward over her feet, her heels will lift off the floor. These movements of the feet are called foot balance reactions. These movements help your child maintain her balance.

Your child will use foot balance reactions more when she is challenged. For example, if she is holding on to a surface with an edge, she will use her hands primarily to balance and will not need to use her feet. However, if she is standing with her hands propped against the refrigerator and needs to reach behind her trunk to get a magnet, she will need to use her feet to help her maintain her balance.

To use foot balance reactions, your child needs to be barefoot and to have her feet in the proper position. If she is wearing shoes, they will tend to hold her feet rigid in one position. If her feet are wider than her hips and turned outward, she will learn to balance herself by using this posture rather than by learning to balance herself properly. Her feet will be blocked from moving when she stands with this posture.

Make sure the height of the table or surface is between nipple level to 3 inches below her nipples. If the height is too short, she will lean over the surface in order to prop on her hands. If the height is optimal, she will stand with her trunk up straight when propping on her hands. With her trunk up straight, she can develop the balance to stand alone.

Choose motivators depending on the standing skills your child is practicing. If she is practicing standing with two-hand support, use toys she can watch. Some examples are: watching and listening to a music box, watching a video or TV, listening to a tape recorder, or listening to your singing or whistling.

When she can stand with one-hand support, have her play with lightweight toys with her other hand. Some examples include: interesting rattles, rings, blocks, push button toys or books, playing a xylophone, popping bubbles, turning pages in a book and pointing to pictures in a book.

When she stands with her hands propping against a surface such as a wall or refrigerator, you can use colorforms or magnets.

When she is standing with support behind her back or standing alone, it is best if you sit on the floor so that you are at eye level or lower. In this position, she can look at you and work to maintain the position and her balance. If you are higher, she will look up at you and lose her balance. You can entertain her by talking to her, singing favorite songs or singing gesture songs like "Itsy Bitsy Spider," "Wheels on the Bus," "If You're Happy and You Know It" and "Pat-a-Cake." Her hands are free to clap or play games like "So Big." She also might like it if you count and show your fingers. This is your chance to be a creative entertainer so she focuses on you rather than thinking about what she is doing. She may stand because she is preoccupied by what you are doing. Later, she will know she can stand and will stand when she wants to.

Provide verbal cues. It is important to say "stand" every time you practice it so she learns what standing is.

Move at your child's pace when developing standing balance. If you force her to stand, she will quickly develop strategies to avoid standing. Try doing it for brief periods and provide entertainment and toys. You need to realize this position may be scary to her. She will be ready to challenge herself when she feels secure in the position and the motivator is worth standing for.

temperament

If your child is an *observer,* she will like to stand with support and play. She will not like to work on challenging her balance because it will feel too risky. In the beginning she will be afraid and will need time and practice to feel secure and develop balance skills. Once she is secure, she will stand and play, balancing herself automatically.

If your child is *motor driven,* she will not want to stand still, so it will be hard to motivate her to stand alone and balance herself. She will develop balance while standing with one-hand support, but when she is ready to stand alone, she will probably try to step to you or will move down to the floor. She will learn further standing balance through stepping activities.

activity #1

Standing with Back Support

1. Place your child standing with her back against the wall or the back of the sofa.
2. Position her legs with her feet under her hips and pointing straight ahead. Position her trunk up straight and watch to make sure she does not arch it.
3. Sit on the floor in front of her so that you are at eye level to her or slightly lower.
4. Entertain her and encourage her to maintain this position for as long as tolerated. You can sing songs, bang blocks, clap hands, and play games like "So Big" and "Pat-a-Cake."
5. When she is familiar with this position, place her standing against the front of the sofa, chair, or toy box. These surfaces will give her less support since they are lower.

activity #2

Supported Standing with Hands Propped on Top of a Surface

1. Place your child standing at a sofa, chair, rectangular storage box with lid, or coffee table and prop her hands on top of the surface. The height of the surface should be within the range of nipple level to 3 inches below.
2. Position her legs with her feet under her hips and pointing straight ahead. Position her trunk up tall and discourage leaning against the surface.
3. Place a bench behind her legs and stabilize it. The bench will give her support and allow her to sit down when she is ready.

4. Entertain her and encourage her to balance herself in the standing position. If she leans in any direction, see if she can move herself back to the centered position. If not, help her.
5. When she is ready, encourage her to let go with one hand and use it to play. Begin by having her play with a lightweight toy in front of her.
6. When she can maintain her balance with one-hand support while reaching for toys in front of her, encourage her to reach to the side of her trunk for a toy. Hold the toy at her side at the level of her middle trunk and have her twist her trunk to reach for it.
7. When she can keep her balance with one-hand support while reaching to the side for a toy, encourage her to reach behind her trunk. Hold a toy behind her at the level of her middle trunk and have her twist her trunk and reach for it.

activity #3   **Supported Standing with Hands Propped against a Surface**

1. Place your child standing with her hands propped against the refrigerator, wall, or kitchen cabinet.
2. Position her legs with her feet under her hips and pointing straight ahead. Position her trunk up tall and discourage leaning against the surface.
3. Place a bench behind her legs and stabilize it.
4. Entertain her and encourage her to balance herself in the standing position. If she leans in any direction, see if she can move herself back to the centered position. If not, help her.
5. When she is ready, encourage her to let go with one hand and use it to play. Begin by having her hold a magnet or colorform placed in front of her. With practice, she will be able to maintain standing with one-hand support for 1 minute or more.
6. When she can keep her balance with one-hand support while reaching for toys in front of her, encourage her to reach to the side of her trunk for a toy. Hold the toy at her side at the level of her middle trunk and have her twist her trunk to reach for it.
7. When she can keep her balance with one-hand support while reaching to the side for a toy, encourage her to reach behind her trunk. Hold a toy behind her at the level of her middle trunk and have her twist her trunk and reach for it.

activity #4   **Standing Alone**

1. Seat your child on a bench in front of you.
2. Sit on the floor so you are at eye level to her or slightly lower when she stands up.
3. Tell her to "stand" and have her pull up to stand holding your thumbs.
4. Position her legs with her feet under her hips and pointing straight ahead.
5. Have her let go of one of your thumbs so she is only holding on with one hand. If she is reluctant to let go, give her a lightweight toy to hold.
6. Entertain her by singing or playing gesture games.
7. When she feels balanced, use your fingers to slide your thumb quickly out of her hand. Entertain her and see if she can stand alone briefly.

8. If she becomes afraid or starts to fall, give her one-hand support.
9. Continue to practice until she becomes familiar with standing alone and learns to maintain her balance without support. Work toward standing alone up to 10 seconds.

Section 2: CRUISING

Cruising is stepping sideways while holding onto furniture. It is generally how a child learns to take his first steps with support. Your child will be ready to learn this skill after she can stand well with one-hand support. The goal is to cruise along furniture and from one piece of furniture to another.

Through cruising, your child will learn to step with one leg at a time and balance herself while stepping, using her arms and stomach muscles. With practice, she will be able to cruise from one end of a table or sofa to the other end by herself. Later, she will cruise from one piece of furniture to another. She will learn to cruise along the wall and will be able to move through the house. The more she cruises, the stronger her legs will become.

To cruise, your child needs to do four steps:
1. **move her hands sideways along the surface and use them to balance;**
2. **"step out" with the leg in the direction she is traveling toward;**
3. **"step in" with her other leg; and**
4. **maintain her balance using her hands and stomach muscles.**

Cruising usually develops before stepping forward with hand support. Cruising prepares your child for stepping forward. When stepping sideways, she needs to learn to shift her weight onto one leg so she can step with the other. In order to cruise to the right, she needs to lean over her left leg in order to step *out* with her right; then she needs to lean over her right leg in order to step *in* with her left. This weight shifting is also needed when stepping forward. By practicing cruising, she learns to weight shift in order to step, balance herself while stepping, and she strengthens critical hip muscles needed for hip stability.

activity guidelines

To motivate your child to cruise, pick the perfect toy and place it just out of her reach. She will need to figure out a way to move to it to play with it. After she is familiar with cruising, use toys to motivate her to cruise longer distances or between pieces of furniture.

Support her arms and have her learn to step with her legs. The most difficult part in cruising is learning to take the first one or two steps. If you support her arms by holding her elbows from behind, she will feel stable enough to move her legs. If she does not initiate moving her legs, you may need to move her legs, one at a time, in the beginning. However, when possible, move toward supporting her arms and having her actively move her legs.

As she learns to cruise, gradually reduce the amount of arm support that she uses. There will be four types of arm support used:
1. leaning over the surface and propping on her elbows;
2. "holding on" to a surface with an "edge";
3. propping her hands *on top of* a surface;
4. propping her hands *against* a surface.

Steps in: Learning to Cruise

Your child will learn to cruise using the following sequence of activities:
1. take 1-2 steps;
2. take 3-4 steps;
3. cruise along the length of the table or sofa in one direction;
4. cruise in both directions;
5. cruise around the "corner" of the table;
6. cruise from one piece of furniture to another, with the surfaces next to each other;
7. cruise from one piece of furniture to another with the surfaces parallel to each other, for example, from the sofa to the coffee table.

Activities #5-8 explain how to practice these steps. As she accomplishes these steps, your child will be able to cruise around the house when and where she wants to. She will not need you to help her. Cruising can be practiced until she has another way to step independently in the house, such as by stepping with a push toy.

She will probably take her first cruising steps by leaning over the surface and propping on her elbows. She will need to feel secure and adequately stable to initiate stepping out with her leading leg. When she is able to step with each leg, she will hold on to a surface with an "edge" and use her arms and stomach muscles to balance herself. With this support, she will develop trunk and leg strength and hold her body upright as she cruises along the surface. She will not need to lean her body against the surface for support. With practice, she will learn to prop her hands *on top of* a surface like a table or the seat of the sofa. Later, she will be able to cruise with her hands propping *against* a surface, like the wall or refrigerator. As she learns to cruise propping her hands *on top of* or *against* surfaces, her stomach muscles will work harder to maintain her balance. As she uses her arms less for support, her stomach muscles will be primarily responsible for controlling her balance.

Make sure her body, and particularly her hips, are parallel to the surface she is cruising along. She needs to practice stepping *out* and stepping *in* to strengthen specific hip muscles. This is the primary skill in which your child uses these muscles and, by strengthening them, she will develop better hip stability for standing balance and stepping. To help her keep her hips parallel to the surface, keep her arms forward on the surface. If you are at her side, do not encourage her to hold one or both of your fingers because then she will turn her trunk and hips to face you. With this support, she will step forward with her legs rather than stepping sideways.

Encourage her to cruise in both directions to see if it is easier for her to move in one direction. If she prefers moving in one direction, let her practice that direction first. When she masters cruising in the favored direction, she will be ready to learn to cruise in the other direction.

Remember that the height of the surface is important in early cruising. It needs to be at the level of her nipples or 1-2 inches lower. When she is cruising well, she will be able to cruise using a surface of any height.

temperament

If your child is an **observer,** she will be *careful* as she is learning to cruise. She may want more arm support or you may need to help her move her legs in the beginning. She will want to feel secure and balanced and will not like to feel off balance. Once she is familiar with cruising and knows how to do it, she will be a pro.

If your child is **motor driven,** she will be *risky* when she is learning to cruise. She will step or fall to the side to get the toy. She may lean her body and not use her hands to hold on to keep her balance. You will need to supervise her to make sure she is safe. When she learns how to do it, she will cruise with control and balance.

activity #5

Beginning Cruising *(see fig. 5.5)*

1. Use a surface with an "edge" or a surface she can lean over and prop on her elbows. The height of the surface should be nipple level or 1-2 inches below her nipples.
2. Have your child pull to stand at the surface.
3. Place a favorite toy on the surface to the right or left side and place it slightly out of reach. Watch her look at the toy and try to figure out how to move to it. If she does not attempt to move to it, try another toy and see if she will try to move to it.

(fig. 5.5)

4. She may have difficulty figuring out how to move to the toy. The first goal is to have her step with the leading leg. Your role is to support her arms so she can step with her leg.
   a. She may try to reach for the toy, lean too far, and lose her balance. If this happens, place your finger under her armpit (on the side she is leaning toward) to support her. Lift upward and see if she will step with her leading leg. If not, help her.
   b. She may lean her head and upper trunk over the surface and prop on her elbows. See if she tries to lean sideways to move toward the toy. If not, support her arms and lean her to the side. Wait and see if she steps with the leading leg. If not, help her.
   c. If she is afraid of being leaned to the side, begin by moving her legs so she is familiar with what she needs to do to move to the toy.
5. Once she tries to move to the toy, let her play with the toy to reward her.
6. Alternate placing the toy on her right and left sides to see if it is easier for her to move to one side than the other. If she can move better to one side, encourage cruising in that direction. Once she does that well, she can learn to cruise in the other direction.
7. When she can cruise three to four steps easily, she can practice cruising the length of the surface, like the length of the sofa. Encourage her to cruise longer distances, with a variety of surface heights, and in both directions.

activity #6   **Cruising with Hands *on top of* a Surface**

(fig. 5.6)

1. When your child can cruise along surfaces with an edge, she is ready to learn to cruise with her hands on top of the surface. Examples include: coffee table or other types of tables, sofa, bed, chairs lined up together, rectangular storage box, or the bathtub.
2. Have her pull to stand at the surface and then place toys at the opposite end of the surface. Encourage her to cruise to the toys.
3. When she is able to cruise along the length of the furniture, you can further challenge her by encouraging her to walk around the corner of the coffee table. This will be more difficult and you will need to help her move around the corner. Use a motivating toy and initially give her hand support to help her balance as she steps around the corner. As she learns what she needs to do, decrease your support until she can do it by herself. *(See figure 5.6.)*

activity #7   **Cruising from One Piece of Furniture to Another**

1. Arrange your furniture so that one piece of furniture is next to another. For example, place a table next to the sofa. Or, place one dining room chair next to another. The surfaces should be approximately the same height. They need to be set up in a line and need to be stable so they do not slide or move. Begin with a 6-inch space between the surfaces.
2. Encourage your child to cruise from one piece of furniture to another. To do this, she will need to let go of the furniture with one hand, balance herself while she places first one hand and then the other on the next piece of furniture. The most difficult part is letting go with one hand as she places it on the next piece of furniture. You may need to help her until she has learned what to do.
3. As she becomes motivated to cruise from one piece of furniture to another, increase the distance between the two pieces of furniture. This will further challenge her balance and control in cruising.

(fig. 5.7)   *(fig. 5.8)*   *(fig. 5.9)*

4. When she can cruise between two surfaces 12-15 inches apart, place the surfaces parallel to each other. For example, place the coffee table in front of the sofa. Place her standing at the sofa and put a toy behind her on the coffee table. Place the toy to her side so she can see it. Encourage her to cruise from the sofa to the table. Begin with the surfaces close together and increase the distance as tolerated. *(See figures 5.7, 5.8, and 5.9.)*

5. This is a risky activity and your child needs to be ready to do it. If she is not ready, she may become frightened and refuse to do it. It is best to move slowly and challenge her when she is willing and ready.

activity #8
Cruising with Hands *against* a Surface

1. Use surfaces that your child will prop her hands *against,* for example, the wall, refrigerator, or cupboards.

2. Encourage her to step sideways and maintain her balance with her hands against the surface. Use magnets or colorforms and place them to her side, just out of reach.

3. If she cannot step sideways with this support, encourage her to stand in the position and play with one-hand support. After she is comfortable in this position, she may take one step sideways to get a toy.

4. When she is comfortable with cruising with her hands against surfaces, she will be able to walk around the kitchen with her hands against the cupboards and walk around the house with her hands against the walls. This will give her a way to step within the house rather than creeping or crawling.

Section 3: PLANTIGRADE & MOVING TO STAND

During this stage, your child will discover and use the plantigrade position— standing with her hands and feet on the floor. First, she will learn to move into the position and, later, she will learn to move from plantigrade to stand.

When she is able to move from plantigrade to stand, she will be able to stand up anywhere and will no longer need to pull up to stand, holding onto furniture or your hands. She will be an independent walker when she can stand up by herself, anywhere in the room, and walk. If she needs to creep over to you or to furniture in order to stand up, she will walk less.

Steps in: Learning the Plantigrade Position

Your child will progress through the following steps:
1. move into plantigrade;
2. move into modified plantigrade;
3. move from modified plantigrade to stand; and
4. move from plantigrade to stand.

moving into plantigrade

Watch her to see when she is ready to move into the plantigrade position. She may be on the floor on her hands and knees and then straighten her knees and lift her buttocks up so she is propping on her hands and feet. She will experiment with moving in and out of the plantigrade position from hands and knees. She also will use the plantigrade position when climbing up stairs. When she is climbing up the stairs, she will start on her hands and knees and then will move onto her feet before she moves her knees up to the next stair.

The plantigrade position is beneficial in building arm strength. To maintain the position, she will need to prop on her hands and hold up her body weight from her buttocks forward.

When she first moves into the plantigrade position, her feet and hands will be far apart. After she practices using the position, she will be able to maintain it with her feet and hands closer together. *(See figure 5.10.)* She will need to be able to do this in order to move from plantigrade to stand.

When she is able to move into the plantigrade position, allow her to play in it and see what she is motivated to do next. She may move around the house on her hands and feet, which is called bear walking. She may use bear walking, in addition to creeping, to move where she wants to go. She may move in and out of plantigrade on her own. She may not realize, however, that she can move to stand from plantigrade. You can teach her the connection between plantigrade and standing and help her learn how to move to stand.

(fig. 5.10)

moving into modified plantigrade

If your child's arms are weak, you can make the position easier by having her prop her hands on the bottom stair or on a sofa cushion placed on the floor. This modified plantigrade position will lessen the weight on her hands until she has adequate arm strength to maintain the position with her hands on the floor.

The modified plantigrade position teaches her to keep her hands and feet closer together and it assists her in moving her buttocks over her feet. From this position, it is easier to balance herself and lift her trunk up to standing. She will learn how to move from modified plantigrade to stand and will use hand support until she can do it by herself.

Once your child is able to move to stand from the modified plantigrade position, you can encourage her to move to stand from the plantigrade position.

(fig. 5.11)

(fig. 5.12)

moving from modified plantigrade to stand

To help your child learn to move to stand, you can start by using the modified plantigrade position. For example, if you sit on the floor with your buttocks on your feet, she can creep to you, move to modified plantigrade with her hands on your thighs, and then you can encourage her to stand up. In the beginning, she will need to hold your hand or prop her hands against your chest as she moves up to stand. With practice, she will use less hand support and ultimately, she will move up to stand from the modified plantigrade position. See activity #9 for more examples. *(See figures 5.11 and 5.12.)*

moving from plantigrade to stand

To move from plantigrade to stand, your child will need to learn to do four steps. *(See figures 5.13, 5.14, and 5.15.)* The steps are:
1. maintain the plantigrade position with her hands and feet close together (approximately 6 inches from toes to wrists);
2. shift her weight back and move her buttocks behind her feet;
3. balance herself in this position;
4. lift her trunk up so she is standing.

(fig. 5.13)   *(fig. 5.14)*   *(fig. 5.15)*

Each step builds on the previous step and each step needs to be done perfectly for her to move up to stand independently. For the first step, if her hands and feet are too far apart, she will not be able to move her buttocks behind her feet. When she is properly postioned, she will find the point where she feels balanced with her buttocks behind her feet. She will hold this balanced position with her legs and buttocks and then lift her trunk up to move to stand. When she first learns to stand up, she will move slowly through the four steps. With practice, she will be fast and the steps will be precise and automatic.

To help her move from plantigrade to stand, you can position yourself in front of her (activity #10) or behind her. If your child prefers support behind her buttocks, she may position herself in plantigrade with her buttocks and feet against the sofa. Or, she may use this same position in the crib or playpen with her buttocks and feet against the crib rails or net of the playpen. You could also provide this support by kneeling behind her. From this position and with the support behind her buttocks, she will feel balanced and able to stand up.

You can help your child learn to move from plantigrade to stand but she will only do it spontaneously when she is ready—when *she* wants to stand. She will choose standing when she knows she can stand well, is comfortable in standing, and is motivated to stand. After she stands up, she will choose what she wants to do next. Her options are: standing for a few seconds, sitting down, singing and dancing, and stepping forward. Your child may learn to move from plantigrade to stand before she takes independent steps or she may take a few independent steps and then learn to move from plantigrade to stand.

activity guidelines

Wait for your child to initiate moving into plantigrade. It is not recommended to try to put her in the plantigrade position. It is awkward to put her in the position and she will probably resist it. Your job is to watch her and notice when she starts incorporating this position into her repertoire of movements.

Expect your child to keep her feet wide apart when she first learns to move from plantigrade to stand independently. By positioning her feet wider than her hips, it will be easier to balance herself as she moves from plantigrade to stand. When she has more strength and balance, she will spontaneously narrow her base. She will learn to stand and balance with her feet under her hips and this will help her narrow her base when moving from plantigrade to stand.

As your child is moving from plantigrade to stand, watch her knees. Look and see whether she holds her knees stiff or bends them. She may hold them stiff in the beginning because this will help her feel more stable. With practice, she will learn to bend her knees. Bending her knees will help her move her buttocks behind her feet and balance in plantigrade as she lifts her trunk up to standing. If she has practiced knee bending through creeping, climbing, and moving from standing to sitting on the floor, she will also figure out how to bend her knees when moving from plantigrade to stand.

temperament

If your child is an *observer,* she will probably learn to move from plantigrade to stand before she takes independent steps. She will approach walking carefully and will want to develop moving to stand and standing balance before she tries to take steps. She may move from plantigrade to stand and then stand alone for 10 or more seconds, or she may move to stand and then sit down again. She will surprise you the first time she does it. She may just stand up, clap, and then wonder what to do next!

If your child is *motor driven,* she will probably take independent steps first (for 2-5 feet) and later, she will learn to move from plantigrade to stand. Since she will like to be risky and move fast, she will take steps, fall down, creep to a table, stand up, and take steps again. She will not be concerned about balancing herself in standing and will prefer to step, even if she falls. Later, when she wants to walk 5-15 foot distances, she will need to learn to balance as she is stepping. When she wants to walk a lot, she will be motivated to learn to move to stand from plantigrade. If you help her learn how to do it at this point, she will learn quickly so she can move to stand and take steps.

activity #9 **Moving from Modified Plantigrade to Stand**
1. Sit on the floor with your buttocks on your heels.
2. Call your child to come to you and have a motivating toy. She will creep over to you.
3. When she is in front of you, pat your thighs and say "come here." She will put her hands on your thighs. Praise her.
4. Hold the toy up above her head and say "stand up."
5. See what she does. You want her to straighten her knees so she moves into the modified plantigrade position with her feet on the floor and her hands on your thighs. From this position, she can prop her hands against your chest to move herself up to standing. If she does not try to move up to stand from the modified plantigrade position, offer her your finger and she can hold it as she lifts her trunk up to standing.
6. When she stands, clap for her and praise her. Give her the toy.
7. The modified plantigrade position can also be done by having her prop her hands on a sofa cushion placed on the floor or prop her hands on the bottom stair. After she creeps over to the surface, encourage her to prop her hands on the surface, move to modified plantigrade and then help her stand up by giving her hand support as needed.
8. When she is familiar with moving from modified plantigrade to stand with hand support, encourage her to stand up without hand support.

activity #10 **Moving from Plantigrade to Stand**
This activity can be done after your child can move from modified plantigrade to stand.
1. Watch your child and when she moves into the plantigrade position, position yourself in front of her. You can sit with your buttocks on your heels, kneel, or stand.
2. Hold a toy above her head and say "stand up."
3. If she is unable to stand and stays in the plantigrade position, offer her your finger to hold onto to help her stand up.
4. Once she is standing, praise her and clap for her. Give her the toy.
5. When she is familiar with moving from plantigrade to stand with hand support, encourage her to stand up without hand support.
6. An alternative method is to provide support behind her buttocks. When she moves into plantigrade, kneel behind her with her buttocks against you. Tell her to "stand up" and assist her by placing your hand on her middle trunk (above her waist) and lifting it up. When she is familiar with standing up, have her do it without your support to lift her middle trunk.

Section 4: CLIMBING

Your child will learn to love climbing. She will see what she can do and where she can go using climbing. She will be able to creep but not yet able to walk by herself, so climbing will be her source of adventure and exploration. She will need to be supervised closely because she will not have the judgement needed for safety. During this stage the goal will be for her to learn to climb safely.

Steps in: Learning to Climb

Your child will learn to:
1. climb up a flight of stairs,
2. climb off the sofa by herself,
3. climb down a flight of stairs, and
4. do other climbing.

You can practice climbing off the sofa and climbing up the stairs at the same time, but you should wait to practice climbing down stairs until she has mastered the other climbing skills.

climbing up stairs

During the previous stage your child learned to climb from the number two stair to the landing. The next challenge is to repeat the sequence of movements to climb up an entire flight of stairs. You can gradually increase the number of stairs when her attention and movement capabilities are sufficiently developed. With practice, climbing up will become automatic for her and she will plan how to move up the whole flight of stairs. She will have achieved the goal of climbing up a flight of stairs when she can do it safely on a consistent basis.

Your child may develop a method of climbing up stairs that is different from the typical method. For example, she may position one leg in the half kneel position rather than get on both knees. Or, she may climb up stairs on her hands and feet and never be on her knees. As long as her method is safe, let her use it.

It is best if you kneel behind her. From this position, you can lean forward to move the toy and then you can lean back and help her as needed. You can also keep her from sitting back on the stair.

climbing off the sofa

To climb off the sofa by herself, your child will need to (*see figures 5.16, 5.17, 5.18, and 5.19*):
1. roll over on her stomach;
2. lean her trunk into the surface and use her arms to control how fast she slides off;
3. slide down until her feet touch the floor.

(fig. 5.16)

(fig. 5.17)

(fig. 5.18)

(fig. 5.19)

Once she knows the steps, she needs to learn how to do them safely by herself. If she is sitting on the sofa and you place a toy on the floor and say "down," will she climb off the sofa safely or will she move after the toy head first because she wants it so much and does not stop to plan how to climb off safely? Once she starts climbing off the right way by herself, you still need to watch her because she will sometimes forget and climb down head first. With practice, climbing off safely will become automatic and she will do it consistently.

When your child has mastered climbing off the sofa, you can practice climbing off other furniture like a chair or bed. Watch the height of the furniture and supervise her until she feels comfortable climbing down. Use a variety of surfaces so she learns to climb down all types.

climbing down stairs

Climbing down stairs develops a few months later than climbing up stairs. Your child will be ready to begin learning this skill after she can climb off the sofa and climb up a flight of stairs by herself. She will probably learn to climb down stairs by sliding on her belly, much as she learned to climb off the sofa. Climbing down stairs will be more difficult because she cannot focus on looking where she is going or she will upset her balance. She will need to keep her head looking forward, with an occasional glance back, while she moves her body down several stairs. She will need to keep her attention focused on moving down all the stairs and then finally will be able to sit and play when she reaches the bottom of the stairs.

To climb down the stairs, she will use one of three methods:
1. **Sliding down on her stomach;**
2. **Climbing down on her hands and knees or hands and feet; and**
3. **Sitting on the stair and "bumping" down on her buttocks.**

You will initially teach her the easiest method, which is sliding down on her stomach. Later, when she wants to climb down the stairs independently, she may use another method from the list above.

To slide down the stairs on her stomach, she will need to:
1. **push off with her hands to push her body down the stairs;**
2. **lean her head and trunk over the stair to keep her balance and control the speed; and**
3. **use her feet to stop herself on the next stair.**

She may prefer to climb down on her hands and knees or hands and feet. To climb down, she will lean her trunk over the stair her arms are on and stabilize herself; then she will slide each knee or foot down to the next stair. With her knees or feet stable on the next stair, she will move her hands down to the stair above her knees. She will repeat this sequence to move down the stairs. *(See figures 5.20, 5.21, and 5.22.)*

Sitting and "bumping" down the stairs is generally used when children are taller. When your child is short, it is scary to fall down to the next stair. She will feel out of control until her buttocks touch the stair. When she is taller, her trunk and legs are longer so she has more balance and control as she "bumps" down. To use this method, she will sit on the stair and slide her buttocks forward to the edge of the stair by bending her knees greater than 90 degrees. Then she will move her feet

(fig. 5.20)

(fig. 5.21)

(fig. 5.22)

so they are below the next stair and bend her knees again to slide her buttocks off the stair and "bump" down to the next stair. *(See figure 5.23.)* She will need to sit with her trunk up straight in order to maintain her balance. Otherwise, she could fall down the stairs.

Begin with only 3-4 stairs, then gradually increase the number of stairs that you ask your child to climb down. Be patient as you help her learn to move down the flight of stairs. She will need to learn how to do it safely and then keep her attention focused to repeat the steps until she reaches the floor at the bottom of the stairs. She will need to be motivated and determined to do it in order to carry it out safely. Keep practicing it until she shows you she is ready to do it independently and consistently.

Position yourself behind her, either sitting or kneeling. Keep her focused on moving down the stairs and make it fun by varying the speed as you slide her down. Do not encourage her to play on the stairs or have conversations; keep her focused on moving down to the bottom and then let her play with her toy.

other climbing

You will be proud to see her move her body and climb so effectively. You will be happy to see her explore, be active, and get where she wants to go. However, it will also be a challenge to keep up with her. For example, Michael wanted to get a cookie from the cookie jar on the kitchen counter. He noticed that the dishwasher door was open, so he climbed onto it so that he could reach the cookie jar. That's where his mother found him, with his hand in the cookie jar!

Once your child wants to climb, think about how you can give her safer, appropriate climbing opportunities. Look for toddler playgrounds or climbing facilities such as at Discovery Zone or McDonald's.

Consider buying some climbing equipment, such as slides, available through Fisher Price, Little Tikes, and other companies. Depending on the size of your house, you can keep them inside or outside. When choosing slides, begin with a slide that has 3-4 stairs. Make sure there is enough room at the top for your child to hold on and sit down safely before she slides down by herself. *(See figure 5.24.)* Good examples are the Little Tikes Tree House, the Little Tikes Activity Gym or the Junior Activity Gym, or the Fisher Price 2 in 1 Adjustable Slide.

If your house does not have any stairs, it is especially important to seek out the types of climbing opportunities described above. You might also wish to ask a friend whether your child can practice climbing the stairs in their house. Climbing is an important skill to work on at this developmental age, and your child will need plenty of practice to master it.

(fig. 5.23)

activity guidelines

Expect your child to go through a four-phase process as she learns climbing skills. The phases include:

1. Practicing the movements needed and using the right sequence;
2. Controlling her body to move safely from one place to the next;
3. Planning how to climb after something; and
4. Using judgement on a consistent basis for safety.

You will see your child go through these phases as she develops each climbing skill. You will need to support her in the beginning and then decrease your support as she learns phases 2,3, and 4.

(fig. 5.24)

Use toys to motivate your child to climb where you want her to go. Place them as described in Activities #11, 12, and 13.

Keep your child moving with momentum and consistency. If she moves slowly or stops to play, she will try to sit back on the stair and will fall backwards, unless you are there to catch her. You want her to learn to keep climbing up or down the stairs when she is on them. She can sit and play when she gets to the top or the bottom.

Remember that your role is to motivate her to climb up and down the stairs, help her move her head, arms, or legs (if needed), and supervise her so she is safe.

Use shorter flights of stairs, if possible. If there are 6-7 stairs to the landing, this is easier to learn to do than a flight of 12-13 stairs.

If your child is short, begin climbing off lower furniture and gradually increase the height when tolerated. If she is short, it will take longer for her feet to touch the ground when sliding off the furniture. This could be scary to her and would make climbing off furniture more difficult. As she gets taller she will be able to climb up on more surfaces, for example, the sofa with the seat cushions in place.

Use carpeted stairs when she is learning to climb the stairs. She will feel more comfortable and you can avoid little accidents, like bumping her head. If only wooden stairs are available, move her slowly and particularly watch her head so she does not bump it. As her climbing skills improve, she will anticipate how she needs to move her head so she does not bump it.

temperament

If your child is an **observer,** she will climb up stairs when she is motivated. You will need to encourage her to keep moving because she will prefer to stop, sit, and play. She will generally be more attentive to being safe, but watch her especially if she tries to sit, rather than continue to climb. When she climbs off the sofa and down stairs, she will be fearful initially and will want to lower herself slowly and carefully. You will need to keep her moving and focused on reaching the bottom of the stairs.

If your child is **motor driven,** she will like to climb up and down stairs. She will like moving fast and will think it is fun. You will need to watch her because she may not pay attention to being safe. She will enjoy the feeling of sliding down as she is climbing off furniture. She will like sliding down the stairs when she is familiar with the movements.

activity #11

Climbing Off the Sofa

1. Place your child sitting on the sofa with the seat cushion in place. Position her with her back against the back cushion. This will give her adequate space to roll over before she slides down to the floor.
2. Place a toy on the floor, approximately 3 feet from the sofa, so she can see it well.
3. Sit on your heels next to the toy. This position allows you to help her if needed but you are far enough away that she will not reach for you or lunge forward and expect you to catch her.
4. Say "down" and see if she will try to climb off the sofa to get the toy.
5. The goal is for her to roll over on her stomach and slide down until her feet touch the floor. Then she can move to the floor and get her toy.
6. If she tries to climb off without rolling to her stomach, tell her to "roll over" or say whatever verbal cue she is familiar with. If she does not roll over after you give her the cue, help her roll over. Then she can slide down to the floor by herself.
7. Continue to practice this activity until she consistently and automatically climbs down safely.
8. When she has mastered climbing off the sofa, have her practice climbing off other furniture—a bed, a variety of chairs in the house.

activity #12

Climbing Up a Flight of Stairs

1. Place your child on the stairs with her hands on the #2 stair (from the top) and her knees on the #3 stair.
2. Place a toy on the landing so it is easy to see but out of reach.
3. Position yourself on your knees on the #4 stair.
4. See if she will try to move to the toy. She will need to do the following steps:
   a. Move onto her feet, one at a time;
   b. Move her hands onto the #1 stair, one at a time;
   c. Move each knee up to the #2 stair;
   d. repeat steps a,b, and c until she climbs up on the landing.
5. Help her move her arms or legs if needed. If her feet slide, block them from sliding. If she tries to sit, encourage her to keep moving forward and discourage sitting on the stairs. Supervise her so she is safe.

6. When she climbs up to the landing from the #3 stair, place her on the #4 stair. Gradually increase the number of stairs she climbs.
7. Work toward climbing up the entire flight of stairs.
8. Continue to practice climbing up the flight of stairs until it is automatic and she consistently climbs up safely.

activity #13

Climbing Down Stairs

1. Place your child on her stomach on the stairs with her elbows on the #4 stair (from the bottom) and her knees on the #3 stair.
2. Place a toy on the floor at the bottom of the stairs.
3. Position yourself on your knees on the #2 stair.
4. Help her move down the stairs using the following steps:
   a. Hold her ankles with her toes pointed down and straighten her knees;
   b. Say "down" and pull her ankles down to the #2 stair until her toes touch the stair;
   c. As she slides down, she will lift her head and move her arms to prop her elbows on the next step;
   d. Repeat steps a, b, and c until her feet are on the floor at the bottom of the stairs. Then let go and let her sit and play.
5. When she is familiar with the movements, set her up on the #4 stair and see if she will climb down by herself. If not, assist her as needed.
6. When she can climb down from the #4 stair by herself, place her on the #5 stair. Gradually increase the number of stairs she climbs down.
7. Work toward climbing down the entire flight of stairs.
8. Continue to practice climbing down the flight of stairs until it is automatic and she climbs down safely.
9. Watch and see if she learns to climb down stairs using methods #2 or #3.

Section 5: WALKING

During this stage, your child will begin walking holding your hands and, by the end of the stage, she will learn to walk by herself. To walk, she will need to develop strength in her stomach and leg muscles, balance, and endurance. However, the key to walking will be her motivation to walk. To help her develop walking skills, you will need to focus on motivating her first. When she is motivated to take steps, you can help her build the component parts needed for walking.

In order to take a step, she will need to shift her weight over to one leg so her other leg has no weight on it and it is free to move. She will initially use arm support to help her balance as she takes steps. Through stepping with support, she will learn to use her stomach muscles to help shift her weight and balance her body so she can step.

walking with two-hand support

Your child will be ready to walk with two-hand support when she can cruise and balance in standing with one-hand support. To see if she will take steps, stand facing her, and have her hold your thumbs and step to you. If she is not able to move her legs with this support, you can help her by leaning her to each side so she can then step with her other leg.

Steps in: Learning to Walk

Your child will need to practice the following steps to learn to walk by herself. They are listed in the order they develop. They are:
1. Walking with two-hand support,
2. Walking holding a push toy,
3. Lunging steps (1-3 steps),
4. Walking with one-hand support,
5. Independent steps, from 2-3 steps to walking 15 feet,
6. Walking within the house (even surfaces), and
7. Walking outside (uneven surfaces).

To teach her to walk properly with two-hand support, you need to:
1. **have your child hold on to your thumbs;**
2. **position her arms with her elbows bent and hands in front of her chest, at shoulder level or lower.**

By holding on to your thumbs, she learns to be responsible for controlling her own balance. If you hold her, she will not have to balance herself and will depend on you to do that for her.

Her hands need to be at shoulder level or lower to enable her to use her stomach muscles for balance. If her hands are higher, she will arch her back and her belly will protrude. In this position, she will not be able to use her stomach muscles and will need to rely on you for balance.

(fig. 5.25)

It works best if you are in front of her and she is holding your thumbs and stepping to you. *(See figure 5.25.)* With you in front of her, you can see how she is doing and can keep her balanced in the forward/backward directions. When she is stepping for distances up to three feet, you can sit on a low chair or the floor in front of her. When she walks for 3-10 feet or more, you can stand in front of her, facing her, and step backwards as she steps forward.

If your child is not motivated to step forward when you are standing in front of her, try standing behind her. She might be more motivated to walk when she can see where she is going or see the motivator she is walking toward. You will need to support her arms properly and lean yourself forward over her so you keep her balanced forward rather than leaning her back toward you.

activity #14   ## Walking with Two-Hand Support
1. To help your child take her first steps with two-hand support:
   a. Place her sitting on a bench, facing you.
   b. Sit on the floor approximately 3 feet away from her.
   c. Have her pull up to stand holding onto your thumbs. From standing, have her hold your thumbs and encourage her to step to you.

     d. When she reaches you, praise her and show your excitement. Hug her and then clap for her, or hold her by the wrists and help her clap her hands together.

     e. An alternative position is to place her standing with her back against the wall or sofa, facing you. Have her hold your thumbs and encourage her to step to you.

2. To help her walk 3-15 feet, follow these steps:

     a. Place her sitting on a bench, facing you.

     b. Stand in front of her.

     c. Have her pull to stand, holding your thumbs.

     d. Check the position of her arms, making sure her elbows are bent and her hands are in front of her chest, at shoulder level or lower.

     e. Set up a distance for her to walk and place a motivator at the endpoint. Pick a motivator that she really likes.

     f. You step backward and encourage her to step forward to the motivator. When she reaches it, praise her, clap for her, and show your excitement.

     g. An alternative starting position is to place her standing with her back against the wall or sofa, facing you. Have her hold your thumbs and continue with steps d, e, and f.

     h. Increase the distance when she is ready. Begin with taking 3-5 steps. Then work toward walking 5-10 feet. The ultimate goal is to walk for distances of 20 feet or more.

     i. If she is not motivated to step forward with you in front of her, stand behind her. Continue to have her hold your thumbs and support her arms properly. You will need to lean your trunk forward to keep her balanced forward.

walking with a push toy

Your child is ready to begin walking with a push toy when she can step well with two-hand support. She will need to know how to hold on so she can hold the handle of the push toy. She will learn to hold on to the handle, control her balance, and take steps. (See figure 5.26.)

     Choose a push toy that your child likes and that works well for her. The push toy needs to:
          1. be stable so it does not tip over easily;
          2. have a bar or edge to hold onto;
          3. be the right height; and
          4. have a base wide enough that your child's feet fit between the wheels.

Examples of push toys that fit these criteria are: Playskool Activity Walker and Toddlin' Train, Little Tikes Play About Walker and Push 'n Ride Walker, the V-TECH Little Smart Talking First Steps, and the Fisher Price Activity Walker. As an alternative, you can use a wagon, such as the Little Tikes 2 in 1 wagon, because it has an edge to hold onto. Generally, lightweight baby strollers and shopping carts do not work well since they tip over easily.

     Practice walking with the push toy on a carpeted surface. If you try it on tile, vinyl flooring, or hardwood floors, the push toy will slip and slide in all directions

(fig. 5.26)

and your child will feel unstable and uncomfortable. On a carpeted surface, the only direction the push toy will move is forward.

When your child is first learning to walk with the push toy, she will lean her body forward. She will be working on holding on and stepping and will not know how to stand tall and balance herself. You will need to hold the push toy and move it forward, controlling the speed and the position of the push toy relative to her body. You want to keep the push toy forward of her body and close enough so she can step. You need to make sure it is not too far forward, causing her to lean excessively forward, because this will make her less stable. With practice, she will learn to stand tall with her body more vertical. At this point, you can try letting go of the push toy so she can try to push it by herself, controlling her own balance.

Do not weight the push toy to provide greater stability. The additional weight will cause your child to lean forward into the toy to make it go, and this will interfere with her development of balance.

As she becomes more skilled, your child will learn to pull to stand at the push toy, first with your support, then without it. This way she will be able to use it spontaneously and whenever she wants to rather than just being able to do it when someone helps her. She will also learn to steer the push toy around furniture and to free it when it gets stuck.

activity #15 Walking with a Push Toy

1. Choose a push toy your child likes. Place it on the carpet.
2. Place your child standing at the push toy and help her place her hands on the handle. You let go and make sure she continues to hold on. Tell her to "hold on."
3. Place your hands on the front of the push toy to stabilize it and slowly move it forward. Your job is to keep it stable, move it forward at the right speed, and keep it the right distance in front of her. Her job is to hold on and step forward.
4. Set up a distance for her to walk and place a motivator at the endpoint. When she reaches it, praise her, clap for her, and show your excitement.
5. Increase the distance when she is ready. Begin with taking 3-5 steps. Then work toward walking 5-10 feet. The ultimate goal is to walk for distances of 20 feet or more.
6. When she is familiar with walking with the push toy and is motivated to use it, encourage her to pull up to stand, holding the bar. You hold the push toy to keep it from moving. Later, have her pull to stand by herself.
7. When she is comfortable and experienced with walking with the push toy, begin to briefly let go and see if she can control it by herself. Begin with short distances, like letting go when she is 3 feet from the sofa so she will automatically stop when the push toy hits the sofa. When she is ready, increase the distance she can walk without your support. Work toward walking across a room by herself.

8. After she has mastered walking with the push toy without your support, teach her to steer it around furniture. When she is stuck against furniture, say "turn" and put your hands over her hands to free it. With practice, she will learn to maneuver it around furniture all by herself.

lunging steps

When she can walk well with a push toy and is beginning to stand alone briefly, you can try lunging steps. Lunging steps are when a child leans forward, props her hands on a support, and then takes a couple steps to stand at the support. For example, you may support your child in standing and have her take lunging steps to the sofa or to another person. When she takes a lunging step, she chooses to move from a supported position to falling forward to another support. Lunging steps get her used to leaning or "falling" forward and experiencing the risk involved in taking a step. This will prepare her to take independent steps.

When you first practice this skill, you can have your child lunge to a horizontal surface such as the sofa. When she can lunge to horizontal surfaces, begin practicing lunging to a vertical surface. For example, have her lunge to a window to look outside, lunge to the refrigerator to play with magnets or colorforms, or lunge to a person kneeling in front of her. Lunging to a vertical surface will teach her to lean forward and balance with her trunk more upright. This practice will help her learn to balance and take independent steps.

When your child is first taking lunging steps, the surface she is moving toward needs to be padded, for your child's safety. If you use a table or firm surface, she may fall or bump into it. It is best to use the sofa, padded chair, or a person's body.

When practicing lunging steps, do not let your child hold your hands. If she is lunging to you, position your hands at your sides or use them to pat the area you want her to move toward. For example, if you are kneeling, pat your belly; if you are sitting on the floor, pat your upper chest area. This will let her know where to prop her hands. If you put your hands out for her to hold, she will depend on you to catch her and help her balance. You want her to learn to fall, prop, and balance herself.

activity #16 **Lunging Steps**

1. Lunging to a horizontal surface:
   a. Place your child in standing, approximately 1½ feet in front of the sofa.

b. If she needs support in standing, position yourself in tall kneeling behind her and support her against your hips and thighs. Make sure you kneel up straight so she is standing up straight. Another alternative is to place a toy box or piece of furniture behind her.

c. Place a book or toy that she loves on the sofa.

(fig. 5.27) (fig. 5.28)

d. Encourage her to move to it. Wait for her to lean forward and prop on the sofa. Then she will step to the sofa to move to the toy. When she reaches the toy, praise her, clap for her, and show your excitement. *(See figures 5.27 and 5.28.)*

e. Do not hold her hand or her body with your hands because she will learn to depend on your support in order to lunge and step.

f. When she does the preceding steps well, place her 2 feet in front of the sofa and repeat steps b, c, d, and e.

g. With practice, she may learn to take a step *before* she props her hands on the sofa.

2. Lunging to a vertical surface

a. Place your child in standing with her back against the wall or furniture.

b. Position yourself kneeling up straight on the floor, approximately 2 feet in front of her.

c. Place a motivator at eye level to her. You can put a toy in your pants pocket or under your belt.

d. Encourage her to lunge and step to you or the toy. Pat your belly or hips and say "come here." Wait for her to lean forward, prop her hands on your hips, and step to you. When she reaches you, praise her, clap for her, and show your excitement.

e. Do not hold her hand or her body with your hands because she will learn to depend on your support in order to lunge and step.

f. With practice, she may learn to take a step *before* she props her hands on you.

g. This activity can also be done between two persons, with both of them kneeling up tall and straight. Place your child standing in front of one person with her back supported against the person's legs. The other person can encourage her to lunge to him. Repeat steps c, d, e, and f. *(See figures 5.29 and 5.30.)*

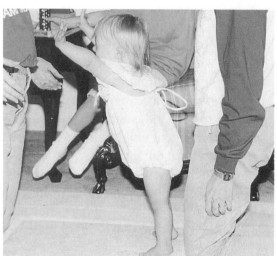

(fig. 5.29)

(fig. 5.30)

walking with one-hand support

When your child can walk well with two-hand support, try letting go with one hand. She will initially resist walking with one-hand support because it will feel unstable to her. She will notice it is much harder to balance and step with only one hand supported. She will prefer holding on with two hands and will reach out for your other hand.

To walk with one-hand support, she will need to balance both sides of her body and step with only one side supported. It will generally be easier to step with the leg on the supported side. When she steps with that leg, she will be balanced in the center by her other leg and the supported hand. However, when she steps with her leg on the unsupported side, her weight will be leaning over the supported side and it will be harder to keep her balance in the center and step. So, when she steps with that leg, she may spin in a circle and fall.

Introduce walking with one-hand support gradually and do it for short distances. Alternate between providing two-hand support and one-hand support. You can walk with two-hand support and when you are 2-3 steps away from the endpoint, let go with one hand. Or, you can have her take 2-3 steps with one-hand support and then have her step toward your other hand so she can walk with two-hand support.

(fig. 5.31)

To teach your child to walk with one-hand support, the proper set-up is critical. Follow the steps in Activity #17. It is best for you to position yourself in front of her, facing her, so you can hold her supported arm and hand at chest level and in the center. This will give her better support to work on balancing herself as she steps. *(See figure 5.31.)* If you stand beside her, facing the same direction as she is, you will have to hold her hand to the side of her body. This will make it harder for her to balance herself and step.

When she can walk well with one-hand support, with you in front of her, you can challenge her balance further by walking beside her. Once she has the balance to do this, you can practice walking longer distances.

activity #17   **Walking with One-Hand Support**

1. To help your child take her first steps with one-hand support:
    a. Position her in standing, facing you.
    b. Sit on the floor or on a low footstool, 2-3 feet in front of her.
    c. Have her hold on to your thumb and position her hand in front of her chest, toward the center.
    d. Encourage her to walk to you, taking 2-3 steps.
    e. If it is helpful, place your free hand in front of her unsupported hand. She will reach for it and step to get it.
    f. When she steps to you, praise her, clap for her, and show your excitement.
2. After she can take 3-5 steps with one-hand support, begin to encourage her to step distances up to 5 feet. Follow these steps:
    a. Position her standing in front of you, facing you.
    b. Position yourself in kneeling or standing.
    c. Have her hold on to your thumb and position her hand in front of her chest, toward the center.
    d. You step backward and encourage her to step forward.
    e. Set up a distance for her to walk and place a motivator at the endpoint. Pick a motivator that she really likes. When she reaches it, praise her, clap for her, and show your excitement.

    f. If it is helpful, place your free hand in front of her unsupported hand to encourage her to keep stepping forward. You can also have her hold a small, lightweight toy in her unsupported hand.

    g. When she is able to walk 5-foot distances without any difficulty, continue to increase the distance she walks, up to 20-30 feet. When walking distances of 10-30 feet, position yourself in standing and step backwards as she steps forward.

    h. When she can easily walk 30-foot distances, you can stand next to her with both of you stepping forward. Make sure her hand is supported at shoulder level or lower.

3. When your child is stepping with one-hand support, try each hand to see if it is easier to balance and step when holding on to a particular hand. If it is easier to use one hand, have her practice using that hand first. Later, when she can walk well with one-hand support, have her practice holding on with her other hand.

independent steps

When your child is beginning to take a balanced step when lunging, she is ready to start learning to change from lunging steps to independent steps. Rather than leaning forward and catching her balance by propping on her hands, she will learn to balance with each step. Her posture will change from leaning forward to standing vertically.

Progressing from taking one step to walking around the house will be a gradual process. She will learn to take independent steps in the following order:

1. walk 1-5 steps,
2. walk 3 feet,
3. walk 3-5 feet,
4. walk 5-7 feet,
5. walk 7-10 feet,
6. walk 10-15 feet,
7. walk 15 feet consistently.

Your child will need to practice each distance until she masters it and then you can move on to the next distance. When she can walk 15 feet consistently, she will be able to learn to walk around the house.

To encourage the first 1-5 steps, you need the ultimate motivator or game. If you are sitting on the floor in front of her, you could have her walk to give you a kiss or touch your nose. You could also partially hide a toy in your shirt pocket or under your collar and have her come and find it. If she is walking to the sofa, you can partially hide a toy in between the cushions and have her come find it. Or, she can walk to a baby doll and touch the baby's eye or put on the baby's hat. Always position the motivator at eye level or lower to help her keep her balance. When she takes a step, praise her, clap for her, and show your excitement and pride.

The activities (Activity #18) for taking independent steps are set up so your child will learn to balance herself before she takes a step and keep maintaining her balance as she steps. This is best achieved by having her balance and take steps to you without holding on to you. This way she learns to balance herself as she takes independent steps rather than holding onto you for balance. (See figure 5.32.)

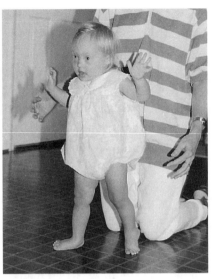

(fig. 5.32)

Practice walking on firm, level surfaces. Try a variety of surfaces such as carpet, tile, vinyl, and hardwood floors to see if she prefers one surface over another. Use the preferred surface consistently to teach her to take independent steps. If she always walks at the same place, she will feel secure and will not be distracted by changes in the environment. Later, when walking is easy and automatic, she will be confident in her ability to walk and will be able to experiment with walking on a variety of surfaces.

When she is taking steps, make sure the area is clear of obstacles that she could trip over, bump into, or be distracted by. If you are sitting on the floor and she is walking to you, make sure your legs are out of her way so she does not trip over them. When she is walking for 5 feet or more, clear out the area so she is safe and will not bump into something and hurt herself. You may need to rearrange furniture so she can practice walking distances of 7-15 feet or walk down a hallway.

As you help your child progress from walking 5-15 feet, watch how she responds to walking and try to see what she needs to help her move to the next level. Possible examples are:

1. Some children are motivated to walk and keep increasing the distance spontaneously. You can help by using the best motivators and increasing the distance appropriately.

2. Some children need incentives to keep increasing the distance. You can help by figuring out what is needed. You can experiment with trying different motivators, giving occasional breaks, giving her more cues, showing more excitement, changing the pace by alternating a slow balanced walk with giving her two-hand support and stepping quickly, and changing the sequence of how you usually practice walking.

3. Some children learn to sit down after taking steps for 3-5 feet. Now they know how to stop walking when they want to and do. Before they learned to sit down, they thought the only way to stop walking was to walk to the destination. You can help increase the distance by using a better motivator to see if they will not pay attention to the distance and keep stepping to get the motivator. If that does not help, you can also help them stand up after a brief break so they can continue stepping to the motivator.

4. Some children need to work on improving their balance and increasing their endurance. A boy named Michael and his father taught me this. Michael could walk independently for 7-10 feet and seemed stuck at that point. He loved to walk and preferred two-hand support. His father started having him practice walking with one-hand support every night when he came home from work. They would walk down their street to a tree that Michael loved and Michael would pick a leaf off the tree. They would take a break and then walk back to their house. Michael was motivated to walk to the tree and back home to see his brother and mother. In the beginning, it took a long time to

walk the distance. With practice, Michael gained the strength and control to do it faster. Within a short time, he was walking by himself in the house.

5. Some children need more practice. They need to walk with support as much as possible to build the strength needed to walk longer distances without support.

6. Some children need more praise or a more outrageous motivator. You need to be creative and keep thinking of possibilities!

Your child *will* learn to move her body and balance herself. Just keep motivating her to walk. With practice, she will take more steps and develop a more efficient pattern of walking.

activity #18   **Independent Steps**
There are many ways to help your child learn to take her first steps and progress to walking for 7-10 feet. Try these set-ups and see what she likes best. When she does take independent steps, praise her, clap for her, and show your excitement and pride.

1. Walking to you
   a. Position your child in standing with her back supported against furniture or the wall. If your child can stand without support, place her standing in the middle of the floor.
   b. Position yourself 2 feet in front of her, at eye level or lower. You can sit on the floor.
   c. Place your hands at your sides or pat your chest and say "come here."
   d. Encourage her to walk 1-2 steps to you. Use a great game or motivator.
   e. As tolerated, increase the distance to increase the number of steps she takes.

2. Walking to the sofa
   a. Position your child standing 2-3 feet in front of the sofa. If she needs support to stand, kneel behind her or place her against furniture.
   b. Place a toy on the sofa and encourage her to step to it.
   c. Position yourself at her side to assist her as needed for her own safety.
   d. As tolerated, increase the distance to increase the number of steps she takes.

3. Walking from one piece of furniture to another
   a. Arrange your furniture so two pieces are facing each other, 2-3 feet apart. For example, place a chair in front of the sofa.
   b. Position your child standing with her back against the chair.
   c. Place a motivator on the sofa and encourage her to walk to it.
   d. Position yourself at her side to assist her as needed for her own safety.
   e. As tolerated, increase the distance to increase the number of steps she takes.

4. Walking from one person to another

        a. Have two people kneel on the floor, facing each other and 2-3 feet apart. Each person needs to kneel up tall and straight.

        b. Position your child standing in front of one person with her back supported against the person's legs.

        c. Encourage her to walk to the other person. Use a motivator and have that person pat her belly and say "come here." Place the motivator at eye level or lower.

        d. As tolerated, increase the distance to increase the number of steps she takes.

5. Move from sitting to standing and then walk

        a. Place your child sitting on a bench, approximately knee height.

        b. Encourage her to stand up and step a distance of 2-3 feet, either to furniture or to you. Use a motivator and place it at eye level or lower.

        c. As tolerated, increase the distance to increase the number of steps she takes.

activity #19

Walking Distances of 10-15 Feet

1. Pick an area in your home that is 10-15 feet long and free of furniture, obstacles, and distractions. Rearrange the furniture if needed.

2. Place your child with her back supported against the sofa or other furniture.

3. Position yourself approximately 7 feet in front of her, sitting on your heels or kneeling.

4. Use a motivator and place it at eye level or lower. Encourage her to walk to you. When she reaches you, praise her, clap for her, and show your excitement.

5. Repeat the above steps until she is stable and can consistently walk within this set-up.

6. When she can do step #5, continue to use the same set-up, and, when she moves close to you, slowly move backward to increase the distance she walks. Continue to do this until she can walk distances of 10 feet.

7. When she can walk 10 foot distances, position yourself 10 feet in front of her. Encourage her to walk to you, and when she is close, slowly move backward to increase the distance she walks. Continue to do this until she walks distances of 15 feet.

8. When she is able to consistently walk 15 foot distances, she is ready to walk around the house on level surfaces.

walking on even surfaces

When your child is able to walk for distances of 15 feet, she is ready to learn to walk everywhere on level surfaces. She has learned by experience how far she can walk. Now, you will need to expand her experience to walk for longer distances. She will ultimately realize she can walk everywhere and can walk all the time. You will rarely see her creep in the house anymore; she will mostly walk. Once she can walk everywhere in the house, you can increase the distance by having her walk in a mall, to church, and everyplace else you go. She will emerge a confident, motivated, exploring walker. It will be automatic for her to walk on level surfaces.

    While practicing walking on level surfaces, she will develop better balance. She will learn to walk faster and will need to learn to balance herself while moving at a faster speed. She will also practice "catching" herself on her hands when she loses her balance and falls forward. She will need to learn to move her arms quickly to catch herself and her arms will need to be strong enough to stop her from falling forward and bumping her face. It is best for her to practice this on a padded surface such as the carpet. Her ability to "catch" with her hands will depend on the speed of the fall. If she falls slowly, it will be easier to "catch" with her arms. If she falls fast and with momentum, she will need more arm strength to stop the fall.

Practice walking on level surfaces at home and other places you go. Try one type of surface at a time so your child learns how to walk on each one. When she first starts walking on a new surface, supervise her until she becomes familiar with it and is safe. Wait to teach her to walk on concrete until she is very stable in walking. It is best to practice walking on concrete with hand support or with a push toy until she is very familiar with walking on it. It is easy to fall and she would be hurt if she did not catch herself effectively with her hands.

When your child walks well on level surfaces, the next challenge is to teach her to pay attention to the floor so she can maneuver herself around obstacles or uneven surfaces. At this point, you can introduce obstacles, as described in Activity #20, and see what she will do. She may notice them and try to walk around them, or she may not see them at all and you will need to point them out and help her move over them.

As your child is learning to walk long distances on level surfaces, it is best if she is barefoot or wearing nonskid socks. When she has mastered walking independently in the house for 1-2 months, you can begin using shoes. The shoes need to have a soft, flexible sole. To test the shoe for flexibility, hold the toe box with one hand and the heel with your other hand. Bend the toe box area and see how easily it moves. You want it to be very flexible so it is easy for your child to bend the shoe as she steps. If you use a shoe with a rigid or firm sole, she will use stiff leg movements, especially at her knees. The shoe also needs to have a rubber or nonskid sole. If it is slippery, she will feel insecure and this will limit her walking and may affect her motivation to walk.

Even if your child has the perfect shoes that pass these requirements, she will need time to adjust to them. Initially, she will compensate by walking with a wider base, stiff knees, and turning her feet outward. She may resist wearing the shoes and want to take them off. Begin using them for brief periods and gradually increase the time as her leg and foot muscles become stronger and she tolerates using them. When she has adjusted to wearing shoes, it is best for her to alternate between wearing shoes and having time barefoot.

activity #20 ### Walking on Even Surfaces

1. Pick an area 15-20 feet long with a consistent, level surface.
2. Encourage her to walk the distance. If she sits or falls, pick her up and place her in standing, and then encourage her to walk again. If she will not walk the distance, begin with a shorter distance and lengthen it by moving the endpoint as she approaches it.
3. Continue to practice until she can walk the distance consistently.

4. Within the same area, increase the distance to 25-30 feet. Encourage her to practice walking this distance until she can do it well.

5. Pick another area to walk on. Either use another type of floor surface or use the same type surface as above but in another location. Practice walking in each area until she is comfortable and competent.

6. Practice walking on a variety of types of floor surfaces in a variety of locations. Do this until she is able to walk on all types of level surfaces.

7. Practice walking from one floor surface to another. Examples are:
    a. walking from an area rug to the hardwood floor and the reverse, where she needs to step *up* and *down*;
    b. walking *over* the threshold between rooms, particularly if it is raised a ½ inch.

    In both examples, if she does not notice the change in surfaces, point it out to her. If she notices and moves down to the floor to climb or creep over it, hold her hand and tell her to walk. Work toward having her learn to notice changes in surfaces and *walk* up, down, and over them.

8. Place obstacles on the floor. Use one obstacle at a time. Examples of obstacles are: string or rope, broom handle or dowel, hula hoop, or toys on the floor. Encourage her to walk around the room, paying attention to the floor, and figuring out how to step over or around the obstacles.

9. Continue to practice until she can walk on level surfaces without tripping or falling, and can maneuver around obstacles safely.

walking on grass

When she can walk on level surfaces with confidence, begin walking on the grass. Changing to this uneven surface will challenge her balance and she will need to use new movements to keep her balance while walking. She will learn to bend her knees and move her feet to use a narrower base.

When your child first steps on the grass, she will know it is different and that she is less stable. She will probably walk 2-3 steps slowly and then fall. You will need to stay close to her so she feels more secure until she is familiar with walking on the grass. As her balance improves, she will be able to take more steps before she falls.

She will need to practice this skill until she can walk across the grass without falling and can move at the same speed as she does on level surfaces. When she is able to do this, she will be ready to practice walking on other uneven surfaces discussed in Chapter 7.

Watch how your child responds to falling when she first starts walking on grass. Some children do not mind and just keep standing up to walk again. Other children get frustrated and overwhelmed and may sit down and decide they do not want to walk on the grass. If your child is frustrated, give her one-hand support to help her become familiar with walking on the grass. When she is ready, decrease your support. Assist your child as needed so she continues to be motivated to walk.

When your child is walking on the grass, experiment with walking barefoot. If she cannot tolerate walking barefoot, have her wear shoes. If she does not mind walking barefoot, have her practice with and without shoes.

activity #21 **Walking on the Grass**

1. Pick an area of the grass that is relatively level.
2. Encourage your child to walk a distance of 5 feet to a motivator.
3. Position yourself near her so she feels comfortable.
4. When she can walk 5 feet, increase the distance to 10 feet. Continue to practice until she can walk around the yard without falling.

activity guidelines **Remember that children vary as to how motivated they are to walk and when they are motivated to walk.** Each child's readiness needs to be understood and respected. Possible reactions to walking are:

1. She may want to step and easily be motivated to do stepping. She may even creep over to you, pull up to stand, and indicate she wants you to walk her around the house.
2. She may feel very independent and want to be independent. Therefore, she will not be interested in walking, which is new and requires someone to help her.
3. She may be efficient in creeping and be able to go wherever she wants. To her, creeping is fast, well established, automatic, and known. She may resist walking because it is new, she is unstable and unbalanced, she cannot do it by herself, and she does not see the value in it.
4. She may fluctuate, wanting to walk sometimes or some days and not wanting to walk other times.

At this point in her life, she is used to choosing what she wants to do and she will decide when she wants to walk. She will choose walking when it has value to her and she is motivated to do it. For example, even though Patrick had mastered the physical skills necessary for walking for some time, he did not decide that it was a worthwhile endeavor until he figured out it was the only way he could carry a book to his mother so she could read to him.

Consider it your job to "turn on" your child to the world of walking. It will be different for her to be stepping rather than moving on hands and knees. It will take time for her to learn to walk with support and feel comfortable with it. Motivators can help to keep her interest. Even if she is not interested in walking, she will want to move to the motivator! Once she uses walking to move to the motivator, she will begin using walking to move from one place to another.

To help her discover the value of walking, make walking activities very familiar to her. Show her what she can do by being able to walk and how she can play. When she is familiar with walking, she will be more cooperative about practicing it. As she practices it, she will do it better and become more motivated to walk. If she is motivated to walk, she will walk more often and her strength, balance, and endurance will improve. By walking more often, she will become confident in her ability to walk. When she is confident, she will be willing to challenge herself. You need to move at her pace and be responsive to her temperament to be successful.

Use a variety of motivators to encourage your child to walk. You can use special new toys, favorite toys, or set up a game. Make the toys and games fun so she wants to play and she will walk to play them.

Some examples of creative games are:

1. She can walk to the phone, walk to a favorite room like the bathroom, or walk to a book.
2. She can walk to a door and knock on it or open and close it.
3. She can walk to a baby doll and feed the baby, put on its clothes or shoes, or show you the baby's nose.
4. She can walk to her mom or dad and give a kiss.
5. She can play "chase" games and try to catch her mom, sister, the cat, or a remote-controlled toy.
6. She can play the game "Where is mom" and walk to find her.
7. You can sit on the floor in front of her and partially hide a small toy in your shirt pocket or under the collar of your shirt and have her come and find it.

The best motivator of all is clapping for your child when she finishes a walk. When she has walked to the motivator at the endpoint, clap for her and praise her. She will love to see you clap for her and she will clap, too. She will see your enthusiasm and excitement. She will feel proud and happy and want to do it again. She will learn walking is great because of what happens when she does it. She will enjoy celebrating her walking successes with you.

Only do walking activities you can motivate your child to do. When you choose each activity, observe how your child is responding. If she dislikes practicing a particular walking activity, try distracting her by using a great motivator or gently tossing her up in the air or tickling her belly. She might forget what she was resisting and walk again. If you try the walking activity again and she still resists it, skip it and try it again later or the next day. If an activity consistently makes your child not want to walk and she sits down, discontinue it. You cannot force her to practice it because she will only resist it more. For example, Sammy was a two-year-old who hated walking with one-hand support. He enjoyed walking with two-hand support, but every time I let go of one hand, he would sit down and refuse to walk. Even if I used great motivators, he would not walk with one-hand support. We continued to practice walking with two-hand support and walking with the push toy so he would be motivated to walk and continue walking. If we had insisted on using one-hand support at that time, we would have decreased his motivation to walk. Later, he did tolerate walking with one-hand support when he was ready.

Provide verbal and visual cues. When you want her to walk, say: "walk." You can also say "walk, walk, walk" as she takes steps. This way she will learn what the word means and will know what you want her to do.

When you are using a motivator to encourage your child to walk, place it at eye level or lower to help her maintain her balance. If it is placed above eye level, her head will tilt back to look at it and she will lose her balance and fall. She needs to be looking forward, not upward.

To encourage her to walk longer distances, you can walk in front of her or beside her and exaggerate your walking pattern so she imitates you. For example, you can do marching steps. She will focus on your legs and try to march, too.

When practicing walking, make sure you do it properly so your child develops good movement patterns or habits. You want to give her the support she needs so she feels comfortable taking steps and develops the strength and balance needed to progress to walking alone. Sometimes, you may need to compromise good habits in order to motivate her to walk. If this happens, resume the good habits as soon as possible. For example, when she is walking with two-hand support, the good movement pattern is to have her hands at shoulder level or lower. However, when you first start practicing this skill, you may need to hold her hands higher to help motivate her to walk. Once she will take steps and shows some motivation to walk, lower her hands to shoulder level.

As she is learning to take steps, don't interfere with her leg and foot movements. If you support her arms properly so she uses her stomach muscles, that is what is most important. When taking steps, her feet will initially be wider than her hips. She will stiffen her knees to feel more stable. You need to let her use her method of moving her legs until she learns to walk. If you focus on changing how she moves her legs, she will feel nagged, her walking will be interrupted, and she will lose her motivation to walk. As she practices walking and it becomes easier, she will bend her knees more. Once she can walk, there are ways to help her learn to walk with a narrower base and bend her knees.

Practice walking on a firm, flat, level surface. The surface needs to be consistent and even so she is familiar with the feeling of the surface and learns by experience how to walk on it. Once she is familiar with the surface, she can focus on balancing herself and walking. A carpeted surface is best if it is not too padded. If it is very padded, she will feel unstable because her feet will rock on the soft surface. Her feet will be more stable on a firm, carpeted surface. You can use hardwood, tile, or vinyl floors if they are not slippery.

Walking will be more complicated and confusing to her if she needs to walk from one surface to another—from a hardwood floor to an area rug. With this set-up, she will need to pay attention to the changes in the surface, plan to step up and down, and plan how to walk on the new surface. Needing to pay attention to the surfaces will challenge her walking skills too much in the beginning.

When she is ready to practice walking longer distances, use an environment with a level surface and a lot of space, like a mall. Go at a time when it is less busy. Pick an area that is relatively quiet. She will get to choose what she is motivated to walk to and can walk from one area to another. Your job will be to keep her standing so she uses walking to explore everything.

Practice walking skills for short periods and repeat several times a day. Practice walking when your child is physically at her best or after she has rested. Do it as long as she is cooperative or until you see signs of fatigue. Common signs of fatigue are: fussiness, rhythmical tongue sucking movements, clumsiness with legs, and resistance to stepping. She needs to be motivated to walk, and, if she is tired or no longer wants to do it, you need to stop and try again later.

Increase the distance your child walks when she is ready. Start with short distances as a warm-up and keep increasing the distance to see how far she can step. When she is practicing walking, set up an endpoint or destination so she knows where she is going. If she sits or falls down before she reaches the end point, quickly stand her up and encourage her to keep walking to the motivator. When she can consistently walk that distance, increase it.

To develop walking skills, simultaneously work on strengthening her stomach and leg muscles, balance, and endurance. You can do this by practicing a variety of walking activities. For example, you can practice walking with two-hand support for longer distances to improve her strength and endurance and you can practice walking with one-hand support for short distances to work on balance. When she can walk with a push toy by herself, she can also practice lunging steps or walking with one-hand support. When she is beginning to take independent steps, she can practice walking for longer distances with one-hand support. Walking for longer distances with two-hand support or the push toy will help improve her strength and endurance. Practicing walking with one-hand support and taking lunging steps and independent steps will help improve her balance.

Practice walking barefoot or with nonskid socks. Walking without shoes helps to optimally develop strength, balance, and controlled movements in her feet and legs. When she is barefoot, it is easier for her to move her feet and she can use her feet for balance.

When wearing shoes, she is unable to move her feet inside them and her muscles are too weak to bend the shoes at her toes when she steps. Since she cannot bend the shoes at the toes, she will compensate by turning her feet outward so she can step by moving over the inside borders of her shoes.

She can wear shoes to dress up and go outside, but when she is home practicing walking, it is best to do it barefoot or with nonskid socks. When she has mastered walking and can walk well, all over the house, you can begin using shoes with flexible soles.

Practice walking in a wide open space rather than a cluttered space. When she is developing walking, she will fall and bump into furniture and toys. Plan ahead by rearranging furniture or having her walk in a particular room that is safer for her.

If she does fall, watch your reaction. You want to calm and soothe her so she is comforted and reassured. Make sure you do not overreact by the facial expression you use or how you initially respond. If you do, this will only upset her more and she may be afraid to try again.

Be patient and remember that timing is everything. The age range in which children with Down syndrome learn to walk is very wide. There are many reasons why some children walk earlier and some later. Their physical skills, temperament, and motivation all play a role. You cannot force it. You will need to wait until your child is ready to walk. There are plenty of other skills to work on while your child is getting ready to walk. Remember that being a late walker does not mean that she will be slower at other things.

temperament

If your child is an **observer,** she will want to feel secure and balanced. She will learn to move to stand from plantigrade and then will take steps. She will step carefully and balance herself with each step. She will resist changes in the type of support provided, for example, progressing from walking with two-hand support to walking with one-hand support. She will not like falling and will work to control her balance so she does not fall. She will notice changes in the floor surfaces and will carefully adjust to each type. To help her learn to walk, focus on:

1. moving slowly,
2. increasing the distance as tolerated,

3. avoiding falls,
4. praising her, and
5. building motivation and confidence.

By understanding how she feels about walking, you can help her develop walking skills in a way that works best for her.

If your child is ***motor driven,*** she will want to move and generally want to step. She may initially resist walking because it will be slower when compared to her fast method of creeping. Once she is motivated to walk, she will surprise you and boldly take steps, whether she is balanced or not. She will step and fall and will not mind falling. She will step first and learn to control her balance later. She will take risks in order to step and you will need to supervise her for safety. She will not be concerned about details, like the type of surface she is walking on. You will need to point out obstacles on the floor or she might trip over them. When she wants to walk all the time, she will learn to move from plantigrade to stand. To help her learn to walk, focus on:

1. stepping quickly,
2. developing balance through walking activities by decreasing the support,
3. supervising her for safety,
4. praising her,
5. building motivation and confidence

By understanding her desire to move, you can help her develop walking skills in a way that works best for her.

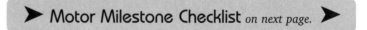

➤ Motor Milestone Checklist *on next page.* ➤

Motor Milestone Checklist

Standing

❑ She stands 3-5 minutes **holding on** with two hands to a surface with an edge

❑ She stands 3-5 minutes **holding on** with one hand to a surface with an edge

❑ While standing **holding on** with one hand, she plays with a toy placed at her side or behind her

❑ She stands with her back against furniture and maintains standing for 3-5 minutes

❑ She stands 3-5 minutes with two hands **propping on top of** a surface

❑ She stands 3-5 minutes with one hand **propping on top of** a surface

❑ While standing with one hand **propping on top of** a surface, she plays with a toy placed at her side or behind her

❑ She stands 3-5 minutes with two hands **propping against** a surface

❑ She stands 3-5 minutes with one hand **propping against** a surface

❑ While standing with one hand **propping against** a surface, she plays with a toy placed at her side or behind her

❑ She stands without support for 2-5 seconds

❑ She stands without support for 10 seconds

❑ She stands without support for more than 10 seconds (optional)

Cruising

❑ She cruises 1-2 steps

❑ She cruises 3-4 steps

❑ She cruises from one end of the sofa to the other

❑ She cruises around the corner of a table

❑ She cruises from one piece of furniture to another, with the surfaces next to each other

❑ She cruises from one piece of furniture to another, with the surfaces parallel to each other

❑ She cruises with her hands against a surface

Plantigrade

❑ She moves into the plantigrade (hands and feet) position on the floor

❑ She bear walks to move around a room (optional)

❑ She moves into the modified plantigrade position

❑ She moves from the modified plantigrade position to standing with one-hand support

❑ She moves from the modified plantigrade position to standing without hand support

❑ She moves from the plantigrade position to standing with one-hand support

❑ She moves from the plantigrade position to standing without hand support

(continued on next page)

Motor Milestone Checklist (continued)

Climbing
- ❑ She climbs off the sofa with verbal cues
- ❑ She climbs off the sofa by herself
- ❑ She climbs up 5-6 stairs
- ❑ She climbs up a flight of stairs
- ❑ She climbs down the bottom 2-3 stairs
- ❑ She climbs down 6 stairs
- ❑ She climbs down a flight of stairs
- ❑ She climbs up a small slide and slides down

Walking
- ❑ She walks with two-hand support for 3-5 steps
- ❑ She walks with two-hand support for 10 feet
- ❑ She walks with two-hand support for 20 feet or more
- ❑ She walks with a push toy with support for 3-5 steps
- ❑ She walks with a push toy with support for 10 feet
- ❑ She walks with a push toy with support for 20 feet or more
- ❑ She pulls to stand at the push toy if it is stabilized
- ❑ She walks with the push toy without support for 3-5 steps
- ❑ She walks with the push toy without support for 10 feet
- ❑ She walks with the push toy without support for 20 feet or more
- ❑ She pulls to stand at the push toy without support
- ❑ She steers the push toy around furniture and obstacles
- ❑ She walks with one-hand support for 3-5 steps
- ❑ She walks with one-hand support for 10 feet
- ❑ She walks with one-hand support for 30 feet or more
- ❑ She lunges to the sofa, props her hands, and then takes 1-2 steps
- ❑ She lunges to a vertical surface, props her hands, and then takes 1-2 steps
- ❑ She lunges to the sofa, a person, or a vertical surface and takes a step **before** she props her hands
- ❑ She takes 1-2 independent steps
- ❑ She walks a distance of 3 feet
- ❑ She walks a distance of 3-5 feet
- ❑ She walks a distance of 5-7 feet
- ❑ She walks a distance of 7-10 feet
- ❑ She walks a distance of 10-15 feet
- ❑ She walks a distance of 15 feet
- ❑ She walks around the house (even surfaces)
- ❑ She walks, paying attention to obstacles on the floor, and does not fall or trip
- ❑ She walks on the grass for 3-5 steps
- ❑ She walks on the grass for 5 feet
- ❑ She walks on the grass for 10 feet
- ❑ She walks on the grass for 15 feet
- ❑ She walks on the grass without falling

PART 2

Post Walking
Skills ▶ ▶ ▶ ▶ ▶ ▶ ▶ ▶ ▶ ▶

CHAPTER 6

Introduction to Post Walking Skills

Once your child has mastered walking, you will have a new set of questions:

◆ When will he walk with his feet closer together like other kids?
◆ He sort of runs, but will he really run fast?
◆ What about stairs? Will he walk up and down a flight of stairs by himself or is he always going to want to hold my hand?
◆ He says "jump," and he wants to jump, but he can't get his feet off the ground. When will he learn to really jump?

The answer is: Yes, your child will learn all of these skills. Part 2 of the book is about Post Walking. It will teach you how to help him learn the skills that develop after walking.

There are nine skill areas to focus on:
1. **Walking on uneven surfaces;**
2. **Kicking a ball;**
3. **Walking up and down inclined surfaces;**
4. **Walking up and down curbs;**
5. **Walking up and down stairs;**
6. **Fast walking and running;**
7. **Balance beam skills;**
8. **Jumping; and**
9. **Riding a tricycle.**

The ages for these skills are generally 2-6 years. Your child will be ready to start practicing these skills when he can walk well in the house and is comfortable walking on the grass.

These skill areas were chosen because they focus on developing:
1. **Increased strength in trunk, leg, and foot muscles;**
2. **Improved balance in standing and walking;**
3. **Narrower base when standing and walking;**
4. **Improved foot posture;**

5. Ability to walk in a variety of environments, including parks, school, and in the community;

6. Increased speed;

7. Increased endurance; and

8. Play and social activities with other kids through running, jumping, riding a tricycle, and kicking a ball.

All of these skill areas will help your child develop better strength in his stomach, leg, and foot muscles. He will develop better balance by practicing the skills of walking on uneven surfaces; kicking a ball; walking up and down inclines, curbs, and stairs; walking across a balance beam; and jumping. With better balance, he will walk with a narrower base. When he can walk with a narrower base, his foot posture will improve. With a more efficient way to walk, he can work on developing speed through the skill of running. As he continues to practice the skills over time, he will increase his endurance. He will have the stamina to keep going when running, walking up and down stairs, jumping, and riding the tricycle. While practicing the skills, he will learn to be independent in a variety of environments and he will have the opportunity to play with his siblings and the neighborhood kids.

This Post Walking phase will be different from the Birth to Walking phase. It will take longer for your child to achieve the goals in each skill area. In the first phase, your child learned many new skills in a two- to three-year period. In the second phase, he will be working on many skills at the same time. He may work on some of them over a period of several years.

FACTORS THAT AFFECT THE DEVELOPMENT OF POST WALKING SKILLS

A number of factors will influence your child's ability to master the nine skill areas of the Post Walking phase of development.

These factors fall into essentially four categories:

1. **Physical problems: including hypotonia, decreased strength, increased joint flexibility due to loose ligaments, short arms and legs, and poor balance;**

2. **Temperament;**

3. **Attention; and**

4. **Readiness and motivation to do a skill.**

physical problems

The typical physical problems were introduced in Chapter 1. Now that your child is older, his hypotonia has improved but it persists in a more subtle way. You may not notice it when you see him doing an established skill such as walking through the park. You will notice it, however, when he is developing a new skill such as jumping. His strength will be decreased, and he will need to work harder to build up the strength necessary to do each skill.

Increased joint flexibility will still be present but you will not see it as much as before during day to day motor skills. You will probably notice the flexibility primarily in his feet. He will have flat feet and may also turn his feet outward, walking on the inside borders of his feet. By practicing the Post Walking skills, his foot posture will change. He will continue to have flat feet but he will learn to walk with his feet closer together and pointing straight ahead.

The length of your child's arms and legs will probably be short relative to the length of his trunk. This will affect walking up and down stairs and curbs and riding a tricycle.

Children with Down syndrome have difficulty balancing on one foot. Balance is important for walking and proper foot posture. They will not learn the skill by practicing standing on one foot because they will not tolerate the exercise. They will learn to do it by practicing skills such as kicking a ball, walking up and down curbs, and walking across a balance beam.

temperament

Whether your child is motor driven or an observer, he will be active during the Post Walking Phase. It is still important to observe which temperament your child tends to be, however, as your role will be different with each type.

If he is *motor driven,* he will prefer vigorous motor activities such as running, climbing, jumping, and riding a tricycle. He will love speed and move quickly. He will not want to move slowly and pay attention. He will be risky and do activities without considering how to do them safely. He will need to be supervised closely to see what he is up to and to make sure he is safe. As he practices the skills, he will learn how to do them safely and he will learn to pay attention.

If your child is an *observer,* he will prefer slower moving skills such as walking on a balance beam and walking up and down stairs. When supported, he will tolerate speed—as when running with support. The speed will need to be slower, however, until he is familiar with it. He will generally pay attention and be careful to do motor activities in a controlled and balanced way. He will generally be safe so you will not need to supervise him closely. He will like you to be there to introduce activities to him so he feels secure. As he becomes competent in a skill, his speed will increase and he will be more vigorous and risky as he practices it.

attention

Certain skills require moving slower and paying attention. When your child walks on uneven surfaces, he will need to look down at the ground to plan how he can walk and avoid falling. When he walks across the balance beam, he will need to watch his feet and stay within the boundary. When walking up and down a 2-inch curb, he will need to be aware of it and plan how to step up and down so he does not fall. By practicing these skills, he will learn to slow down and pay attention to what he is doing.

If your child is an observer, he will pay attention more easily than a child who is motor driven. The child who is motor driven will learn to pay attention by practicing the skills that require it.

You will need to help your child focus his attention. You can get his attention by setting up an activity properly or showing him an activity and having him imitate you. For example, if you practice balance beam skills by walking across a 10-inch wide piece of wood placed on the floor, your child will notice if he steps out of the boundary. This set-up will more effectively get his attention than walking between two pieces of tape. With each skill, there are ways to help your child pay attention in order to learn how to do it. You will learn to be creative in finding ways to get his attention.

readiness

Your child will not tackle a skill until he is physically and psychologically ready. For example, you can help him become interested in jumping by turning on music and helping him bounce on his legs. But he will only learn to lift his feet off the ground when he is physically ready and has become curious about how to do it. Your job is to help him practice what he likes and help when he is ready and willing to try the next level of a skill.

guidelines for practicing post walking skills

Provide an environment that is safe and has a variety of activities to do. Now that your child can walk, he will want to be independent and explore more than ever before. To encourage his independence, you will need to select or set up environments where he can play with little intervention from you. You can set up a room in your home or use your backyard. You can go to the park or a toddler playground. You can go to Discovery Zone or to community toddler programs, such as Gymboree or the YMCA. You can take walks around the neighborhood, at the zoo, or at the mall. With these environments, he can choose where he wants to walk and what he wants to do. You can let him be the leader and supervise him so he is safe.

Introduce all the skill areas and see what he is interested in doing. Let him focus on the skill areas he likes so they become familiar and routine. Gradually add in other areas as tolerated. Over time, he will be motivated to practice all of them.

Let your child choose the order of activities he wants to do. After you have selected or set up an environment, let him move from one activity to another in the order he chooses. Let him repeat each activity as long as he is interested. You can help him practice activities that are hard for him to do by himself.

Guide your child to alternate hard and easy activities. Watch your child and see which skill areas he finds easy and which are hard. Look for a pattern and see if he prefers vigorous activities, like running and jumping, or slower moving and attentive activities, like walking across a balance beam. Once you figure out which skill areas are easier for him, guide him to try a "hard" one after he has done a couple easy skills. You can say "try this" and do it yourself and he may follow you. Let him practice it as long as he wants to and then let him do easier skills again.

In the beginning of this phase, the easier skills are kicking a ball, walking on uneven surfaces, beginning running, and walking across a 10-inch wide balance beam. The intermediate level skills are walking up and down inclines, curbs, and stairs, running, jumping, and walking across a 6-7-inch wide balance beam. The advanced level skills are walking across a 4-inch wide balance beam and riding a tricycle.

Follow the sequence of steps within each skill area. Each skill area will have goals, and there will be a list of steps to practice to achieve the goals. You will determine what your child can do and what is next for him to learn to do. Begin at his level and, when he is ready, help him practice what is next.

Motivate your child to practice the skills. The best motivator will be to watch another child do the activity and then say "your turn." Your child will be motivated to play with his brother or sister or other kids in the neighborhood. His body will be strong enough to try doing what they are doing. He will challenge himself to do what they are doing. He will enjoy imitating them and taking turns with them.

Provide visual cues and simple verbal instructions. Your child will learn by watching. He will watch other kids climbing up the slide or jumping on the trampoline. Then he will try to imitate what they are doing. If there is a special way to do an activity, show your child's playmate how to do it so your child imitates doing it the right way. Since your child will be watching what his playmate is doing, it will help to exaggerate certain areas you want your child to focus on. For example, when walking across the balance beam, the playmate can march across it and stomp his feet to draw attention to his feet on the board. You can also add words like "walk, walk, walk" as he walks across the balance beam.

With each skill, give him the name for what he is doing. For example, say "kick," "jump," "walk" (on the balance beam, on gravel or sand), "run," and "up" or "down" (stairs or curbs). Do not give him complicated verbal instructions because they will be hard for him to use and understand. If you show him and name what he is doing, he will be ready to practice the skill.

Do activities for short periods. Your child will show you how long he is motivated or physically able to practice an activity. Typically, he will begin practicing activities for two to three repetitions and then move on to another activity. Later, as he gains strength and balance, he will practice for longer periods. Remember, certain skills such as running and jumping make you tired more quickly.

Be prepared for toddler experiences. Your child will use his newly developed skills wherever he is. He may use his new running skills to run away from you when you are in the grocery store or department store. He may use his climbing skills to get something you never imagined he could reach. For example, Elizabeth was in her bedroom which had been "child proofed." She figured out if she moved the hamper over to the dresser, she could climb on the hamper and up on her dresser to get the Balmex cream. She did this and had a few seconds of fun putting Balmex on her face and on the mirror before her mother found her!

Alternate using shoes and being barefoot. Your child will continue to benefit from walking barefoot. Without shoes, he will be better able to actively move his feet. By alternating walking barefoot with wearing shoes, his leg and foot strength and balance will improve and his foot posture will change a lot.

Monitor your child's foot position and provide the appropriate support. To monitor the changes in his foot posture, watch him walk when he is barefoot. Observe him from behind to monitor the width of his base by observing how close together his heels are. Observe him from the front to see if his feet point straight ahead or turn outward. The goal is for his feet to point straight ahead and for his base to be narrower than his hips. Monitor his foot position yearly.

Your child's shoes should always have a flexible sole. You should be able to easily bend the shoe at the ball of the foot. *(See figure 6.1.)* If the soles are stiff, his walking pattern will be distorted because his feet will not be strong enough to bend them. Likewise, high top shoes tend to limit ankle mobility, which can interfere with skills such as running and walking up and down curbs, stairs, and inclines. For this reason, choose low top shoes whenever possible.

Once your child is familiar with wearing shoes, arch supports should be added. You can purchase supports at some children's specialty stores such as Stride Rite. Some stores require a doctor's prescription, so call ahead to find out whether you need a note from your pediatrician. *(See figure 6.2.)* Children with Down syndrome tend to have flat feet, but arch supports will maintain their feet with an arch while they are wearing shoes. Lifting the arch transfers weight to the outside borders of the feet and helps the feet point straight ahead. You and your physical therapist or orthopedist can decide if arch supports are adequate or

(fig. 6.1)

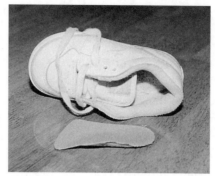

(fig. 6.2)

(fig. 6.3)

if more foot support is needed. If more support is needed, plastic foot supports, called orthotics, can be made. Orthotics will need to be prescribed by your physician or orthopedist. *(See figure 6.3.)*

Be aware that up to 20 percent of children with Down syndrome have a condition called atlantoaxial instability. This refers to a weakness or instability of the upper two bones of the spinal column in the neck. In extreme cases, the condition can lead to spinal cord damage. Because of this danger, you want to prevent wild or sudden movements of the head, either forward or backward. For more information, refer to *Babies with Down Syndrome: A New Parents' Guide* (second edition), pages 77-78 or *Medical and Surgical Care for Children with Down Syndrome: A Guide for Parents*, pages 193-199.

HOW TO USE CHAPTERS 7-15

Each of the chapters will focus on one of the nine skill areas of the Post Walking phase of development. There will be a goal or goals for each skill area. The steps needed to achieve each goal will be explained, along with instructions on how to practice the steps properly. Tips or guidelines will be provided to let you know how to practice the skills most effectively.

Each chapter ends with a checklist of motor milestones. Using it, you can keep track of what your child can do in each skill area. Since you will be practicing many of the skill areas at once, the checklist will help you keep track of what has been accomplished and what to focus on next.

CHAPTER 7

Walking on Uneven Surfaces

Your child has learned to walk on level surfaces and is comfortable walking on the grass. The next skill for her to master is walking on all types of surfaces, for example, on a mattress, sand, gravel, wood chips, and a concrete sidewalk. You can practice on any surface your geographic location has to offer, including snow. The goal will be to walk on all types of surfaces and to walk smoothly from one type of surface to another.

Now that she has learned to walk, you cannot change how she walks on level surfaces because she has an established pattern. That pattern usually includes a wide base and walking on the inside borders of her feet with her feet turned out. **To change this pattern, you need to change the surface she walks on.** By doing this, you will challenge her to find a new way to move her body and balance herself with each step.

As she takes a step, her foot will be in an unfamiliar position due to the uneven nature of the surface, and she will need to learn how to move her foot, leg, and body to take another step without falling. Initially, she will meet the challenge by stiffening her knees and continuing to use a wide base. With practice, she will learn to shift her weight from the inside borders of her feet to the outside and to position her feet to point straight ahead rather than turning out. By learning to walk with her feet in this position, she will use a narrower base. Using a narrower base, it will be easier to bend her knees as she walks.

SEQUENCE OF SURFACES

This is the typical sequence in which children learn to walk on surfaces, from easier to harder. Each surface requires different movements and strategies for balance.

(fig. 7.1)

Steps in: Learning to Walk on Uneven Surfaces

Your child will learn to achieve the goal in this skill area using the following steps:

1. walking on a variety of surfaces:
   A. walking on a mattress (or some other kind of soft, squishy surface like an exercise mat, a sofa bed mattress, a futon, a float, or a water bed;
   B. walking on sand;
   C. walking on a sidewalk with cracked uneven pavement;
   D. walking on wood chips;
   E. walking on gravel or rocks.

2. walking from one surface to another

When your child is beginning to practice walking on a new surface, think about how it feels to her as she takes each step. It would be similar to you suddenly stepping onto a new surface, such as ice. You might take 1 or 2 steps and fall. Then you would know to pay attention to the new surface. You would move your body differently than how you ordinarily walk. You would be conscious of each step and would constantly work to maintain your balance. You would learn how big a step to take and how fast to move. Initially, you would move stiffly, and, with practice, would move more freely. Your child will go through this learning experience with each surface she walks on.

mattress   When your child walks on a mattress, her foot will sink into the surface and she will need to actively push off to take a step. The softer the surface, the more she will sink in. It will be easier if you begin with a firmer surface and then gradually try softer surfaces when she is ready. You will need to use a surface large enough so she can take several steps before she reaches the edge. For example, use a sofa bed mattress rather than a sofa cushion because the cushion would not be large enough. *(See figure 7.2.)* Keep the surface close to the floor for safety. You can help your child step up or down with hand support. Remember, whatever you practice walking on, your child may try repeating it when you are not there if she is able to get to it.

(fig. 7.2)

sand

Walking on sand will be similar to walking on a mattress, but more difficult. Your child's foot will sink deeper into the sand and then she will need to push off with her foot and leg to move forward and take another step. She will be able to practice walking on wet and dry sand. When she is comfortable walking on sand, the next challenges will be to walk longer distances and faster.

sidewalk

Walking on a sidewalk with cracked, uneven pavement will combine walking on even and uneven surfaces. Your child will need to pay attention to when the sidewalk is uneven and plan how to walk on it. She may need to step up or down a crack or the sidewalk may slant up or down. Initially, you will need to point out the changes and, later, she will notice them by herself.

woodchips, gravel, & rocks

Walking on wood chips, gravel, and rocks will require your child to learn to walk on hard, uneven surfaces. As she places her foot on the surface, her foot position will change. Her ankle will be turned and she will need to move her leg and body to balance over her foot in this new position. With each step, she will make new adjustments due to the inconsistency of the surfaces.

(fig. 7.3)

Depending on where you live and where your child plays, you may have additional types of surfaces to walk on. You may have snow, beaches, ice rinks, or nature trails. Your toddler playground may have a large tunnel to walk through or a "swinging bridge" to walk across. *(See figure 7.3.)* Be on the lookout for all kinds of surfaces. Encourage your child to walk on each type of surface because each will teach her new ways to move her body and balance herself while walking.

walking from one surface to another

When she is comfortable walking on new surfaces, you can challenge her to walk smoothly from one surface to another. For example, walk from the sidewalk to the grass at your home or walk from the grass to the sand to the wood chips at the park. When she first does this, she will probably trip as she takes a couple of steps on the new surface. You can help her by giving her hand support until she learns what she needs to do. With practice, she will know how to step from one surface to another. *(See figure 7.4.)*

(fig. 7.4)

Practice within your child's tolerance. She will need to adjust to walking on uneven surfaces. See how she responds and help her be successful. When she begins walking without hand support, she may fall a lot and may get tired of falling. The falls will tend to have a cumulative effect and she may get upset and frustrated. To minimize the stress, alternate walking with support and without support.

Motivate your child to walk by having her walk to someone or something she wants. She will not want to practice walking on a new surface for the exercise or challenge of it. She will need to be motivated. For example, have her walk on the wood chips at the park to get to the swing.

Begin with hand support and then let go when she is ready. Gradually increase the distance walked as her strength and balance improve.

Choose relatively flat, rather than inclined surfaces. If a surface is uneven and inclined, you will be challenging her to do two hard motor skills at once. She will need to practice each skill area separately, walking on uneven surfaces and walking up and down inclines (Chapter 9). She can practice walking on uneven surfaces that are flat, and, at the same time, she can practice walking on even surfaces that are inclined. When she is familiar with both, you can combine them and have her walk up an uneven surface that is inclined, like a sand dune or a grassy hill.

Prepare for falls. Your child will fall when she is learning to walk on uneven surfaces without your support. She will use her hands to "catch" herself and prevent falling forward. She will not mind falling on the grass or other soft surfaces, but probably will not like to fall on hard surfaces. When she is first practicing on hard surfaces, stay close by so you can help her until she walks better and falls less.

Use different footwear for different surfaces. It is best for your child to go barefoot on soft or squishy surfaces, such as grass and sand. On hard surfaces such as concrete, gravel, rocks, or wood chips, use appropriate shoes that your child is comfortable with. If your child is walking in the snow with boots, she will first need to learn to walk using boots and then she will need to learn how to walk in snow.

If your child is an *observer,* she will notice the new uneven surface and step slower. She will tolerate it when holding your hand and you will need to be responsive to the pace she chooses. When it is time for her to walk by herself, she may stand still or sit down, if she does not want to walk on a particular surface. She will not want to fall, and so may refuse to walk on a surface if she feels too threatened. When she walks from one surface to another, she will take her time and try to do it without falling. With practice, she will learn how to walk on each surface and from one surface to another.

If your child is *motor driven,* she will walk on the uneven surface at full speed and then fall. She may tolerate holding your hand or she may let go because she wants to do it by herself. She will learn how to walk on the new surface through trial and error. She will learn she has to slow down in order to walk without falling. When she is familiar with the surface, she will learn to walk on it using her regular "fast" speed. When she walks from one surface to another, she will initially fall. Later, she will learn to move her legs quickly to stagger and recover her balance.

activity #1   **Walking on Uneven Surfaces**

1. Pick one surface at a time.
2. If the surface is soft, have your child walk on it barefoot. If not, wear flexible sole shoes that she is comfortable walking in.
3. Have your child hold your hand and walk on the surface for approximately 10 feet. Continue to practice this distance until she is familiar with it.
4. Increase the distance when she is ready and continue providing one-hand support. When possible, walk together for distances of 100 feet.
5. When she can walk on the surface comfortably with hand support, let go and begin practicing walking for short distances without hand support. Position yourself squatting or kneeling 5 feet in front of her. Encourage her to walk to you without support.
6. Continue to increase the distance she walks by herself when she is ready.
7. Practice the selected surface until she knows how to walk on it and can do it without falling.
8. Repeat steps 1-7 on all types of surfaces until she can walk on them confidently and comfortably.

activity #2   **Walking from One Surface to Another**

1. Pick two adjacent surfaces, for example, the sidewalk and grass, and make sure your child is comfortable walking on each surface.
2. Position your child on the sidewalk, standing with her feet perpendicular to the edge of the sidewalk.
3. Stand next to her or kneel on the grass in front of her and let her hold on to your thumb.
4. Encourage her to walk from the sidewalk to the grass.
5. When she is familiar with walking from the sidewalk to the grass with hand support, try doing it without hand support. Kneel in front of her on the grass and encourage her to walk to you. When she does that well, let her spontaneously walk from the sidewalk to the grass while playing—for example, when chasing a ball.
6. When she walks from the sidewalk to the grass by herself consistently, begin practicing walking from the grass to the sidewalk.
7. Practice on all types of adjacent surfaces. Practice moving in one direction until she masters it and then begin moving in the opposite direction.

► Motor Milestone Checklist *on next page.* ►

Motor Milestone Checklist

Walking on uneven surfaces
- ❑ She walks with hand support on a mattress
- ❑ She walks by herself on a mattress

She walks with hand support on the following surfaces:

	10-20 feet	100 feet
sand	❑	❑
sidewalk (with cracks)	❑	❑
wood chips	❑	❑
gravel or rocks	❑	❑
other:_____	❑	❑

She walks without hand support on the following surfaces:

	10 feet	50-100 feet
sand	❑	❑
sidewalk (with cracks)	❑	❑
wood chips	❑	❑
gravel or rocks	❑	❑
other:_____	❑	❑

- ❑ She walks on all types of surfaces by herself without falling

Walking from one surface to another
She walks from one surface to another with hand support:
- ❑ sidewalk to grass
- ❑ grass to sidewalk
- ❑ grass to gravel
- ❑ gravel to grass
- ❑ other:_____

She walks from one surface to another without hand support:
- ❑ sidewalk to grass
- ❑ grass to sidewalk
- ❑ grass to gravel
- ❑ gravel to grass
- ❑ other:_____

- ❑ She walks from one surface to another by herself, using all types of surfaces

CHAPTER 8

Kicking a Ball

Your child is ready to learn a new game using a ball. He has probably enjoyed playing with a ball and is familiar with rolling it back and forth with someone, sitting on the floor. Now you will teach him the skill of kicking the ball. The goal will be to kick the ball 20-30 feet by swinging his leg with his knee straight.

Learning this skill will improve his foot posture, standing balance, and leg strength. He will learn to stand and walk using a narrower base, with his feet pointing straight ahead.

Learning to kick the ball will be a two-step process. First, your child will need to develop the strength and balance to stand on one leg, while lifting his other leg to kick. Second, he will need to maintain his balance while he swings his kicking leg.

The first challenge will be teaching your child how to balance on one foot. His typical standing position will be with his feet under his hips, his feet turning outward, and his weight on the inside borders of his feet. This foot posture will make it difficult to balance on one foot.

To stand on one foot, your child will need to lean his hips over that foot and shift the weight from the inside border to the outside border of his foot. To shift his weight, his foot will need to be pointing straight ahead. *(See figure 8.1.)* If his foot is turned outward significantly, it will prevent him from shifting his weight and he will be stuck with his weight on the inside border of his foot. Learning the proper foot position in standing will be critical in learning to balance on one foot.

Steps in: Learning to Kick a Ball

Your child will learn to achieve the goal in this skill area using the following steps:
1. Kicking a ball if provided with two-hand support and assistance to swing his leg (if needed);
2. Kicking a ball with one-hand support;
3. Kicking a ball without support;
4. Kicking a ball by swinging his leg and keeping his knee straight when his foot hits the ball.

As he is learning to kick in steps 1-3, he will kick the ball with his hip and knee bent. *(See figure 8.2.)* Later, in step 4, his balance will improve and he will be able to kick the ball by swinging his leg keeping his knee straight when his foot hits the ball. *(See figure 8.3.)*

Your first job will be to introduce your child to the game of kicking a ball. You will show him the object of the game is to move his foot to hit the ball. When he does this, the ball will move. You will need to say "kick" as his foot touches the ball so he begins to identify what the game is. When he has kicked the ball, praise him and clap for him.

You will need to provide two-hand support until your child learns how to kick (Activity #1). With this support, you will direct his attention to kicking the ball and prevent playing catch. You will also control his balance so he can focus on moving his leg.

(fig. 8.1)

(fig. 8.2)

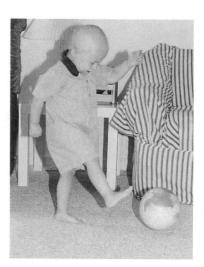

(fig. 8.3)

When he knows the "game" and kicks the ball with two-hand support, begin giving him one-hand support (Activity #2). With one-hand support, you will help him balance while he focuses on kicking the ball. When he kicks the ball, he will lift his leg with his hip and knee bent. With the ball placed in front of his foot, this leg movement will make his foot hit the ball and the ball will move forward. This will be the beginning method he will use to kick the ball. With practice, he will kick the ball a longer distance because he will begin swinging his leg forward when he kicks.

When he is ready, see if he will kick the ball without holding your hand (Activity #3). He may kick the ball or he may squat down and hit the ball. He may also pick up the ball and throw it. Since you are not holding his hand, he will be free to choose if he wants to kick the ball or play another game with the ball. If he is not interested in kicking the ball at that time, play another game and practice kicking the ball another time. Continue to practice until he kicks the ball without hand support.

By now, he has developed the balance and strength to stand on one leg in order to lift his other leg to kick. He will be confident in his ability to kick and will enjoy the game. Now, he will be ready to focus on swinging his kicking leg and maintaining his balance while he does it. He will learn to swing his leg from the hip and keep his knee straight as he kicks the ball (Activity #4). He will be able to kick the ball harder and farther using this new method. It will also require him to work harder to maintain his balance because he will need to balance on one foot longer and maintain the balance of his body while he swings his kicking leg with momentum and speed. Using this method, he will be able to kick the ball 20-30 feet. When he can do this, he has achieved the goal of this skill area.

activity guidelines

Choose a ball with the appropriate size and weight. In the beginning, use a ball that is 10-16 inches in diameter and lightweight. You can use a beach ball or inflated rubber ball from the toy store. If the ball is big, lightweight, and soft, it will be easier to hit with his foot, it will roll farther, and it will be comfortable to his foot as he kicks it. When he is familiar with kicking and is motivated to kick, you can use smaller balls, approximately 8 inches. When he kicks well, you can vary the weight of the ball and use a heavier ball, such as a soccer ball or kickball. He will need to swing his leg with strength, momentum, and speed to kick these balls any distance.

Practice kicking when your child is motivated. He may want to throw the ball or play catch rather than kick the ball. If he is not interested, try again another time. Your child will show you when he wants to do it. It will help if he watches his brother or sister do it and they play the game together. For example, when Blaine watched his brother play soccer with his friends, he became motivated to kick the ball, too. His brother would also play with Blaine and kicking the ball in the back yard became a favorite activity for Blaine. On the other hand, Matthew watched his brother play basketball so he was more motivated to catch, throw, dribble, and shoot into the hoop. Matthew would practice with his brother and his brother's friends when they came over. Your child *will* learn to kick the ball. It is your job to see when he is ready to practice and to give him role models to imitate.

Let your child kick with the leg he chooses. As your child practices kicking the ball with hand support, place the ball in front of each foot to see if he kicks the ball better with one foot or if he prefers to use one leg more than the other. If he uses or prefers one leg more than the other, let him practice kicking with that leg. Your child will learn to have a dominant leg, just as he develops a dominant hand. He will show you which leg is easier to kick with, and, in most cases, it will be his dominant leg.

Provide verbal, visual, and tactile cues. Give verbal cues by saying "kick" to identify the game to him and to tell him what to do with his leg. You want to say it every time either of you does the kicking motion or kicks the ball. Saying "kick" will help him focus on the action of kicking the ball.

Give him visual cues. He will watch you or a sibling do the kicking motion with your leg or kick the ball. After he watches you, he will be motivated to imitate what you did. When you do the kicking motion, you will need to exaggerate it and say "kick" so he pays attention. He will imitate what he paid attention to and what he can physically do.

Provide tactile cues to help him feel the motion or action you want him to do. For example, when you give him two-hand support and help him move his kicking leg, move it fast and hit the ball with impact. If you move his leg slowly and gently touch the ball with his foot, he will barely notice what he needs to do to kick. By moving his leg fast and with impact, the action will get his attention and he will feel what he needs to imitate. When he is ready, you will also give him the tactile cue of swinging his leg with his knee straight to kick the ball with momentum and force.

Choose the right surface and space to practice kicking. When your child is first learning to kick, it will be easier for him to balance on a firm, even surface like the surfaces found inside the house (tile, hardwood, and carpeted floors). When he is familiar with kicking and is motivated to kick, you can use uneven surfaces like the grass. When kicking is a game for him and he likes to chase the ball and kick it again, you will need to use a large area like a big backyard, park, or playground area.

Use appropriate footwear when practicing kicking. When your child is practicing kicking a lightweight ball in the house, he can be barefoot. To learn to balance on one foot, it is best to be barefoot since he can move his foot more easily. When he practices kicking the ball outside on the grass or concrete, he can wear shoes or sneakers with flexible soles. When he kicks a heavier ball, he will need to wear shoes to support and protect his foot as it hits the ball.

temperament

If your child is an **observer,** he will feel secure when learning to kick the ball with hand support. When you let go, he will be careful to control his balance and will kick gently. When he is learning to walk to the ball and kick it, he will be upset if he trips over the ball a lot. You will need to help him until he learns to do it without falling. If he becomes frustrated, he may temporarily stop kicking the ball and choose to squat and hit the ball with his hand. When he is comfortable kicking the ball, he will play kick ball until he is tired or bored with it.

If your child is **motor driven,** he will progress to kicking the ball without hand support more easily. He will trip when kicking the ball without support because he will be moving too quickly. The tripping will not bother him and eventually he will plan how to kick the ball without tripping. He will be motivated to kick the ball even if he trips. He will enjoy playing kick ball and will like the combination of running and kicking the ball.

activity #1

Kicking the Ball with Two-Hand Support
1. Have your child stand on a flat, even surface.
2. Position yourself standing behind him.
3. Have him hold your hands or you hold his hands. Position his hands at shoulder level (or lower) and in front of his chest.
4. Place the ball in front of one foot.
5. Use your leg to move his leg forward to kick the ball. As you do this, say "kick." After the ball moves, clap for him.
6. An alternative method to help him kick is to hold both of his hands in one of your hands and use your other hand to swing his leg forward to kick. After you have helped him move his leg to kick the ball a few times, see if he will move his leg by himself. Praise him if he uses any leg motion at all.
7. When he understands how to move his leg forward to kick, just hold his hands and let him kick. Continue to place the ball in front of his foot, say "kick," and clap when he does it.

8. Place the ball in front of each foot to see if one is easier or preferred. Continue to practice using the easier leg.
9. Practice until he can consistently kick with two-hand support.
10. When he is ready, try it on a variety of surfaces, like grass.

activity #2 **Kicking the Ball with One-Hand Support**

1. Have your child stand on a flat, even surface.
2. Stand next to him.
3. Have him hold your hand. Position his hand at shoulder level (or lower) and in front of his chest.
4. Place the ball in front of one foot.
5. Say "kick" and clap for him when he kicks the ball.
6. Place the ball in front of each foot to see if one is easier or preferred. Continue to practice using the easier leg.
7. Practice holding on with each hand to see if one hand is preferred. Continue to practice using the preferred hand.
8. Practice until he can consistently kick with one-hand support.
9. When he is ready, try it on a variety of surfaces, like grass.
10. When he can kick the ball well with one-hand support on the grass, begin practicing walking to the ball and kicking it again. Repeat as tolerated. This will teach him where to position his body relative to the ball so he can kick it. He will learn when to stop as he approaches the ball. This will prepare him to continuously kick the ball while playing in the yard.

activity #3 **Kicking the Ball without Support**

1. Have your child stand on a flat, even surface.
2. Place the ball in front of his preferred foot.
3. Say "kick" and clap for him when he kicks the ball.
4. Practice this method until he kicks the ball easily.
5. When he kicks the ball easily on an even surface, practice on a variety of surfaces, like grass.
6. When he can kick the ball on the grass, practice kicking the ball and then walking or running to it and kicking it again. Repeat as tolerated. Through practice and experience, he will learn where to stop in front of the ball in order to kick it rather than trip over it. He will learn to effectively position himself and swing his leg to play kick ball.

activity #4 **Kicking the Ball 20 Feet**

1. Position your child on the grass in your backyard or at a park.
2. Stand next to him and place the ball in front of your foot. Swing your leg with your knee straight as it hits the ball, and say "kick."
3. Place the ball in front of his foot and say "kick."
4. Praise him when he kicks the ball. See if he imitated how you kicked.
5. Continue to practice until he can swing his kicking leg with momentum and speed. Watch and see if his knee is straight as his foot hits the ball. Work toward kicking the ball 20-30 feet.

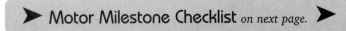

► Motor Milestone Checklist *on next page.* ►

Motor Milestone Checklist

He kicks the ball with two-hand support when the ball is placed in front of his foot:
- ❏ on even surfaces
- ❏ on the grass

He kicks the ball with one-hand support when the ball is placed in front of his foot:
- ❏ on even surfaces
- ❏ on the grass

- ❏ With one-hand support, he kicks the ball, walks or runs to it, and kicks it again

He kicks the ball without support when the ball is placed in front of his foot:
- ❏ on even surfaces
- ❏ on the grass

- ❏ Without support, he kicks the ball, walks or runs to it, and kicks it again without tripping
- ❏ He kicks the ball for 20 feet by swinging his leg with his knee straight
- ❏ He kicks the ball for 30 feet by swinging his leg with his knee straight

CHAPTER 9

Walking Up and Down Inclined Surfaces

Walking up and down inclined surfaces is an important skill to learn. This skill will improve your child's walking pattern and help her be more independent when walking in the community. Examples of inclined surfaces are: inclined sidewalks or driveways; ramps; and sloped areas in yards, playgrounds, parks, malls; school or church hallways; and nature trails. You will need to look around and see what is available in your community. You will need to find small (2-4 degrees), medium (5-10 degrees), and large (15-20 degrees) inclines for your child to practice on. The goal will be for your child to walk up and down all types of inclined surfaces by herself.

Practicing walking up and down inclines will improve her walking pattern, particularly her use of knee bending. Her early walking pattern on level surfaces will be with her knees stiff and straight and her trunk vertical. When she walks up or down an inclined surface, her whole body position will change, and she will learn how to balance herself in forward and backward directions.

Your child will need to become familiar with the feeling of walking up and down inclined surfaces. When she first tries walking up a small inclined surface, her feet will be angled upward and this will feel very different to her. Initially, she will not know how to move her trunk, hips, and knees to walk. Her habitual walk-

Steps in: Learning to Walk on Inclined Surfaces

To achieve the goal of this skill area, your child will practice these steps in the following order:

1. walking up and down small inclines with and without support;
2. Walk up and down medium inclines with and without support; and
3. Walk up and down large inclines with and without support.

(fig. 9.1)

ing pattern with her feet flat, knees fairly straight, and trunk up straight will no longer work. She will need your hand support until she figures out how to move her legs and trunk. She will learn she has to bend her hips and knees a lot and maintain that position with each step. She will also need to keep her hips forward, in front of her feet (looking from the side view), rather than over her feet. When she is familiar with these leg movements, you can let go and let her figure out how to maintain her balance as she walks up. She will learn to balance by leaning her trunk and hips forward in front of her feet. She will need to concentrate on maintaining her body in this new position until she reaches the top of the incline. If she forgets or stops paying attention, she will lose her balance.

Your child will adjust to walking up inclined surfaces with hand support fairly easily. The real challenge is for her to walk up without hand support. She will need to practice a lot. She will be wobbly at first and will waiver forward and back until she figures out how to position her body for balance. You will need to be close enough to give her support when needed. With practice, she will find the position of her trunk and hips where she is balanced. She will learn to automatically move to her point of balance when she feels her feet angled upward. *(See figure 9.1.)*

Walking down a small inclined surface will require a different strategy than walking up. Her feet will be angled downward and she will need to learn how to move her body to maintain her balance and how to control her speed. She will need hand support while she learns how to move her legs and trunk. *(See figure 9.2.)* She will learn she has to bend her hips and knees, but to a lesser degree than when walking up an incline. She will also need to keep her hips behind her feet (looking from the side view) to control her speed. When she can walk down the incline with hand support, you will let go so she can learn how to balance herself. She will learn she needs to straighten her trunk and lean it back to keep her balance and control her speed.

When your child begins walking down the inclined surface by herself, she will not be able to control her speed. You will need to be close to help slow her down. With practice, she will show you the speed she is comfortable using. Her temperament will influence her preferred speed.

When your child is able to walk up and down small inclines without support, you will progress to medium and then large inclines. The same principles of learning to walk up and down will apply, but the foot, leg, and trunk movements will be more dramatic. She will need a lot of practice to develop the strength, balance, and endurance needed to walk up and down large inclines. Continue to practice this skill area until she can walk up and down all kinds of inclines automatically without hand support.

(fig. 9.2)

activity guidelines

Vary the angle of the incline and the length. It will be helpful to measure the angle of the incline so you know which size incline you are using. To measure the incline you can use a tool called an angle finder. Roofers use it to determine the slope of a roof and it can be purchased in a hardware store. Another easy method is to use a level and tape measure. Measure and mark 12 inches (30.48 cm) on the level. Place the level on the incline. Raise one end of the level until it is level. Measure the distance from the 12 inch mark on the level to the incline. See figure below.

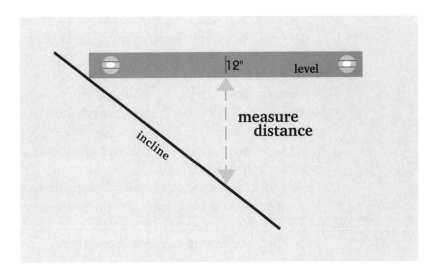

Then use the following table to determine the angle of the incline.

If the distance is:	the angle is:
.210 inch/.533 cm	1 degree
.420 inch/1.07 cm	2 degrees
.630 inch/1.60 cm	3 degrees
.840 inch/2.13 cm	4 degrees
1.050 inch/2.67 cm	5 degrees
1.260 inch/3.20 cm	6 degrees
1.476 inch/3.75 cm	7 degrees
1.686 inch/4.28 cm	8 degrees
1.902 inch/4.83 cm	9 degrees
2.118 inches/5.38 cm	10 degrees
3.216 inches/8.17 cm	15 degrees
4.368 inches/11.09 cm	20 degrees
5.598 inches/14.22 cm	25 degrees
6.930 inches/17.60 cm	30 degrees
8.400 inches/21.34 cm	35 degrees
10.068 inches/25.57 cm	40 degrees
12.000 inches/30.48cm	45 degrees

You will probably tend to overestimate the angle of an incline. You will see a 2 degree incline and you will think that it is 10 degrees. However, when you actually measure the inclines you and your child use in your community, you will see small ones are 2-4 degrees, medium ones are 5-10 degrees, and large ones are 15-20 degrees. You will begin with small inclines and gradually progress to medium and large inclines when your child is ready.

Each incline will have its own particular length. The shorter the length, the easier it will be to walk up and down. To develop the strength and balance needed to walk up and down inclines, you can start with inclines that are 5-10 feet long and progress to inclines that are 40 feet or longer. As your child learns to walk up and down each grade, the next challenge is to increase the length. For example, when your child can walk up and down a 5-10 foot medium incline, try a 20 foot medium incline; when she can do that, try a 40-50 foot medium incline. Continue to practice on medium inclines until she is ready to try large inclines.

Practice walking up first before beginning to work on walking down. Walking up is generally easier than walking down. Walking up an incline is easier because the pace is slower and the ground is closer. Your child will feel more in control, and, if she does fall, can more easily catch herself with her hands because the ground is closer than usual. When she walks down an incline, the tendency is to move faster and feel out of control. It is easier to fall and this could make her more fearful.

Use surfaces that are familiar and safe to your child. Familiarize her with walking on a particular type of surface before you add walking up and down an incline on that surface. For example, after she is familiar with walking on the grass, then she can practice walking up and down a grassy incline. If she is not ready to walk on uneven surfaces such as grass, use an even surface such as a carpeted or tile floor. You may be able to find small inclines with carpet or tile surfaces in churches, schools, or malls. Concrete driveways can be used with close supervision to avoid falls.

Begin with hand support and then let go. Hand support will be needed until she learns how to move her legs and balance herself. When providing hand support, have your child hold your hand or finger. If you hold her hand and pull her, she will not figure out how to balance herself. You will be controlling her trunk rather than having her learn how to lean to control her own balance.

When walking up or down inclines, you will begin with two-hand support, progress to one-hand support, and work toward no support. With two-hand support, it is best if you are in front of your child, facing her and stepping backwards as she steps forward. Two-hand support can also be provided with one person on each side of her and the three of you stepping forward. Using either method, her hands need to be positioned in front of her chest and below her shoulders. When she is ready, let go of one hand and continue to use the methods and positioning described above. When she is ready to walk without support, squat or kneel in front of her. Use a motivator or have her walk to you. Increase the distance as tolerated. When she can walk up or down the small incline, have her walk to a motivator with you walking beside her. When she can do it well, she can chase you or a sibling.

Encourage her to walk up and down the incline rather than climb. Your child will naturally prefer to climb rather than walk, particularly with the medium and large inclines. To move up the incline, she will use the plantigrade position and to move down, she will try to sit and scoot (or slide). She will use these climbing methods when she is playing by herself or when you do not give her hand support and she does not feel ready to walk. When you are practicing the inclines with her, encourage her to walk up and down and give her one-hand support until she will do it by herself.

Provide verbal and visual cues. As she is walking up or down the incline, pick an appropriate verbal cue to say. You can say "walk," "up," or "down." To keep her focused, you can repeat the word with each step she takes. She will also pay attention to visual cues, such as watching another child walk up and down the incline. To make it more exciting to watch, you can think of different ways to walk up and down. For example, you can march up and run down and say "whee." If it looks like fun, she will want to try to do it.

Wear appropriate footwear. In the beginning, try walking barefoot on suitable surfaces. It will be easiest to move her ankles and knees if she is barefoot. When she is familiar with walking up and down, she can wear shoes with flexible soles. High top shoes are not recommended because they will make it harder for her to bend her ankles. This will influence hip and knee bending.

temperament

If your child is an ***observer,*** she will feel the change in the surface and become alert and cautious. She will want to move slowly so she feels in control. She will prefer hand support until she feels comfortable doing it by herself. When she first does it without support, she may sit or stop walking if she feels she will fall. With practice, she will become confident and walk up and down, maintaining a careful speed.

If your child is ***motor driven,*** she may not notice the incline, or if she does, it will not stop her. With her adventuresome nature, she will continue to walk at her regular speed, whether she falls or not. She will need hand support, particularly when walking down the incline, to slow down her speed. With practice and when she is motivated, she will learn to walk up and down maintaining her balance, while moving at her normal fast speed.

activity #1

Walking Up and Down Inclines *(see figs. 9.3, 9.4)*

1. Pick a small incline (2-4 degrees) to walk up and down. Make sure the surface is familiar and she is comfortable walking on that surface.
2. Give her two-hand support by standing in front of her and stepping backwards or by using two persons, with one on each side, and stepping forward. Have her hold your hands or fingers. Make sure her hands are positioned in front of her chest and below her shoulders. When she is walking down, she may step faster and you will need to slow her down.
3. Provide verbal and visual cues when walking up and down.
4. Clap and praise her when she reaches the top or bottom of the incline.
5. When she is familiar and confident with two-hand support, begin one-hand support. Stand beside her and walk forward or stand in front of her, stepping backwards. Have her hold your hand or fingers and position her hand in front of her chest and below her shoulder.
6. When she can walk well with one-hand support, begin practicing without hand support. In the beginning, squat or kneel in front of her and encourage her to take 1-2 steps to you. Increase the distance as tolerated. When she can walk without support, walk beside her and assist her as needed. When she can do it well, you can run up and down and have her chase and follow you.

7. When she can walk up a small incline on one type of surface, try it on a variety of surfaces.

8. When she can walk up and down mild inclines for 5-10 foot distances, try longer inclines.

9. Follow these steps using medium and large inclines when she is ready.

(fig. 9.3)

(fig. 9.4)

➤ **Motor Milestone Checklist** *on next page.* ➤

Motor Milestone Checklist

❏ She walks up small inclines with two-hand support
❏ She walks down small inclines with two-hand support
❏ She walks up small inclines with one-hand support
❏ She walks down small inclines with one-hand support
❏ She walks up small inclines without support
❏ She walks down small inclines without support
❏ She walks up medium inclines with two-hand support
❏ She walks down medium inclines with two-hand support
❏ She walks up medium inclines with one-hand support
❏ She walks down medium inclines with one-hand support
❏ She walks up medium inclines without support
❏ She walks down medium inclines without support
❏ She walks up large inclines with two-hand support
❏ She walks down large inclines with two-hand support
❏ She walks up large inclines with one-hand support
❏ She walks down large inclines with one-hand support
❏ She walks up large inclines without support
❏ She walks down large inclines without support
❏ She walks up and down all types of inclined surfaces by herself

CHAPTER 10

Walking Up and Down Curbs

Now that your child can walk well on even surfaces and he has practiced paying attention to the floor to step over obstacles, he is ready to learn the skill of walking up and down "curbs." For the purposes of this chapter, a curb is defined as any single step or raised surface from 1-8 inches in height. The goal is to walk up and down a curb (about 8 inches) without hand support. Examples of curbs are: an exercise mat or board on the floor, a step at the front door of your house to the front porch, railroad ties at a playground or park, or any place where there are two adjacent surfaces with one higher than the other.

Learning to handle curbs will improve his walking pattern and foot position because it will develop his leg strength and balance on one foot. When he walks, he will use a narrower base and will bend his knees. His foot position will change so that his feet point straight ahead rather than out. This skill will also prepare him for walking up and down stairs as he becomes familiar with the leg motions and gradually builds up the strength he will need.

A prerequisite for this skill is your child's ability to *notice* and *pay attention* to obstacles on the floor or changes in the floor surfaces. If he is not able to do this, he will not notice the curb and will trip and fall. You will need to give him cues to point out the changes in the surfaces. With experience, he will learn to pay attention. When he notices that one surface is higher or lower than the other, he will need to stop and plan how to step up or down.

In the beginning, it will be hard for your child to judge the height of the curb. When he is standing, looking down, he will not know how far up or down to step. He will learn by trial and error and repetition. When stepping up, he may trip because he does not lift his foot high enough or he may lift his foot too high and take a huge step when it was not necessary. When stepping down, he may lunge and trust you will catch him or he may step down slowly. If he chooses the careful, slow method, he will move one foot slowly forward off the curb until his toes touch the ground and he knows how far to step.

Your child will learn how to plan to walk up and down curbs.

To walk up a curb, he will need to *(see figure 10.1)*:

1. **Balance on one foot;**
2. **Maintain his balance while he lifts the other foot up on the curb;**

3. Maintain his balance with one foot on the curb and his other foot on the ground;
4. Lean over the foot on the curb and lean his trunk forward;
5. Straighten the hip and knee of the leg on the curb and lift his body up on the curb; and
6. Place his other foot on the curb.

To walk down a curb, he will need to (*see figure 10.2*):

1. Balance on one foot;
2. Straighten his trunk over the leg he is balancing on and lean back slightly;
3. Step out with his other leg;
4. Maintain his balance while slowly bending the hip and knee of the leg on the curb to lower his body weight until his other foot touches the ground; and
5. Move the foot on the curb to the ground.

He will first develop the *leg strength* needed to walk up and down curbs using hand support. Later, he will learn how to *balance* himself when he is practicing without hand support. Your child's short stature, particularly his short leg length, will influence his ability to do this skill area without hand support. He will be able to do 1-3" curbs with practice. The higher curbs, 4-8", will be more difficult, and he may need to grow taller, as well as gain leg strength and balance, to walk up and down them. You can determine whether a curb is too high for your child by looking at his

(fig. 10.1)

leg position from the side. When he places one leg up on the curb, where is his knee relative to his hip? If his knee is lower than hip level, it will be appropriate to practice a curb with that height. If his knee is at or above hip level, he will probably need to grow taller to do it without hand support. *(See figure 10.3.)* To understand the leg strength and balance needed, try stepping up onto a surface where your knee is at or above hip level.

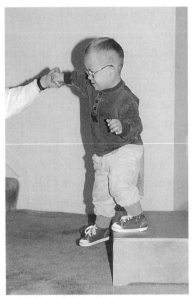

(fig. 10.2)

(fig. 10.3)

activity guidelines

Let your child lead with the foot he chooses. As he practices walking up and down curbs, he may frequently step up with one foot and step down with the other foot. When walking up a curb, the leg that steps up on the curb is the stronger leg. When stepping down a curb, the leg that stays on the curb is the stronger leg. He may figure out which leg is stronger and automatically use that leg when walking up and down. For example, if his right leg is stronger, he will step up leading with his right foot and step down leading with his left. With practice, you will see which leg is dominant.

Begin with hand support and then let go. Your child will begin with one- or two-hand support. You will need to position yourself in front of him, whether he is walking up or down. When he needs hand support, he can hold your finger or hand and you can position his hand in front of his chest, below shoulder level. This will support him to be balanced in the center. If you were behind or beside him, you would probably lean him back or to the side without knowing it. This would set him up to learn to depend on your support because he would feel off balance. By positioning yourself in front of him, you will prepare him to balance himself from the centered position as he steps up or down.

When he is ready to walk up and down without hand support, you will need to squat or kneel in front of him so you are at eye level to him. This positioning will help him maintain his balance when he is looking at you. If you are above eye level, he will look up at you and probably lose his balance. With you in front of him, he will also feel more secure. He will know he can hold on to you if he needs to and you will catch him if he falls.

Watch to see whether walking up or down is easier for your child. You will need to practice both, but it is helpful to know which is easier. This way you can be sensitive to his reactions to walking up and down and effectively help him learn the parts that he perceives as difficult.

Walking up the curb is generally tolerated with hand support. Your child will feel comfortable learning to use the necessary leg motions with hand support. He will be challenged when he needs to walk up without hand support.

Walking down curbs is either viewed as fun or is met with resistance. For some children, walking down is easy at first because they "fall off" the curb. They quickly step off the curb with one leg and then try to recover their balance when their feet land on the ground. For other children, walking down is harder because they resist bending the hip and knee and then they cannot step down. They may resist the movement because they do not feel stable.

Provide verbal and visual cues. You will need to look at the set-up when you practice this activity.

1. **Make sure the curb is noticeable.** You can point it out to your child by patting or slapping the surface with your hand. He may also notice it because the color of the curb is distinct and different than the ground surface.

2. **Let him know what you want him to do.** You will need to tell him "up" or "down" and demonstrate it so he can imitate you. If you exaggerate the motions by marching, he will see what you are doing with your legs and imitate you.

3. **Make sure he is motivated to walk up or down and feels secure enough to try it.** Provide a motivator so it is worth challenging himself to walk up or down. For example, he may step up or down to get a ball, read a book, or pop bubbles. You will need to hold the motivator at eye level to him so he must be standing to get it. If you are practicing walking up the curb and you place the motivator on the curb, he will climb to get it rather than try to walk. If you position yourself in front of him with the motivator, he will also feel secure enough to practice walking up or down.

Choose adjacent surfaces that are firm and level. When your child is first learning to walk up and down curbs, he needs to feel secure and stable when walking from one surface to another. He will feel most stable on surfaces that are firm and level. After he learns to step up and down a particular height curb, you can then challenge him by using uneven surfaces. For example, at first, he will feel more stable using tile, carpeted, or concrete curb surfaces. Later, he can practice walking from a grass surface to a raised surface with wood chips. When he is using uneven surfaces, it will be harder to balance on one foot as he is stepping up or down. His foot will rock and be in a less stable position to balance himself than when he is on a flat, even surface.

Select adjacent surfaces that are the appropriate size. Each surface should be a minimum of 3 feet wide by 3 feet long when he is learning to step up or down without hand support. After he steps up or down with both legs, he will need to take 2-3 more steps to regain his balance. He could stagger in any direction and the surface must be large enough to allow him to take the additional steps. When he develops better balance and control, he will not need to take additional steps.

Encourage walking up and down curbs rather than climbing. *(See figure 10.4.)* Your child will want to be independent, so, when he approaches a curb, he

(fig. 10.4)

will spontaneously move to the plantigrade position to climb up or down the curb. He will know this is his safe method to move from one place to another if he is not able to walk. First, you will teach him to walk up or down 1-2 inch curbs and then he will no longer climb when he approaches curbs of this size. But, with every increase in the height of the curb, he will always spontaneously climb when he feels the curb is too high to walk up or down. So, with each increase in the height of the curb, you will need to teach him to walk rather than climb.

Practice walking up and down a variety of heights of curbs. While your child is learning to walk up and down a 2" curb without hand support, you can also practice walking up and down 4-6" curbs with hand support. You will be teaching him to walk rather than climb. When you are at the park, walking in and out of your house, or walking up and down a standard curb, give him the hand support he needs and encourage him to walk up or down the curb. After a while, help him figure out how to walk up or down by himself when possible. For example, when walking up or down a step at the front door, help him learn to hold on to the door frame with both hands to balance himself. By practicing with a variety of heights of curbs, his strength and balance will improve and walking up and down curbs will become easier for him.

temperament

If your child is an **observer,** walking up a curb will be easier than walking down. He will feel comfortable using the leg motions to walk up the curb, especially with hand support. The leg motions needed to walk down the curb will feel very different. He will generally be careful, fearful, or resistant when walking down. He will notice the change in the surface and will move slowly to lower his foot down to the ground so he is in control. When he is on a 1-2" curb, he will keep his heel on the curb and slide his toes forward until they touch the ground. Then he will feel comfortable stepping down with each foot. With practice, he will become familiar with what he needs to do and will move faster.

He will prefer to climb or walk up and down with hand support so he is safe. You will need to wean him from the support when he is ready and show him he can do it by himself. When you are weaning him, you can hold the sleeve of his shirt or slide your finger out of his hand as he is walking up or down the curb. He will move slower when he does not have hand support and he will be cautious. You will need to move at his pace so he continues to build confidence rather than lose it. When he is successful with a particular curb height, gradually increase the height of the curb, giving him time to adjust. With practice, he will walk up and down with control.

If your child is **motor driven,** walking down the curb will generally be easier than walking up. He will need to develop the leg strength to walk up the curb but will be willing to just step off the curb without control. He will tend to move fast, so you will need to give him the support he needs to be safe. He may try to climb up the curb, or he may walk and trip over the curb, or he may step up and need room to recover his balance. You will need to position yourself to give him hand support if it is needed to walk up the curb. To walk down the curb, he probably will just step down by "falling off." On 1-2" curbs, he may be able to take steps to regain his balance after he steps down to the ground. You will need to be positioned in front of him to slow him down, give him hand support to help him lower himself down to the floor, or catch him. With practice, he will learn to plan how to step down with balance and control.

activity #1   **Walking Up and Down Curbs**

1. Pick two firm adjacent surfaces with one surface raised 1 inch. Make sure the surfaces are stable and will not slide or move. Examples of how you can create 1-2 inch curbs are:

    a. Use a wooden board that is 1 to 1½ inches thick, 10-12 inches wide, and at least 3 feet long. Place it on the floor and have your child approach it from the side. Have your child step up, walk across the width of the board, and then step down. It is best if the board is on a carpet so it does not slide. The carpet needs to have little or no padding. If it is padded, the board will rock and feel unstable.

    b. Use a firm, densely padded exercise mat on the floor.

    c. Use the sidewalk, particularly if there is a crack in the sidewalk or if there are two adjacent squares with one higher than the other.

    d. Look everywhere for 1-2 inch steps, for example, from the sidewalk to the grass, from the driveway to the grass, or from the garage to the driveway.

2. Kneel, squat, or sit on a low bench in front of your child.

3. Provide one- or two-hand support. Have him hold your finger or hand and make sure his hand is in front of his chest, below shoulder level.

4. While holding your hand, have him step up or down. Say "up" or "down." If necessary, pat the curb to get his attention.

5. Praise him and clap for him when he walks up or down.

6. When he is ready, encourage him to walk up or down without hand support. *(See figures 10.5 and 10.6.)*

    a. Position yourself in front of him, at or below his eye level. Be close enough so he feels secure.

    b. Hold his sleeve if needed. Or, have him hold your finger but you slide it out after he starts stepping up or down the curb.

    c. Use a great motivator, such as bubbles.

    d. When he is practicing walking up the curb, begin by placing him just in front of it. When he is practicing walking down the curb, place him at the edge of it.

    e. When he can walk up and down the curb when placed in front of it or at the edge, place him 10 feet from the curb and have him walk and then step up and down. If needed, get his attention to show him where the curb is so he can plan how to do it rather than tripping.

(fig. 10.5)

(fig. 10.6)

   f. After he can walk up and down two firm surfaces, try on a variety of 1" curbs, using even or uneven surfaces.

7. When he is ready, try a 2" curb. Follow steps 1-6.

8. Continue to increase the height of the curb, as tolerated, up to 8 inches. Follow steps 1-6. You can make a curb with a 3 foot by 3 foot piece of plywood. You can block the corners to the desired height. You can also purchase an aerobic step.

9. While you are practicing walking up and down a low height curb (1-3"), working toward doing it without hand support, assist your child in walking up and down 4-8 inch curbs with hand support. Begin with having him hold your hands and work toward having him do it by himself, by holding a door frame, a rail, or something similar.

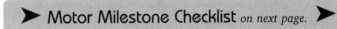

> ➤ Motor Milestone Checklist *on next page.* ➤

Motor Milestone Checklist

❏ He walks up 1" curb with support
❏ He walks up 1" curb without support
❏ He walks down 1" curb with support
❏ He walks down 1" curb without support

❏ He walks up 2" curb with support
❏ He walks up 2" curb without support
❏ He walks down 2" curb with support
❏ He walks down 2" curb without support

❏ He walks up 3" curb with support
❏ He walks up 3" curb without support
❏ He walks down 3" curb with support
❏ He walks down 3" curb without support

❏ He walks up 4" curb with support
❏ He walks up 4" curb without support
❏ He walks down 4" curb with support
❏ He walks down 4" curb without support

❏ He walks up 5" curb with support
❏ He walks up 5" curb without support
❏ He walks down 5" curb with support
❏ He walks down 5" curb without support

❏ He walks up 6" curb with support
❏ He walks up 6" curb without support
❏ He walks down 6" curb with support
❏ He walks down 6" curb without support

❏ He walks up 7" curb with support
❏ He walks up 7" curb without support
❏ He walks down 7" curb with support
❏ He walks down 7" curb without support

❏ He walks up 8" curb with support
❏ He walks up 8" curb without support
❏ He walks down 8" curb with support
❏ He walks down 8" curb without support

CHAPTER 11

Walking Up and Down Stairs

Your child will be ready to practice the skill of walking up and down stairs after she is able to walk up and down 4- to 8-inch curbs with hand support. The curbs will prepare her to use the leg motions and to develop the strength needed to walk up and down stairs. Walking up and down stairs uses the same physical skills, but requires more leg strength because stairs are higher and several must be climbed in a row. First, your child will learn to walk up and down using a marking time pattern; that is, two feet on each stair. Later, she will learn to use an alternating pattern; that is, one foot on each stair.

Your child will have the following four goals to achieve in this skill area:
1. **Walk up a flight of stairs holding the railing with two feet on each stair (marking time);**
2. **Walk down a flight of stairs holding the railing with two feet on each stair (marking time);**
3. **Walk up a flight of stairs holding the railing with one foot on each stair (alternating);**
4. **Walk down a flight of stairs holding the railing with one foot on each stair (alternating).**

These goals will take a long time to achieve. Your child will begin practicing walking up and down stairs after she learns to walk. She will probably achieve the first two goals around the ages of 3-4 years, the third goal at 4-5 years, and the fourth goal at 6-7 years. You will have lots of time to practice the goals since stairs are everywhere. When your child learns to walk up and down stairs by herself, she will be independent at home, school, and in the community.

To walk up and down stairs, your child will need to develop:
1. **Leg strength to lift and lower her body weight up and down stairs;**
2. **Arm strength for balance and to assist her legs with lifting and lowering her body weight;**
3. **Growth of her arms, legs, and overall height so that she is able to reach the railing and manage walking up and down a standard size stair;**

Steps in: Learning to Walk Up and Down Stairs

To achieve the goals of this skill area, your child will practice the following steps:

1. Walk up and down stairs, marking time, holding onto an adult with two hands;
2. Walk up and down stairs, marking time, holding onto an adult with one hand and to the railing with her other hand;
3. Walk up and down stairs, marking time, stepping sideways and holding the railing;
4. Walk up and down stairs, marking time, with one hand holding the railing;
5. Walk up stairs, alternating feet, with one hand on the railing and one hand holding onto an adult;
6. Walk up stairs, alternating feet, with one hand holding the railing;
7. Walk down stairs, alternating feet, with one hand on the railing and one hand holding onto an adult;
8. Walk down stairs, alternating feet, with one hand holding the railing

4. **Ability to plan and carry out the sequence of steps necessary to walk up and down a flight of stairs;**
5. **Judgement to walk up and down the flight of stairs safely on a consistent basis.**

Each physical skill is necessary to achieve the goals. You will need to be patient and help your child develop each skill. At times, you will need to wait for her to grow since her size will be critical in being able to climb stairs by herself. For example, if she has adequate arm and leg strength but is still too short to reach the railing, it will be almost impossible for her to progress any further until she grows.

The terms for the various parts of stairs can be confusing, so for the purposes of this chapter, we will use the following definitions:

1. **Banister:** the handrail or the horizontal bar that everyone uses.
2. **Spindles:** the vertical posts that hold up the banister.
3. **Railing:** the place your child holds on; it could refer to either the banister or the spindles.

It will be important to use a railing that your child can reach and hold onto. When your child is young, spindles will be easier because they are often narrow enough for her hand to grasp and she can choose the height that works best for her. The banister is usually too high and so wide that it is hard to hold onto. You will need to find a railing your child can use so she is successful in learning to walk up and down stairs. For example, Allison's father added a lower and smaller railing to help her master the stairs.

Our discussion will presume that your child is stepping up leading with the right leg and stepping down leading with the left. This presumes that the right leg is the dominant or stronger leg, which is most common. If your child is left leg dominant, you will need to adjust the instructions accordingly.

walk up stairs, marking time, stepping forward

To walk up stairs, your child will need to:
1. **hold on with one or both hands**
2. **lift her right foot up on the stair and balance using her arms**
3. **lean her trunk forward over the stair and over her right foot**
4. **straighten her right hip and knee and lift her body weight up on the stair. She will simultaneously use her arms for balance and to pull her body weight up on the stair.**
5. **place her left foot on the stair so both feet are together**
6. **repeat these steps until she walks up the flight of stairs.**

(fig. 11.1)

She will begin by holding an adult's hand with each of her hands. She will progress to holding an adult's hand with one hand and a railing with the other. *(See figure 11.1.)* The hand holding the adult's hand needs to be positioned in front of her chest, at or below shoulder level. A common mistake is to hold the child's hands above her head and to pull the child up on the next stair. When this is done, the child is lifted and she does not develop the arm and leg strength needed to do it by herself. Therefore, the proper position of your child's arms and hands is critical in developing the physical skills needed to walk up stairs.

When providing hand support, watch your child's legs and make sure she is using a marking time pattern. If she alternates her legs, you may be giving her too much support or holding her hand above her shoulder. It will be better for her to establish the marking time pattern first. After she can walk up the stairs marking time, holding the railing only, then she will be ready to work on using the alternating pattern.

When your child easily walks up the stairs, marking time, with one hand on the railing and one hand holding an adult's hand, she may be ready to walk up by holding only the railing. When she first tries to walk up the stairs using only the railing for support, she may compensate by propping one hand on the next stair. If she does this, continue to let her hold your hand with her other hand until she will walk up by herself with one hand on the railing. You can help prepare her by lowering the hand you are supporting. If you lower her hand to her waist level, it will provide minimal support compared to holding it at shoulder level. When she is comfortable with this support, you can hold the sleeve of her shirt, rather than having her hold your hand.

walk down stairs, marking time, stepping forward

To walk down stairs, she will need to:
1. hold on with one or both hands
2. straighten her trunk over her legs and lean back slightly
3. step out with her left leg and balance using her arms
4. slowly bend her right hip and knee to lower her body weight until her left foot touches the next stair. She will simultaneously use her arms for balance and to lower herself.
5. step down with her right leg using her arms for balance
6. repeat these steps until she walks down the flight of stairs.

To walk down stairs, she will follow the same progression of hand support as explained for walking up stairs. There will be one significant change in how the support is provided. Rather than positioning yourself behind your child, you will be in front of her. You will need to stand two stairs below her, facing her, and you

(fig. 11.2)

will step backwards down the stairs. You can lean against the railing so you feel stable. In this position, you will be able to support her hand(s) in the proper position. You will also block her view down the flight of stairs, which will allow her to focus on one stair at a time.

After you support her hands in the proper position, you will need to wait for her to bend her hip and knee and lower herself down to the next stair. By practicing in this way, she will learn how to move down the stairs with balance and control. If her hands are positioned above her shoulders and she is allowed to lean forward a lot, she will try to step down without bending her knees and will be out of control.

When your child can walk down the stairs easily, marking time, with one hand on the railing and one hand holding your hand, she will be ready to practice walking down stairs with only one hand on the railing. *(See figure 11.2.)* She will either try to do it holding the railing, or she will refuse and "sit and bump" down the stairs. If she will not try walking down the stairs, continue to let her hold your hand for support until she is ready. You can decrease your support gradually by lowering her hand to waist level and work toward only holding her sleeve. When she knows how to walk down the stairs with the railing, you can walk beside her and let her get used to the view and not be afraid of it.

walk up and down stairs, marking time, stepping sideways

Walking up and down stairs sideways can be practiced if your child is tall enough to reach a banister or if you have spindles. It can be practiced at the same time as walking up and down stairs, marking time and stepping forward, with one hand on the railing and one hand holding an adult's hand.

To walk up the stairs, she will need to:
1. hold onto the spindles or banister with both hands and stand sideways, facing the railing. (She will hold the railing on the left side of the staircase so her right leg can lead.)
2. lift her right foot up on the next stair and balance using her arms
3. lean her trunk sideways over her right foot

4. straighten her right hip and knee and lift her body weight up on the stair. She will simultaneously use her arms for balance and to pull her body weight up on the stair.
5. place her left foot on the stair so both feet are together
6. re-position her hands on the railing
7. repeat these steps until she walks up the flight of stairs

To walk down the stairs, she will need to *(see figs. 11.3, 11.4):*

1. hold onto the spindles or banister with both hands and stand sideways, facing the railing. (She will hold the railing on the right side of the staircase so her left leg can lead.)
2. lean her trunk over her right foot
3. step out with her left foot
4. bend her right hip and knee and lower her body weight until her left foot touches the stair below. She will simultaneously use her arms to lower herself and for balance.
5. step down with her right leg, using her arms for balance
6. re-position her hands on the railing
7. repeat these steps until she walks down the flight of stairs.

(fig. 11.3)

(fig. 11.4)

At first, you will need to hold your child's hands on the railing and advance them as she walks up or down. When she is walking up the stairs, you will position yourself behind her so you can easily reach her hands. When walking down the stairs, you will position yourself two stairs below her, facing her. When she is ready, you will decrease your support.

You will need to supervise your child until she learns to do this skill safely on a consistent basis. When she is ready, she will spontaneously let go with one hand and begin stepping forward with only one hand on the railing. By practicing walking up and down sideways, she will learn what she needs to do to control her own body rather than learning to do it with another's support.

walk up stairs, alternating feet

To walk up stairs, she will need to:

1. hold on with one or both hands
2. lift her right foot up on the stair and balance using her arms
3. lean her trunk forward over the next stair and over her right foot
4. straighten her right hip and knee and lift her body weight up on the stair. She will simultaneously use her arms for balance and to pull herself up on the stair.
5. hold on and balance while lifting her left leg up two stairs from where it was

6. re-position her hand on the railing
7. lean her trunk forward over the next stair and her left foot
8. straighten her left hip and knee and lift her body weight up on the stair. She will simultaneously use her arms to pull herself up on the stair and for balance.
9. hold on and balance while lifting her right leg up two stairs from where it was
10. re-position her hand on the railing
11. repeat steps 3 to 10 until she walks up the flight of stairs.

Your child will generally show you she is ready to practice this variation by spontaneously using an alternating pattern as she walks up the top one or two stairs. She will need to be independent walking up stairs, marking time, and holding the railing by herself. She will also need to have the strength and height to alternate her legs on the stairs. Each leg will need to have adequate strength to lift her body weight up onto the next stair. When marking time, only one leg, the leading leg, needed to have that degree of strength.

If your child continues to use the marking time pattern when she is 4-5 years old, it means that leading with her dominant leg has become a habit. You need to help her learn to alternate her legs. You will need to help her strengthen her other leg so she can learn to use an alternating pattern. You can begin by encouraging her to walk up curbs or stairs leading with her non-dominant leg. You can also help her practice using an alternating pattern when she is walking up a flight of stairs by lifting her non-dominant leg. For example, if her right leg is dominant, after she places her right foot on the next stair, you will lift her left foot up two stairs by lifting under her thigh. Then she will practice lifting her body weight up with her left leg. After she does that, she will step up with her right again and you will repeat lifting her left leg.

walk down stairs, alternating feet

To walk down stairs, she will need to:
1. hold on with one or both hands
2. straighten her trunk over her legs and lean back slightly and to the right
3. step out with her left leg and balance using her arms
4. slowly bend her right hip and knee to lower her body weight until her left foot touches the next stair. She will simultaneously use her arms for balance and to lower herself.
5. straighten her trunk and lean over her left leg
6. step out with her right leg and lower it down two stairs from where it was. To lower it, she will slowly bend her left hip and knee until her right foot touches the next stair.
7. re-position her arms
8. straighten her trunk and lean back and over her right leg
9. step out with her left leg and lower it down two stairs from where it was
10. repeat steps 4 to 10 until she walks down the flight of stairs.

Walking down stairs using an alternating pattern will be harder than walking up stairs and she will develop it significantly later. Your child will need to have additional leg strength and height in order to do it. Some children will be fearful of the combination of lowering the body so far with each leg and visually looking down the flight of stairs. You will need to be sensitive to your child's reaction and phase in this skill when she is ready.

If your child is still using the marking time pattern when she is 7 years old, you need to help her learn to alternate her legs. Watch to see which leg she prefers to lead with when she walks down stairs. Begin by encouraging her to lead with the other leg when walking down stairs or curbs. You can also help her practice using an alternating pattern when she is walking down a flight of stairs by moving the leg she does not lead with. For example, if she generally leads with her left leg, after she places her left foot on the next stair, you will move her right foot two stairs below where it was. As you move her right foot, she will practice lowering herself using her left leg. You will keep repeating this down the flight of stairs.

Your child will need to practice this activity many times before she learns to do it quickly and automatically. At first, she will need to move slowly and focus on one stair at a time. For example, Jawanda was tall and strong enough to walk down stairs using an alternating pattern. She needed to be reminded do this, however, rather than use the marking time pattern. She could use an alternating pattern if she used a smooth, slow rhythm. It helped her stay focused and keep moving if we counted each step. With practice, she became faster and learned to do it automatically.

activity guidelines

Let your child lead with the leg she chooses. As discussed in the last chapter, your child will generally prefer to lead with a particular leg when stepping up and use the opposite leg when stepping down. If she does not show a preference, watch her to see if she develops one. Generally, she will learn to step up leading using her stronger, dominant leg and step down leading with her other leg.

Allow her to lead with the leg she chooses so she feels stable walking up and down the stairs. Later, when she is ready to learn to use the alternating pattern, you can encourage her to do the opposite of what she is familiar with in order to strengthen her non-dominant leg.

Observe your child and see if walking up or down stairs is easier. Up is generally easier because she is more familiar with straightening her hip and knee and she feels secure with the next stair being so close that she could prop on it if she needed to.

Down is generally harder because she needs strength to lower herself to the next stair. A standard size stair will seem like a long way for her to have to lower herself. It will also require more control than stepping off the curb since she cannot "fall off" and then catch her balance. Stepping down is hard for many children, but particularly those who have tended to move with stiff knees.

Be sensitive to your child's reactions to walking up and down the stairs and provide the support she needs to be comfortable learning these skills.

Give your child hand support and, when she is ready, let go. She will need your hand support until she can walk up and down by herself, holding the railing. The type of hand support required is outlined in the Activity section below.

When your child has mastered walking up and down stairs with her hand on the railing, I continue to recommend using the railing for safety. Do not practice walking up and down stairs without the railing because your child may try to do that in a crowded setting, like at school, and might fall.

Give verbal, visual, and tactile cues. When your child is learning to walk up and down stairs, you will say "up" or "down" with each stair. When she is practicing walking up or down a flight of stairs, you can focus her on each stair by counting. When she is ready to learn to alternate her legs, you can say "big step." She will probably repeat the words you say and this will help her focus on what she is doing.

To visually get her attention, have her watch someone, like a sister, walk up the stairs in front of her. Or, her sister can stand at the top of the stairs and hold a toy for motivation. To help her hold the railing or move her hands forward on the railing, you can slap the railing with your hand (or tap your ring on a metal railing for the sound effect). This will focus her on where you want her to put her hand. When she is ready to alternate her legs, you can stand beside her and she can watch you do it and then imitate you.

You will initially provide tactile cues by giving her hand support so she feels the motions needed for walking up and down stairs. Later, you can give specific cues to her hands to help her hold onto the railing and to her legs to help her use an alternating pattern.

(fig. 11.5)

If spindles are available, use them first. *(See figure 11.5.)* Look for stairs with spindles. Or, if your stairway has them on only one section, use that section to initially practice walking up and down stairs. It will be easier to hold the spindles because she will be able to reach them at a height that is comfortable for her. When she is taller and can comfortably reach the banister, she will use it instead of the spindles.

Use a railing that is small enough for your child to grasp. Your child probably has short fingers and small hands, which will make it hard for her to hold onto many railings. If you can find a railing that is small enough for her to hold and grip with her hand, she will be more successful. With a small railing, she will be able to use her arms more effectively to pull up, lower, and balance herself when walking up and down stairs. If she cannot hold onto the railing, she will need to hold onto your hands to effectively use her arms. Some examples of where to look for small railings are: stairs at toddler playgrounds and spindles on front porch stairs. Later, when her legs are stronger and she only needs to use her arms for balance, she will be able to use the standard banister because she will be able to prop on it rather than grip it tightly and her hand will be larger.

Begin with walking up and down a few stairs and work toward doing a flight of stairs. When possible, begin with a set of three to six stairs so she is successful in reaching the top or bottom before she is fatigued. You can also use the top three to six stairs when walking up a flight of stairs or the bottom three to six when walking down. When she is ready, gradually increase the number of stairs until she can walk up and down the entire flight of stairs.

Use carpeted stairs if available. Your child will generally feel more secure on carpet because it will not be slippery. You will probably feel more comfortable, too, knowing she will not hurt herself if she falls. When she is not using a carpeted surface, supervise her more closely until you feel comfortable with her ability to walk up and down the stairs safely.

Use stairs with a height of 3-6 inches if available. Your child will be ready to walk up and down stairs earlier if she can use shorter stairs with a lower railing. *(See figure 11.6.)* The major difficulty in using standard size stairs is your child's height and short leg length relative to the 8-inch high stair and the standard height banister. If shorter stairs are available, she will be able to practice walking up and down stairs by herself at an earlier age. If they are not available, she will need to practice on standard size stairs with support until she has adequate strength, balance, and height to use them by herself. Some brick front porch stairs are shorter, and you may also find sets of shorter stairs at toddler playgrounds, at parks, and in your neighborhood.

Provide supervision appropriate to your child's skill level. In the beginning, you may be reluctant to practice walking up and down stairs due to your fear of your child falling down the stairs. You will realize that once she has the idea of standing on the stairs, she may try it when you are not there. So, once you start practicing walking up and down stairs, you will need to set up the house so your child is safe. You can use gates so she can only be on the stairs when you are with her. You will need to manage her safety on the stairs until you know she has developed the physical skills and judgement to walk up and down the flight of stairs safely on a consistent basis.

When stepping sideways up or down the stairs, set her up to lead with her preferred leg. She will need to use the railing on a particular side of the staircase in order to lead with her preferred leg. For example, if she prefers to lead with her right leg, she will need to use the railing on the left. If there is only one railing for the staircase and it is not on the side your child needs it to be, she will not be able to practice walking up and down sideways on that staircase. You will need to practice walking up and down, facing forward, with one hand holding the railing and her other hand holding your hand.

Encourage your child to carry a small toy in one hand when she is ready to use one hand on the railing. Your child will be reluctant to have you let go of her hand. When she is ready to learn to walk up and down the stairs with only one hand on the railing, give her a small, lightweight toy to hold in her other hand. This may help her forget about holding your hand. You can play a game where she needs to take the toy and give it to someone at the top or bottom of the stairs.

Remember that your child will learn to walk up and down stairs when she is physically ready and when she wants to do it. Watch to see *what* she likes to practice: walking up or down or both. Also observe *when* she wants to practice. It will help to incorporate it into her schedule for specific fun activities. For example, Blaine was motivated to walk up the stairs every night to take a bath and walk down the stairs in the morning to see the school bus. Sarah was motivated to walk down the stairs in the morning to see her brothers and sisters.

(fig. 11.6)

temperament

If your child is an *observer,* she will want to feel safe, secure, and in control. She will prefer her old methods of climbing up and down the stairs because she will know how to do that, and it will be easier for her. She will need to be motivated to walk up and down the stairs. With hand support, she will cooperate with walking up and down the stairs. She will pay attention to each stair and will be careful with each step she takes. She will intuitively focus on being safe and you will need to focus on helping her learn the movements efficiently and with ease.

After she has learned to walk up and down the stairs with hand support, she will be reluctant to change to only holding the railing. She will prefer holding your hand because she will feel more stable and safe.

When it is time to learn to use an alternating pattern, your child will probably need to be taught. Walking up and down the stairs using a marking time pattern will be effective so she may not initiate using an alternating pattern.

Taurean could walk up the stairs well using an alternating pattern. He was 7 years old, very tall, and ready to learn to walk down using an alternating pattern. When I first began teaching him to walk down the stairs, he told me "I'm scared." He would step down with his left foot easily and then I would move his right foot down to the next stair. Every time I moved his right foot, he said "hurts." We kept repeating the leg motions together and after several repetitions, he no longer said "hurt" or "I'm scared." Then I started counting "1, 2" and, on "1," he would move his left foot, and on "2," I would move his right foot. By practicing this way, the movements were tolerated and became familiar. He learned he was safe and could trust what I was doing to his right foot. With practice, he learned to alternate his legs by himself.

When the *motor driven* child is learning to walk up and down, she will generally move her legs fast but may not pay attention to where she places her feet. She might move her feet up two stairs or she might put her foot on the edge of the stair, where it could slide off. She will need to learn how to move so she is safe.

You will need to supervise her closely until she learns how to move her legs safely. She will learn to walk up the stairs safely before she learns to walk down safely. When she first begins to walk down, she may use the strategy she used to step down a curb. She may move fast and "fall off" the stair. You will need to slow her down so she learns to lower herself safely and with control.

When it is time to take away your hand support, she will not mind. She may spontaneously let go of the railing when she should be holding on. Watch what she does and help her when she gets into predicaments.

She probably will initiate using an alternating pattern. She may even try it early, when walking up stairs, before she is able to use a marking time pattern, holding the railing. She will tolerate practicing using an alternating pattern more easily than a child who is an observer.

activity #1

Walking Up Stairs, Marking Time, Stepping Forward

1. Place a motivator at the top of the stairs.
2. Position your child at the base of the stairs. Begin with a short set of stairs or use the top half of the flight.
3. Position yourself behind her, leaning your trunk forward, over her.
4. Have her hold your hands and position her hands in front of her chest, at or below shoulder level.

5. Using your hands, lean her forward over the next stair.
6. Give verbal (say "up") and visual cues.
7. Wait for her to step up with one leg.
8. Encourage her to walk to the top of the stairs to the landing. Clap for her, praise her, and give her the motivator.
9. Alternative: Rather than one person standing behind her, position one person on each side of her.
10. Continue to practice the above steps until she can walk up the entire flight of stairs easily.
11. When she can do #10, help her hold the railing with one hand and hold your hand with her other hand.
     a. Use a railing that she can reach, for example spindles or a low banister.
     b. Position yourself behind or beside her.
     c. Assist her hand holding the railing. At first, help her grasp the railing and advance her hand forward with each stair. Later, see if she can do these actions by herself.
     d. Follow steps 1, 3-8, and 10, except she will only hold on to one of your hands.
12. When she can do #11, try having her only hold onto the railing.
     a. If she is not ready to do this, hold her sleeve or shoulder and see if she will walk up without holding your hand. She may feel secure enough with this amount of support.
     b. If she holds the railing with both hands, let her. Later, she will let go with one hand.
     c. Try giving her a small, lightweight toy to hold in her free hand.
     d. To help her feel secure, assist her hand holding the railing. If she feels stable with that hand, she may be able to walk up the stairs.
     e. Position yourself behind or beside her. Follow steps 1, 6, 7, 8, and 10.
     f. Continue to practice until she can walk up stairs by herself, safely, on a consistent basis.

activity #2   Walking Down Stairs, Marking Time, Stepping Forward

1. Place a motivator at the bottom of the stairs.
2. Position your child at the top of the stairs. Begin with a short set of stairs or use the bottom half of the flight.
3. Position yourself two stairs below her, facing her.
4. Have her hold your hands and position her hands in front of her chest, at or below shoulder level.
5. Using your hands, lean her trunk forward a little bit, keeping her buttocks over her feet.
6. Give verbal cues (say "down") and visual cues.
7. Wait for her to step down with one foot. Assist her, if needed, to stay balanced and move slowly.
8. Encourage her to walk to the bottom of the stairs. Clap for her, praise her, and give her the motivator.
9. Alternative: Rather than one person standing in front of her, you could position one person on each side of her.

10. Continue to practice the above steps until she can walk down the entire flight of stairs easily.

11. When she can do #10, help her hold the railing with one hand and hold your hand with her other hand.
    a. Use a railing that she can reach, for example spindles or a low banister.
    b. Position yourself two stairs below her, facing her, or stand beside her.
    c. Assist her hand holding the railing. At first, help her grasp the railing and advance her hand forward. Later, see if she can do these actions by herself.
    d. Follow steps 1, 3-8, and 10, except she will only hold onto one of your hands.

12. When she can do #11, try letting go with one hand.
    a. If she is not ready to do this, hold her sleeve or shoulder and see if she will walk down without holding your hand. She may feel secure enough with you giving her this amount of support.
    b. If she holds the railing with both hands, let her. Later, she will let go with one hand.
    c. Try giving her a small, lightweight toy to hold in her free hand.
    d. To help her feel secure, assist her hand holding the railing. If she feels stable with that hand, she may be able to walk down the stairs.
    e. Position yourself two stairs below her, facing her, or walk beside her. Follow steps 1, 6, 7, 8, and 10.
    f. Continue to practice until she can walk down stairs by herself, safely, on a consistent basis.

activity #3   **Walking Up Stairs, Stepping Sideways**

1. Place a motivator at the top of the stairs.
2. Position your child on the bottom stair, facing the railing. Use spindles or a low banister so she can hold on and reach the railing. Begin with a short set of stairs or use the top half of the flight. If she has a foot she prefers to lead with, place her on the side of the staircase to lead with that leg.
3. Position yourself behind her.
4. Help her place her hands on the railing and provide support to help her hold on, if needed.
5. Give her verbal cues (say "up") and visual cues.
6. Wait for her to step up with each leg.
7. Help her to advance her hands on the railing.
8. Encourage her to walk to the top of the stairs to the landing.
9. Continue to practice until she can walk up the entire flight easily using the arm and leg motions required.

activity #4   **Walking Down Stairs, Stepping Sideways**

1. Place a motivator at the bottom of the stairs.
2. Position your child on the top stair, facing the railing. Use spindles or a low banister so she can hold on and reach the railing. Begin with a short set of stairs or use the bottom half of the flight. If she has a foot

she prefers to lead with, place her on the side of the staircase to lead with that leg.

3. Position yourself two stairs below her, facing her.
4. Help her place her hands on the railing and provide support to help her hold on, if needed.
5. Give her verbal cues (say "down") and visual cues.
6. Wait for her to step down with each leg.
7. Help her advance her hands on the railing.
8. Encourage her to walk to the bottom of the stairs.
9. Continue to practice until she can walk down the entire flight easily using the arm and leg motions required.

activity #5 **Walking Up Stairs, Alternating Her Feet**

1. Place a motivator at the top of the stairs.
2. Position your child at the base of the stairs. Begin with a short set of stairs or use the top half of the flight.
3. Position yourself beside her.
4. Have her hold the railing with one hand and hold your hand with her other hand. Position her hand in front of her chest, at shoulder level.
5. Give her verbal cues (say "up" or "big step") and visual cues.
6. Wait for her to step up with each leg.
   a. If she uses a marking time pattern, help her use an alternating pattern. Have her step up with her dominant leg and you move her other leg up to the next stair. Stand next to the leg you need to assist. Place your hand under her thigh and lift it until her foot is on the next stair. When she is familiar with alternating her legs with support, just tap the thigh of her non-dominant leg to cue her to step up with it.
   b. If she uses an alternating pattern, practice this variation until she uses it well.
7. Encourage her to walk to the top of the stairs to the landing. Clap for her, praise her, and give her the motivator.
8. Continue to practice until she can walk up the entire flight of stairs easily, alternating her legs, with one hand on the railing and her other hand holding your hand.
9. When she can do #8, see if you can let go and have her only hold on the railing.
   a. If she is not ready to do this, hold her sleeve or shoulder and see if she will walk up without holding your hand. She may feel secure enough with you giving her a little support even if she is not holding your hand.
   b. If she holds the railing with both hands, let her. Later, she will let go with one hand.
   c. Try giving her a small, lightweight toy to hold in her free hand.
   d. To help her feel secure, assist her hand holding the railing. If she feels stable with that hand, she may be able to walk up the stairs.
   e. Position yourself beside her and give her the visual cue of watching your feet. Say "big step" or count "1, 2."

f. Practice walking up the flight of stairs.

g. Clap for her and praise her when she reaches the top of the stairs.

h. Continue to practice until she can walk up the stairs, alternating her feet, with her hand on the railing, safely and consistently.

activity #6   Walking Down Stairs, Alternating Her Feet

1. Place a motivator at the bottom of the stairs.
2. Position your child at the top of the stairs. Begin with a short set of stairs or use the bottom half of the flight.
3. Position yourself beside her.
4. Have her hold the railing with one hand and hold your hand with her other hand. Position her hand in front of her chest, at shoulder level.
5. Give her verbal cues (say "down" or "big step") and visual cues.
6. Wait for her to step down with each leg.
    a. If she uses a marking time pattern, help her use an alternating pattern. Have her step down with the foot she likes to lead with and you move her other foot down to the next stair. Stand next to the leg you need to assist. Let her hold one of your hands and use your other hand to move her leg. Begin by holding her calf or foot and slowly move it down to the next stair. When she is familiar with alternating her legs with your support, just tap her lower leg to remind her to step down to the next stair with it.
    b. If she uses an alternating pattern, practice this variation until she uses it well.
7. Encourage her to walk to the bottom of the stairs. Clap for her, praise her, and give her the motivator.
8. Continue to practice until she can walk down the entire flight of stairs easily, alternating her legs, with one hand on the railing and her other hand holding your hand.
9. When she can do #8, see if you can let go and have her only hold onto the railing.
    a. If she is not ready to do this, try the tips in Activity #5, 9a-e.
    b. Practice walking down the flight of stairs.
    c. Clap for her and praise her when she reaches the bottom of the stairs.
    d. Continue to practice until she can walk down the stairs, alternating her feet, with her hand on the railing.

➤ Motor Milestone Checklist *on next page.* ➤

Motor Milestone Checklist

❑ She walks up stairs, marking time, stepping forward, holding onto an adult with both hands

❑ She walks down stairs, marking time, stepping forward, holding onto an adult with both hands

❑ She walks up stairs, marking time, stepping forward, with one hand on the railing and one hand holding an adult's hand

❑ She walks down stairs, marking time, stepping forward, with one hand on the railing and one hand holding an adult's hand

❑ She walks up stairs, marking time, stepping sideways, with both hands holding the railing

❑ She walks down stairs, marking time, stepping sideways, with both hands holding the railing

❑ She walks up stairs, marking time, stepping forward, with one hand holding the railing

❑ She walks down stairs, marking time, stepping forward, with one hand holding the railing

❑ She walks up stairs, alternating her feet, with one hand on the railing and one hand holding an adult's hand

❑ She walks up stairs, alternating her feet, with one hand on the railing

❑ She walks down stairs, alternating her feet, with one hand on the railing and one hand holding an adult's hand

❑ She walks down stairs, alternating her feet, with one hand on the railing

CHAPTER 12

Fast Walking and Running

As your child's walking pattern becomes secure and established, he will experiment with stepping at a faster pace. At this point, he will be ready to begin practicing the skill of fast walking. Gradually, over time, he will progress to running fast, just like the other neighborhood children. Running is defined as moving swiftly on foot so both feet leave the ground for an instant during each stride. The goal for this skill area is to run 100 feet in 15 seconds or less. Once your child achieves this goal, he can continue to practice, increasing his speed and distance.

Practicing fast walking will help change his early walking pattern. In his early walking pattern, he will stand vertically, take short steps, use a wide base, and take weight mainly on the inner borders of his feet. By using fast walking, he will learn to rotate his buttocks independent from his trunk. As he learns to move his buttocks and leg separately from his trunk, his walking pattern will become more efficient, having a longer stride, narrower base, and faster speed. *(See figure 12.1.)*

(fig. 12.1)

Learning to run will provide many additional benefits for your child. He will develop a more efficient pattern of walking and will learn the concept of speed and moving fast. He will learn to move his body in a coordinated way to generate increased speed. With regular practice, running will improve his overall level of fitness. He will enjoy running while playing games like chase, tag, sports, and races with friends and siblings. He will be motivated to run and will enjoy the experience of moving fast.

As he is learning fast walking, the first shock will be the experience of moving so fast. He will not be familiar with walking with speed. At first, he will grapple with moving his legs fast enough to keep up with you. Once he is familiar with the experience, he will enjoy it and find it exhilarating. You will need to constantly move him to the next level of speed so he learns there is "faster to go." Once he experiences fast walking with support, he can try to imitate it by himself.

Steps in: Learning Fast Walking and Running

To achieve the goal of this skill area, your child will need to practice the following steps:

1. Fast walking with two-hand support on level surfaces;
2. Fast walking down an incline with hand support, then without hand support;
3. Fast walking with one-hand support;
4. Fast walking swinging one or both arms for momentum;
5. Fast walking for 100 feet in 25-30 seconds;
6. Running 100 feet in 10-15 seconds, swinging arms with elbows bent.

Your child will develop these components of fast walking and running as his skill increases:

1. **Move his legs fast to step quickly;**
2. **Take long steps or lengthen his stride;**
3. **Swing his arms for momentum and speed;**
4. **Lean his body forward, particularly his trunk and hips, so he takes weight on the balls of his feet;**
5. **Increase leg strength and leg length to use a long stride effectively;**
6. **Develop endurance and stamina to move over long distances at a fast speed.**

fast walking with two-hand support on level surfaces

Your child will need hand support so he can focus on stepping fast with his legs. He will need both hands supported so he is stable and balanced and can move both legs effectively. If only one hand is supported, he will not be able to move the leg on the unsupported side as well and that side will hang back.

You can provide two-hand support with one person on each side of him *(see figure 12.2),* or one person can do it, standing in front or behind him. When one person does it, it is best to stand in front of your child, facing him, and to step backwards as he steps forward. With this support, he is better balanced in the center and easily leaned forward. When you are behind him and lean over him, it is harder to make sure he is balanced and leaning forward. The tendency is to lean him to one side and not forward enough. Your child will feel off balance and this will compromise his ability to step quickly.

The best way to provide hand support is to have your child hold your thumbs. After he grasps your thumbs, put your fingers on top of his hand to give him extra support in case his grip loosens. When he is able to hold on consistently, stop providing the additional support. With this hand support, your child will learn to hold on when he wants to step

(fig. 12.2)

quickly and he can let go when he wants to stop. When he is holding your thumbs, you will position his arms so his hands are at or below shoulder level and in front of his chest. When two people are providing support, make sure both of the child's arms are positioned the same, rather than each of you doing it differently.

Once you have provided the proper support, you will be ready to focus on speed. At first, you will move slightly faster than your child's regular speed. You want to move fast enough so he feels what it is like to move at that faster speed but not so fast that he cannot keep up with you. You want him to feel challenged and be able to enjoy it, too. After you practice the increased speed for a few repetitions, let go and see if he will try to imitate moving faster without support.

At this time, your child will also enjoy fast walking on his own, using a push toy, the handle of a riding toy, or the back of a wagon. He will hold on with both hands and experiment with moving fast. You can encourage him to move faster by playing chase.

fast walking down an incline

When your child is familiar with fast walking on level surfaces and can move his legs fast, try inclined surfaces. The incline will help him step faster than his usual speed. To use inclines, he will need to already be familiar with walking up and down them with control (Chapter 9).

You will introduce him to a new way to move down inclines. You will say "whee" and teach him to step quickly down the inclines. You will begin with two-hand support, and, when he is ready, decrease the support until he will do it by himself. He can practice with you using small, medium, and large inclines. He can practice on his own with a push toy down a small incline of a driveway or sidewalk.

fast walking with one-hand support

When he knows how to step quickly and easily with two-hand support and can keep up with you, try one-hand support. Stand beside him and have him hold your fingers or thumb. As before, position his arm in the proper position, making sure he is balanced in the center rather than leaning toward you. Have him hold on with each of his hands to see if he does better with a particular hand supported.

You can only find out if he is ready to do this step by trying it. If his unsupported side hangs back and his speed slows down a lot, he is not ready and needs two-hand support. If he can move both legs quickly and can maintain the same speed or needs to slow down just a little, then he is ready to use one-hand support. When he can step quickly with one-hand support, practice increasing his speed. You can continue to use one-hand support when he is doing Steps #4 and #5 to help him practice moving at faster speeds.

fast walking swinging one or both arms for momentum

As you keep practicing fast walking with hand support, you will notice your child spontaneously stepping faster while playing. He will step fast to catch his sister or to run to someone or something he wants. He will be motivated to move faster and will experiment with his body to see how to move faster. You will notice he will lean his body forward a little, take longer steps, and begin to swing one or both arms for momentum. *(See figure 12.3.)*

Usually, he will swing one arm first. His arm will be positioned with his hand at his side and his elbow fairly straight. He will swing it forward and back from his shoulder as he is fast walking. He will generally keep his other arm stable and it could be held in any position. He will practice swinging one arm and, later, he will swing both. When he begins swinging his arms for momentum, see how far he will go. Encourage him to step quickly for longer distances. Begin with 25 feet and increase the distance to 100 feet.

(fig. 12.3)

fast walking for 100 feet in 20-30 seconds

At this point, your child has developed the components needed to step quickly. He will be able to move his legs fast, lean his body forward a little, swing his arms for momentum, and take longer steps. He will now be ready to practice using this pattern for increased distances. You will gradually increase the distance to 100 feet. You will work toward having him step quickly for the whole distance, without stopping.

When he can step quickly for 100 feet, you will focus on improving his speed. You will give him one- or two-hand support and help him learn how to move faster. One person can stand on each side of him for two-hand support or you can stand beside him for one-hand support. You will practice with and without hand support so he has the opportunity to see how he needs to move his body to move fast (with support) and then has the chance to imitate it on his own.

He will be motivated to step faster when he has hand support. He will need to be motivated to move faster when he is doing it by himself. You can play chase games or have races with him and his siblings. You can generate excitement by saying "Ready, set, go" or "1, 2, 3, go." Your child will try to move faster to keep up with you or his siblings.

running 100 feet in 10-15 seconds

To move 100 feet in 10-15 seconds, your child will use a running pattern. He will need to be able to use a long stride, lean his body forward so he takes weight on the balls of his feet, and swing his arms forward and back with his elbows bent in approximate right angles. By the time he is ready for this skill, his legs will be longer, which will help him lengthen his stride. He will have increased leg strength to push off with each leg to propel his body forward. With practice, he will learn to use his body in a coordinated way to move faster. Once he is able to run, he will continue to practice to run farther and faster. He will need a motivator to challenge himself to generate more speed and move over longer distances.

activity guidelines

Use even surfaces and wide open spaces. At first, your child will need a flat, even surface so he can focus on moving fast. You can use the sidewalk, driveway, a school gym, or a long hallway. If the surface is uneven, like grass, he will fall more and will not increase his speed because he will feel unstable. Once he can step quickly and does it spontaneously, you can practice on uneven surfaces. Try your backyard, parks, playgrounds, golf courses, or football fields.

He will do best in large, wide open spaces. This will encourage him to move over longer distances. He will be free to explore and you will not need to supervise him closely. He can take turns, alternating walking and fast walking or running.

Alternate using hand support and providing no support. When your child is learning to step quickly, he will need hand support until he can move fast by himself. The hand support will help him learn the motions needed and then you can let go and see if he can imitate them on his own. Even after he is familiar with moving faster, you should still sometimes provide hand support to further develop increased speed and distance. The hand support will teach him what is required for the next level of the skill. He will need practice using hand support and then trying it on his own. You will continue alternating hand support and no support until he is using the running pattern and has speed.

Use the proper hand and arm position. Since your child's hands and fingers are small, it is best if he holds your thumbs or one or two of your fingers rather than your hand. He will need to hold on tightly and your hand will be too wide to hold onto. In the beginning, if he is having difficulty holding your thumbs, put your fingers over the top of his hand to give him extra support until he can hold on by himself. If he cannot hold on tight, he will not be secure enough to step faster.

After he holds on, you will need to position his arms to provide the appropriate "pull." You will want him to feel a *forward pull* rather than an *upward pull.* To give him the *forward pull,* his arms will need to be forward in front of his chest and at or below shoulder level. With the forward pull, he will learn the actions of leaning forward, having his weight over the balls of his feet, and stepping fast with his legs. If his arms are held upward with his hands above his shoulders, you will be providing an upward pull. This will not be effective in teaching him to step quickly or run, as you will be lifting him and controlling his balance. His trunk will be fairly vertical and he will step at a slower speed. Depending on your height and your child's, you may need to bend down to provide the *forward pull.*

Motivate your child to step quickly and run. Many games can be used to motivate your child to step quickly or run. *(See figure 12.4.)* The best motivator will

be his brother, sister, or friend. If they will run, your child will, too, in order to keep up with them. They can run while playing together or when playing games like chase, tag, and races. When you want to challenge your child's speed and distance, a race will motivate him to do his best. Later, a variety of sports can be used that combine running and ball skills.

Provide verbal cues. You will use a wide assortment of verbal cues depending on what you want your child to do. To cue him to go, you can say "ready, go," "ready, set, go," or "1, 2, 3, go." To cue him into the fun of moving fast, you can say "whee." To cue him to move faster, you can say "go, go, go" or "faster, faster, faster." To cue him to stop, say "stop". These cues help him focus on what he needs to do now. They need to be simple and clear and be said when you want him to do the action.

Use fast walking and running for breaks between other activities. Your child will love to practice fast walking and running after he has been doing something hard or requiring concentra-

(fig. 12.4)

tion, or has been sitting for awhile. Taking a running break will release any stored up energy or frustration and help him feel alert, awake, and energized. Your child may even initiate running to get away from something he does not want to do!

Build speed, distance, and endurance. As your child is practicing fast walking and running activities, he will work to develop increased speed, distance, and endurance simultaneously. At first, you will work toward having him use the speed of fast walking for the distance of 100 feet. Then you will focus on increasing his speed over the 100 foot distance until he uses a running pattern and speed. Once he can run 100 feet in less than 15 seconds, he can continue to challenge himself by increasing the distance and speed. While he practices improving his distance and speed, his endurance will improve.

Be prepared for your child to spontaneously use fast walking and running. Your child will go through four stages in learning to move fast. First, he will experience moving fast with your support and he will enjoy the feeling. Second, he will gain the strength and motions to move fast. Third, he will see how to move fast when playing games, like chase. Fourth, he will spontaneously move fast when he is motivated. At this point, he will realize what he can use fast walking or running for in his own life! An early sign is running away from you in a store, particularly when you are in the check-out line. He also will use running to get something he wants but probably is not allowed to have. Now you will be challenged to keep up with him!

Wear appropriate footwear. Your child should wear flexible sole sneakers to practice fast walking and running. Since he will need to lean forward onto the balls of his feet, he needs shoes that bend easily to allow that foot position. Shoes with stiff soles would limit his foot motion. High top shoes are not recommended because they will limit bending at the ankle, which will make it harder to lean forward over the balls of his feet.

temperament

If your child is an **observer,** he will prefer to start out at a slower speed. He will need support to tolerate the new experience of moving fast. After some practice, he will smile, showing you he likes it because it feels good. He will like practicing with hand support and will be willing to gradually increase his speed and run down inclined surfaces. When he does not have hand support, he will gradually increase his speed on his own. He will tend to move slower because he will try to balance control with increased speed.

He will practice fast walking and running for a few repetitions but then will need to be motivated to continue. He will use running for a particular game or to get to something he wants. When he is tired or bored or not motivated to run, he will stop. You will need to set up motivators to help him increase his distance and speed.

If your child is **motor driven,** he will love fast walking and running from the very beginning. Since he will love to move fast, he may spontaneously initiate it after you show him or he may say or sign "more" so you can help him do it again. He will practice fast walking on his own and will like to do it with hand support or down inclined surfaces in order to move faster. He will be motivated to increase his speed, even if he feels out of control. When he is out of control, he will try to regain his balance by stepping faster. He will step fast and adapt when needed rather than plan ahead.

He will practice fast walking and running until he is fatigued. He will not necessarily need a game in order to practice. He will be self-motivated to move fast and run and will easily tolerate increasing his distance and speed. Later, when he is 4-5 years old, he may use it to run away or initiate chase games and you will need to run to catch up with him!

activity #1   **Fast Walking with Support**

1. Use a flat, level surface with a distance of 50 feet or more. It is best if it is straight rather than curved.
2. Stand in front of your child, facing him. Or, if two persons are available, position one person on each side of him.
3. Have your child hold your thumbs. Position his arms so they are in front of his chest, at shoulder level or lower. If needed, put your fingers over his hand to assist his grip.
4. Give verbal and visual cues. Use a motivator if needed to encourage him to move a particular distance and speed.
5. Step quickly at a speed faster than his usual speed. He will need to hold on and step fast to keep up with you. When he is tired or does not want to do it anymore, he can let go.
6. Alternative set-up: He can step quickly holding on to a push toy. Make sure that the handle is about chest high so that he can hold on without bending over.
7. When he is ready, increase the distance to 100 feet.
8. As tolerated, increase his speed over the 100-foot distance.
9. When he is familiar with inclines (Chapter 9) and fast walking, begin practicing fast walking down small and medium inclines. Provide two-hand support initially and then decrease your support to one hand. When he is ready, try it without support. He can also use his push toy or wagon and step quickly down a small incline.
10. When he can step quickly for 80-100 feet and keeps up with you easily with two-hand support, try providing only one-hand support. Stand beside him, have him hold your finger, and position his arm in the proper position. Continue to increase his speed over the 100-foot distance.

activity #2   **Fast Walking and Running**

1. Use a flat, level surface with a distance of 100 feet or more.
2. Either you or a sibling stand beside your child.
3. Motivate your child to run as fast as he can by setting up a favorite game like chase or races.
4. Say "ready, go."
5. Encourage him to step quickly for a distance of 50-100 feet without stopping.
6. As he tries to move faster, see if he swings one or both arms.
7. When he steps quickly for 100 feet and swings one or both arms, see if he is standing vertically or if he is leaning forward with his weight over the balls of his feet. If vertical, provide two-hand support with one person on each side of him or one-hand support. When he holds your fingers or thumbs, make sure his arms are forward but no higher than shoulder level. As he holds on and you run with him, he will lean forward and experience this new position for running.
8. Have him practice running by himself at his own speed and running with hand support to experience running at a faster speed. Continue to practice increasing his speed for the 100-foot distance until he can do it in 10-15 seconds.

> ► Motor Milestone Checklist *on next page.* ►

Motor Milestone Checklist

- ❑ He fast walks for 25-50 feet with two-hand support
- ❑ He fast walks for 100 feet with two-hand support
- ❑ He fast walks down a medium incline with hand support
- ❑ He fast walks down a medium incline without hand support
- ❑ He fast walks with one-hand support for 50 feet
- ❑ He fast walks with one-hand support for 100 feet
- ❑ He fast walks for 50 feet, swinging one or both arms for momentum
- ❑ He fast walks for 100 feet, swinging one or both arms for momentum
- ❑ He fast walks for 100 feet in 20-25 seconds
- ❑ He runs 100 feet in 10-15 seconds

CHAPTER 13

Balance Beam Skills

When your child is walking well on level surfaces, she will be ready to learn to walk on a balance beam. For the purposes of this chapter, a balance beam will be defined as a board that is ¾ to one inch thick and comes in a variety of widths, particularly 10 inches, 7 inches, 5½ inches, and 4 inches. The board will be approximately 6 feet long and will be placed on the floor. The goal will be for your child to walk across a 4-inch wide balance beam without hand support.

Walking on a balance beam will help to change your child's early walking pattern. In her early walking pattern, she will use a wide base, her hips will rotate outward causing her knees and feet to turn out, and she will take weight on the inside borders of her feet. By practicing walking on a balance beam, she will learn to walk with her legs and feet in a new position. She will learn to rotate her hips so her knees and feet point straight ahead. She will need to position her feet closer together and will learn to balance herself using this narrower base. With her feet in this position, she will take weight on the outside borders of her feet.

To achieve the goal of this skill area, your child will practice walking across progressively smaller balance beams (10, 7, 5½, and 4 inches). You will provide hand support until she learns how to move her legs and feet to walk on the balance beams. When she can walk within the width of the balance beam, let go so she can work on developing the balance needed to walk with the narrower base.

Your child will learn two methods to walk across the balance beams, depending on the width of the board. For the 5½- to 10-inch wide balance beams, she will step by placing one foot next to the other. The narrower the balance beam, the closer together her feet will be. For the 4-inch wide balance beam, she will step by placing one foot in front of the other so the heel of one foot is in front of the toes of the other foot. As the width of the balance beam narrows, she will be challenged and may try her own unique methods to walk across it. She may turn her body sideways and step sideways across the balance beam. Or, she may step with one foot on the balance beam and one foot on the floor. You will help her learn to step forward with both feet on the board.

Using boards that are ¾ to 1-inch thick as balance beams will help your child learn to pay attention to walking within a boundary. She will feel the edge of the board and will feel a consequence when she steps off the board with one foot. This will get her attention but not scare her. When balance beams that are raised 6

Steps in: Learning to Walk across a Balance Beam

To walk across the balance beam, your child will need to:
1. Understand she needs to step within the boundaries (width) of the balance beam;
2. Pay attention in order to keep her feet on the balance beam as she walks from one end to the other;
3. Take steps and balance with her feet closer together.

inches or more off the floor are used, children become frightened of falling off. It is better to place the balance beam on the floor so she notices the boundary but is not frightened by the height of the board.

walking across 10-inch wide balance beam

Your child will adjust easily to walking across a balance beam with this width. You will use this time to teach her how to walk across balance beams. You will teach her to pay attention to the board and step within the boundary. You will hold her hand so she practices walking on the board and becomes familiar with it. You will also show her how to step on and off the board. When she is ready, you will encourage her to do it by herself.

When she is walking across the balance beam by herself, she will be more attentive to where her feet are placed on the board. *(See figure 13.1.)* At first, she will position her feet just close enough to fit within the 10-inch width. With practice, she will place her feet closer together so the outside borders of her feet are 1-2 inches from the edge of the board and the inside borders are 3-5 inches apart. When she is comfortable walking across the board, she will know how to step within the boundary and will not need to watch her feet. Then she will be ready to use a 7-inch wide balance beam.

walking across 5½-to7-inch balance beams

Once your child knows how to walk across a balance beam, challenge her by using narrower ones, first 7 inches, then 5½ inches. She will need hand support to adjust to the narrower boundary. She will need to learn how to move her legs and feet to consistently walk within the smaller space. When she can do this, you can let go.

When she is walking across the balance beam by herself, she will develop the balance to walk with her feet very close together. *(See figure 13.2.)* With the 7-inch balance beam, the inside borders of her feet will be approximately 2-3 inches apart. With the 5½-inch balance beam, the inside borders of her feet will be 1-2 inches apart. The inside borders of her feet may even touch as she walks from one end to the other. When she can walk across the 5½-inch wide balance beam by herself, she will be ready to use a 4-inch balance beam.

walking across 4-inch wide balance beams

To walk across the 4-inch wide balance beam, your child will first need to learn a new way to move her legs and feet. She will not be able to use the old method of placing one foot next to the other because they will not fit within the width of the board. She will need to place one foot in front of the other so the heel of one foot is in front of the toes of the other foot. *(See figure 13.3.)* She will need hand support and a lot of practice to prepare for doing it by herself.

To walk across the 4-inch wide balance beam by herself, she will need to:
1. **Lean over her right foot and balance herself;**
2. **Lift and place her left foot in front of her right foot;**
3. **Maintain her balance with her legs and feet in this position;**
4. **Lean over her left foot and balance herself;**
5. **Lift and place her right foot in front of her left foot;**
6. **Maintain her balance with her legs and feet in this position;**
7. **Continue steps 1-6 until she walks across the length of the balance beam.**

This activity will challenge her balance and her ability to keep her attention focused on the activity until it is completed. She will need to move slowly and with control. She will need to concentrate and pay attention as she takes each step. If she becomes distracted, she will lose her balance. If she is no longer motivated to do it, she will step off. You will need to see when she is ready to practice this activity. She will need a lot of practice and motivation to accomplish it.

(fig. 13.1)

(fig. 13.2)

(fig. 13.3)

activity guidelines

Set up the balance beam so your child feels stable on it and is comfortable using it. Your child will be focusing on balancing herself so she will need to feel safe enough to practice. She will feel more comfortable using a balance beam placed on the floor rather than raised off the floor. You will need to put it on a firm surface such as a vinyl or hardwood floor or an unpadded carpet. On a padded carpet, it will rock from side to side with each step and she will feel unstable on it. The balance beam will need to be stabilized to prevent sliding in any direction. The easiest way to do this is to use your weight to stabilize it. Also make sure the bal-

balance beam is not warped. If it is warped, your child will feel the unevenness in the board and it will tilt her off balance.

Provide hand support, and, when she is ready, encourage her to do it by herself. Hand support can be provided in two ways:

1. She can hold your finger;
2. She can prop her hand against the wall.

Holding your finger will provide more support because you will automatically assist her if she is off balance. When she props her hand against the wall, she will need to control her own balance.

When she holds your finger, you will need to position her arm in front of her chest with her hand below shoulder level. You will also need to make sure you do not lean her toward you because then she will be off balance.

To prepare your child to walk across the balance beam by herself, you can begin by letting her hold your finger and, later, prop her hand against the wall for support. When she can walk across the balance beam with her hand against the wall, you can re-position the balance beam so half is next to a wall (or furniture) and the other half is in open space with nothing for her to prop against. You can position yourself in front of her and encourage her to take steps to you without holding on to anything or anyone.

It will be a challenge for your child to walk across the balance beams without hand support. She will feel stable with support and will prefer to hold on. As soon as possible, you will need to experiment with letting go. When she does not have support, she will need to grapple with balancing herself with her feet closer together. When she learns how to balance herself using a narrower base, she will learn to walk better.

Provide verbal and visual cues and motivate her to walk across the balance beam. You will need to set her up so she knows what to do and is motivated to do it. You will give her simple verbal instructions, have her watch or follow someone else doing it, and have a motivator, if needed, at the end of the balance beam. You can tell her "walk on the board" or "walk like Katie." If she walks with one foot on the board and one on the ground, tell her "both feet on the board" or "two feet on the board." She will enjoy watching her sister or parent walk across the board and then you can say "your turn." You can help her focus her attention on your feet by marching or stomping your shoes as you walk across. She may also like counting each step she takes. Your child may like walking across the balance beam because it is a game to do with her siblings or friends. If she is not motivated to walk across it, hold a motivator at the end of the beam or put one on a chair. If you are holding it, kneel on the floor so you are at eye level to your child.

Walk across the balance beam barefoot. Your child needs to be barefoot so she can freely move her feet to effectively balance herself when walking across the balance beam. If she is barefoot, she will also learn to turn her feet straight because she will not like how it feels with her feet turned out so her feet or toes are on the outer edges of the board.

If your child is reluctant to walk across the balance beam, let her practice standing on it while you entertain her. You can blow bubbles or sing songs while she practices balancing herself with her feet closer together and pointing straight ahead. When she is comfortable standing on it, you can practice stepping on and off it. Have her approach the balance beam from the side and help her step up on the balance beam and then step off. When she can do this, she will be ready to walk across the length of the balance beam.

(fig. 13.4)

Leave the balance beam on the floor in the middle of the family room or play area. With the balance beam readily available, your child will explore it on her own. She will practice stepping on and off it and across the length of it. During her playtime, she will be able to choose when and how she wants to play with it.

When practicing walking across the balance beam without hand support, begin with a couple of steps and increase the distance as tolerated. At first, she will take small steps, but her steps will get bigger when she is familiar with the activity. After she takes a couple of steps without support, try walking across half the length of the balance beam. When she is ready, encourage her to walk across the full length of the balance beam.

Use a variety of balance beam activities in your community. Once your child is familiar with and enjoys walking across balance beams, find new ways to practice these activities. You can walk across railroad ties or other wooden borders at playgrounds, parks, and gardens. *(See figure 13.4.)* Since these examples will be raised off the ground, your child will need support initially to learn to walk on them. She will enjoy playing Follow the Leader with the other kids.

Sarah's family invented another way to play with their 10-inch wide balance beam. Sarah loved walking across it and quickly learned to do it without hand support. So they set up the balance beam like an incline. They placed one end on a child's chair (approximately 11 inches high) and they stabilized the other end. Then Sarah would walk up and down the incline.

temperament

If your child is an **observer,** she will like doing balance beam activities when she is familiar with them. She will move slowly and carefully and focus on staying within the boundary. She will prefer hand support, so you will need to encourage her to let go and do it by herself. She will need to be motivated by someone or by a favorite toy to take on the challenge of walking across the balance beam without hand support. Once she feels comfortable using the balance beam, she may practice it for fun.

Your jobs will be to:
1. Assist her until she learns the leg and foot motions and balance needed to walk across the balance beam by herself;
2. Leave the balance beam set up so she can practice it when she wants to.

If your child is **motor driven,** she will want to use her usual fast speed to practice balance beam activities. She will probably learn to walk across the balance beam without hand support at a fast speed. She will take steps and try to adjust her balance as she is stepping on the balance beam or else she will step off. To move quickly, she may choose to step with one foot on the balance beam and one on the ground.

Your jobs will be to:
1. Slow down her speed;
2. Get her to look at and pay attention to her feet;
3. Keep both feet on the balance beam.

You will need to plan the right time to practice balance beam activities. As the width of the balance beam becomes narrower, it will be more difficult to do and your child may not be interested in practicing it. Try it for brief periods to see when she is ready and willing to do it.

activity #1   Walking Across a Balance Beam

Follow steps 1-6 using balance beams with the following widths: 10", 7", 5½", and 4". Begin with the widest balance beam. Then, once she can walk across it without support, try the next width. To create balance beams with these widths, begin with a 10" wide piece of shelving (6 feet long). You can cut it down (or have it cut) to the next size width when your child is ready. For the 5½" wide balance beam, you can also use a 1"x 6" piece of wood.

1. Have your child step up on the balance beam. Assist her if needed.
2. Stand beside her and have her hold your finger. Position her arm in front of her chest and below shoulder level. (You can also stand in front of her, facing her, and step backwards if your child prefers this support in the beginning. You can place your feet on the floor rather than trying to step backwards on the balance beam! When she is ready, change your position to standing beside her.)
3. Give her verbal and visual cues. Encourage her to walk across the balance beam. Use motivators if needed.
4. When she walks to the other end of the balance beam, have her step off. Praise her and clap for her.
5. When she can walk across the balance beam holding your finger, try having her prop her hand against the wall for support. Place the balance beam next to the wall, approximately 12-15 inches away from the wall. Encourage her to put her hand on the wall for support.
6. When she is ready, encourage her to walk across the balance beam without hand support. Begin with a couple of steps, then half the length of the balance beam, and then increase the distance until she can walk across the full length.

➤ Motor Milestone Checklist *on next page.* ➤

Motor Milestone Checklist

❑ She walks across a 10" wide balance beam with one-hand support
❑ She walks across a 10" wide balance beam without hand support
❑ She walks across a 7" wide balance beam with one-hand support
❑ She walks across a 7" wide balance beam without hand support
❑ She walks across a 5½" wide balance beam with one-hand support
❑ She walks across a 5½" wide balance beam without hand support
❑ She walks across a 4" wide balance beam with one-hand support
❑ She walks across a 4" wide balance beam without hand support

CHAPTER 14

Jumping

When your child can walk and is comfortable standing on soft, squishy surfaces, he will be ready to practice the skill of jumping. He will first practice bouncing up and down on a springy surface (such as a bed or trampoline). Once he knows how to bounce, he will learn to push off with his toes to lift his body upward. He will need to have adequate strength in his legs and feet to lift himself off the ground.

The jumping goals will be to:
1. **Jump in place (on the floor) one time;**
2. **Jump off the bottom stair with both feet together.**

By achieving these goals, he will learn to jump in two directions: vertically and forward.

Some of the benefits of learning to jump are:
1. Your child will strengthen his calf muscles, which tend to be weak in children with Down syndrome. His calf muscles need to be strong so he can stand on tiptoes. His walking and running skills will also improve because he will have better toe push off.
2. Jumping will help him learn to shift the weight to the outside borders of his feet. To jump, he will need to position his feet closer together, pointing straight ahead, and he will be on his tiptoes with the inside borders lifted with a little arch. Practicing these foot motions in jumping will help him use a better foot posture when standing and walking.
3. He will learn to use a combination of bending and straightening movements with his hips and knees while practicing bouncing. He will develop a balance between both movements rather than predominantly using the straightening movements. This will help him with other skills such as walking up and down inclines, stairs, and curbs and riding a tricycle.

Remember that jumping will take time to develop. On average, a child with Down syndrome learns to walk at 2 years of age and to jump at 4 years of age. (See Appendix for detailed information on average ages and the range of ages for vari-

Steps in: Learning to Jump

To achieve the goals of this skill area, your child will need to practice the following steps:

1. Bouncing up and down on a springy surface with hand support with his hips and knees bent and feet flat;
2. Bouncing, as above, but on tiptoes;
3. Jumping on a springy surface and lifting his feet off the surface, with and without hand support;
4. Jumping on the floor and lifting his feet off the floor, with and without hand support;
5. Jumping off a 4-8 inch step with both feet together, with and without hand support;

Your child will begin the jumping experience by learning and enjoying the sensation of bouncing up and down. When he is comfortable with it, he will try to imitate it and repeat it without your help. Then he will expand it by moving up on his tiptoes. The next level will be to learn how to lift his body up and clear his feet off the surface. Eventually he will be able to do it without hand support.

ous skills.) Your child will learn to jump on the floor first and later learn to jump off of a stair. Be patient: it is a skill that takes time.

bouncing with flat feet

Your first job will be to introduce your child to bouncing and make it fun so that he is interested and willing to participate. You will try a lot of variations to see which ones he feels comfortable doing. Later, you can use specific variations that help him learn to bounce properly.

You will need to watch your child and see how he responds to the experience of bouncing. You want to make sure he feels safe. He may love the vigorous action of bouncing right away or you may need to start slowly and gently and build up his tolerance. Initially, he will need to get used to: standing on the springy surface and the action of bouncing. You will need to set up the experience with an eye to how he feels about it.

Your child will need two-hand support, either holding your thumbs or holding onto something he can grip easily. *(See figure 14.1.)* The support will need to be at chest or shoulder level. At first he will prefer to hold your thumbs because he will be more stable. Once he is familiar with bouncing, encourage him to hold onto something he can grip easily so he becomes responsible for balancing himself and learns to use his arms to help lift himself.

(fig. 14.1)

To begin practicing bouncing, you can place him on the springy surface and bounce him or you can stand on the surface and gently bounce up and down with him. Some ways to do this:

1. Bounce up/down on a small trampoline with your child using these positions:
    a. stand on the trampoline, with him facing you, and hold his hands above his head;
    b. stand on the trampoline, with him facing you, and hold him under his armpits.
2. Help your child bounce up/down on the trampoline by:
    a. providing hand support while you are standing on the floor;
    b. sitting on the floor and holding his lower legs while he holds onto the back of a chair;
    c. supporting his hips or legs while you straddle the chair and he holds on to the back of the chair;
    d. positioning the armrest of the sofa in front of the trampoline so he can lean over it while he tries to bounce or you support his legs to assist him.

At first your child may prefer to have you bounce him by holding his hands above his head or by holding him under his armpits. You can do this in the very beginning to help him learn that bouncing is fun, but it will not teach him the leg movements needed for bouncing. When you provide this support, he will hold his hips and knees straight as you bounce him on his feet. He will rely on you to bounce him and he will not learn to bend his hips and knees to generate bouncing by himself. So, once he likes the bouncing feeling, lower the hand support to shoulder or chest level and work on the hip and knee bending motions needed for bouncing.

When he is familiar with bouncing and likes it, see if he will try to move his legs to bounce by himself. He can try to do it by:

    a. bouncing in the crib holding the rail;
    b. bouncing on the bed holding the headboard;
    c. bouncing on the seat cushion of the sofa while holding the back of the sofa;
    d. bouncing on the seat cushion of the sofa placed on the floor under the armrest;
    e. bouncing on a trampoline holding your hands.

When he tries to jump by himself, he may rock from side to side, move one leg at a time, or rock forward and back with his knees stiff. Discourage any of these movements and continue to help him bounce up and down with his legs together.

Work toward having him generate the bouncing for more repetitions, using a rhythm. When he can bounce repeatedly, begin to encourage more energetic and vigorous bouncing so he depresses the springy surface 2-3 inches. Until now, he has primarily used the *lift* provided by the springy surface to bounce up and down. Now we want him to push into the surface to generate more lift and bounce. To do this, he will need to increase the strength in his legs and feet and begin using speed and momentum as he is bouncing up and down.

bouncing on tiptoes

By now, your child knows the bouncing routine and regularly bends his hips and knees with his feet flat to bounce on a springy surface. The next physical skill to focus on is rising up on his tiptoes. He first needs to learn to move his feet to the position and then he will need to learn to use this position to push against the surface to lift himself up off the surface. To push off on his toes effectively, he will modify his bouncing motions. To move upward, he will straighten his hips and knees and push off on his tiptoes. As he moves back downward into the springy surface, he will bend his hips and knees with his feet flat.

To familiarize your child with rising up on his tiptoes, you can encourage him to reach upward when standing. He may already do this while he is playing and encouraging him to do it a lot will build up calf muscle strength. He can do it holding onto a surface or without support. For example, Elizabeth had a kitchen set with the microwave on top. She had to rise up on her tiptoes to reach the microwave. Her mother encouraged her to play with the microwave, putting food in and taking it out. By playing this way, she spent a lot of time on her tiptoes. She would move up on her tiptoes, stay in the position for awhile, and then move her heels down to the floor again. *(See figure 14.2.)*

(fig. 14.2)

(fig. 14.3)

Once your child can stand on his tiptoes on the floor, the next step is teaching him to do this on the springy surface. You can hold his ankles and bounce him on his toes while he holds onto the back of a chair or you can hold his arms to help him stand on his tiptoes. To help him do it by himself, have him hold onto a chair with a higher back, so it is at the level of his face. He will hold on and use his arms to help lift himself onto his toes. *(See figure 14.3.)*

With practice, your child will learn to use the new bouncing method and to stand on his tiptoes. He will need to practice these motions, use them repeatedly in an up/down rhythm, and do them fast to prepare for jumping.

jumping on a springy surface

Your child is now ready to learn to jump on a springy surface and lift his feet off the surface with two-hand support. You will need to teach him what "lift off" is so he feels what you want him to imitate. Once he understands what he is supposed to do, it will be up to him to experiment and grapple with doing it.

"Lift off" may be difficult because he will need to add a new physical skill to his bouncing repertoire. He will need to add speed and momentum to his bouncing rhythm when he is doing the upward motion. He will not be able to lift his feet off the surface by merely rising up on his toes. He will need to figure out a way to boost himself upward to lift his feet off the surface. To do this, he could help by pulling with his arms or pushing off on his toes.

To help him learn what "lift off" is, you can:

1. Show him by having him watch your feet as you jump on the trampoline, holding a chair. Exaggerate how high you raise your feet when you are jumping to draw attention to your feet.
2. Hold his lower legs and raise them up off the surface, while moving within his bouncing rhythm. He will be holding the chair for support and you can sit on the floor.
3. Hold him under his armpits and lift him up so he raises his feet off the surface, while moving within his bouncing rhythm. He can hold the chair and you can straddle it, facing him.
4. Use a higher chair (at the level of his face) for him to hold on to while bouncing. He can use his arms to help lift his body up so his feet are off the surface.

You will continue to help him learn how to lift his feet off the surface until he begins to do it by himself.

At first, he will accidentally lift his feet one time while doing a series of bounces. Or, he might lift one foot but not the other. When he feels the lift and sees your excitement and praise, he will keep trying to do it again. With continued practice, he will learn to jump and lift his feet off the surface each time.

He will need two-hand support until he can jump on a consistent basis. The hand support will be needed to help him balance as he is gaining the leg and foot strength needed to jump. Even when he jumps consistently, it is recommended that he continue holding on for safety when jumping on a springy surface.

jumping on the floor

Once your child can jump on a springy surface, he will be ready to learn to jump on the floor with two-hand support. The springy surface helped lift him upward. He will now need to learn how to jump using a surface that has no spring. To jump on the floor, he will need to push off with his toes against the surface with enough strength and speed to lift his body upward.

While he is gaining the leg and foot strength, he will use two-hand support to help lift himself up and for balance. With practice, he will be able to jump on the floor with two-hand support. Then he can try to do it without hand support. He will need to use his legs and feet to land effectively and maintain his balance. He will enjoy practicing jumping because it is fun and he will be proud to be able to jump by himself.

jumping off

Your child will be ready to learn to jump off a 4-8 inch step when he knows how to jump on the floor without hand support and he is able to walk down a 4-8 inch curb without hand support. He needs to be comfortable with each skill and then he will be able to combine them to learn to jump off. To jump off, he will also need to combine jumping upward and forward.

You will first practice jumping forward with two-hand support. He will need to jump forward about 6-9 inches to jump off a step. To help him jump forward, you will kneel in front of him and he will hold your thumbs. You will pull him forward toward you as he jumps upward. Your hand support will teach him the direction to move and keep him balanced. Once he is familiar with moving forward, you can make up games. You can teach him to jump over something like tape or rope on the floor, or from the carpet to the hardwood floor. You can also have him jump into or out of a hula hoop. When he is ready, he can try jumping forward without hand support. You can stand beside him and jump over the rope and then have him imitate you.

Once he is comfortable with jumping forward, you can work toward jumping off a 4-8 inch step. You will start with a 1-2 inch step and gradually increase the height of the step to 4-8 inches. He will need hand support to adjust to the motion of jumping off the step and to regain his balance when he lands. You will continue to provide hand support until he jumps off easily. Whatever surface he uses to jump off will need to be stable. He will feel insecure if it rocks, wobbles, or slides.

When he is ready, he can try jumping off by himself. You can stand beside him and jump off and then encourage him to jump off. At first, he may step off with one foot at a time. He may even step off quickly and think that passes as jumping off! If he keeps stepping off with one foot at a time, stand beside him and hold one hand and jump off together. With one-hand support, he will be able to jump off with both feet together. Gradually decrease your support, working toward having him jump off with both feet together, without hand support.

other jumping activities

When your child achieves the goals in this skill area, he will have learned the basics of jumping. It is recommended that jumping activities be continued through a physical education program at school, community recreation programs, or at home with his siblings. Examples of advanced jumping activities are:

1. jumping in place for multiple (20-50) repetitions;
2. broad jump;
3. successive jumps across a room (10-30 feet) using big jumps; repeat using small jumps;
4. hopping on one foot;
5. jumping forward and then backward over a line; when he can do that sequence once, repeat up to ten times without pausing in between jumps;
6. jumping side to side over a line; when he can do that sequence once, repeat up to ten times without pausing in between jumps;
7. jumping in a square:

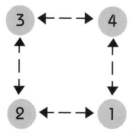

Have your child stand at number 1, facing number 4. Have him jump sideways to number 2 (always continuing to face forward), then forward to number 3, sideways to number 4 and then backwards to number 1. Do in one direction and then repeat in the opposite direction.

8. jumping jacks, with or without arm motions;
9. hopscotch;
10. jumping rope.

These activities will continue to improve your child's strength, balance, coordination, and endurance.

activity guidelines

Use the best motivators, which are music and other children. When your child is first learning to bounce, he will automatically bend his hips and knees to dance if he hears music. The livelier the music, the more energetic he will be. When he is able to bounce and is working on jumping, you can use songs that include the word "jump," such as "Five Little Monkeys Jumping on the Bed." You can also use action songs such as "Pop Goes the Weasel."

Your child will love bouncing and jumping with his siblings and friends. He will see it as fun, practice longer and more vigorously, and will try to imitate what they are doing. The best set-up is to take turns, first the sibling or friend, and then your child. You can say "your turn" to prompt each child when it is his turn to jump. You can have the sibling or friend do what you want your child to practice, such as bouncing on the trampoline while holding the chair. Or, you can have the other child do it in an exaggerated way to encourage your child to learn a new variation; for example, jumping with feet off the surface. By taking turns, your child will get a break but will stay engaged watching the other child. He will be ready for his next turn and will probably continue practicing for several repetitions.

If you are practicing when siblings or friends are not available, use a video that shows kids jumping. For example, Jennifer learned to jump while watching a Barney show where kids were jumping and singing a jumping song.

With all jumping activities, praise your child and clap after each series of bounces or jumps. If he is doing it with siblings and friends, both you and your child will clap for them, too. The praise and clapping will let everyone know they are doing a great job and will motivate them to do it more!

Provide verbal, visual, and tactile cues. You will need to provide all these cues for your child to fully understand each jumping activity.

Verbal Cues: Whether your child is bouncing or jumping, say "jump" to help him learn the word and what it means. At first, it will mean the up/down motion and later it will mean lifting his feet off the surface.

You will need to see what verbal cues work best for your child as he does each of the jumping activities. Your child may like you to count while he is bouncing or jumping. He also may like you to be a cheerleader. For example, Lily loved her mother to say or sing "jump, Lily, jump" as she was practicing jumping. You also can use other words to engage your child in the jumping activities. For example, Elizabeth would jump her best if her mother said "Jump like Charlie" (her brother) or "show me how Charlie jumps." When your child is practicing jumping forward or jumping off, you can say "Ready, go" or "1, 2, 3, jump."

Visual Cues: Your child will need to *see* each jumping activity in order to practice it. He will imitate what he sees and you will need to help him *see* and *pay attention* to what you want him to imitate. For example, it will be easy for him to see bouncing up and down with feet flat. It will be harder for him to focus on his brother's feet when he needs to pay attention to bouncing on tiptoes or jumping up and lifting his feet off the surface. To get his attention, his brother can exaggerate how he moves his feet to draw attention to them. For example, he can jump very high and you can say "Look at Charlie's feet" or "Big jump."

Since your child will imitate what he sees, whoever is jumping needs to do it the way you want him to do it. If you want your child to jump on the trampoline, holding the chair, his sibling needs to do it that way when he is jumping. Your child will also enjoy watching himself jump by watching himself in a mirror. He will see what he is doing and then may try new or more vigorous movements.

Tactile Cues: Your child will need to *feel* the movement you want him to imitate. Each jumping activity will have new movements to experience. He will need to feel bouncing with feet flat, bouncing on tiptoes, jumping up and lifting his feet off the surface, landing on his feet after he jumps up, jumping forward, and jumping off. After he feels the movement, he can then try to imitate it. Examples of how to provide the tactile cues are included in the Steps and Activities sections of this chapter.

Use a springy surface to practice bouncing and jumping. The springy surface is needed to:

1. Give your child the feeling of moving up and down a greater distance than if he did it on the floor;
2. Assist with propelling him upward.

A springy surface will help him feel the up/down motions more dramatically and he will practice repeating them. As he practices, he will increase the distance he moves up and down, increase the number of repetitions he can do within a set of bounces, and he will use the spring to lift himself up to jump. He will feel successful because he is generating the movements.

The springy surface needs to be firm and taut. Your child will be able to adjust more easily to the way a taut surface feels (or "gives") when he first stands on it. He will also need to move his legs more actively to make the surface move when he is bouncing. When he bounces on it, he will learn to move up and down rhythmically. Examples of surfaces to use are:

1. Small round trampoline (38-40 inches in diameter) or small rectangular trampoline with handle;
2. Bed or crib;
3. Sofa;
4. Sofa cushion or mattress placed on the floor;
5. "Swinging bridge" playground equipment.

Whether you want him to practice jumping activities on furniture or on a small trampoline will be your choice. One advantage to using the trampoline is that you can easily put it away to store it in between practices.

Make sure that your child's neck is maintained in the normal, upright position when he is practicing bouncing and jumping. Since children with Down syndrome are at risk for atlantoaxial instability, they need to be constantly supervised when using a trampoline or other springy surfaces. You need to prevent wild, sudden movements of the head, either forward or backward. This means you need to make sure he learns to use the springy surface safely. Since he will imitate what others do, you will need to make sure his siblings and friends use it safely also. You will need to set up the rules early so only standing, bouncing, and jumping are allowed, with no roughhousing. For more information on atlantoaxial instability, refer to pages 77-78 in *Babies with Down Syndrome: A New Parents' Guide* (second edition) and pages 193-199 in *Medical and Surgical Care for Children with Down Syndrome: A Guide for Parents.*

Large trampolines are not recommended and are considered dangerous. Children tend to move wildly with the increased space and spring provided by the

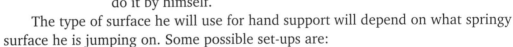

surface. A child will jump and land on his head, buttocks, and back and can easily bump into other children. Children may even fall off the trampoline and injure themselves. It is hard to manage children on a large trampoline and accidents happen easily. These possibilities are even more dangerous for a child with Down syndrome, so use the smaller size recommended above.

Provide two-hand support while your child is learning each jumping activity. With hand support, he will be able to use his hand and arm strength to *hold on, pull himself upward or forward,* and for *balance.* Once he is familiar with a jumping activity, he will feel comfortable moving his legs more vigorously and challenging himself if he has hand support. *(See figure 14.4.)* For example, if he can bounce on the trampoline, he will try to bounce harder if he has hand support. Later, when he does the activity well with hand support, he can begin practicing it without hand support.

(fig. 14.4)

At first, he can use your fingers or thumbs for support. When he is ready, it will be best for him to hold onto a bar, chair, or other stable surface. When he holds onto you, he will depend on you to assist him. When he holds onto a surface, he will need to do it by himself.

The type of surface he will use for hand support will depend on what springy surface he is jumping on. Some possible set-ups are:

1. Use a trampoline with a bar attached to it;
2. Place the back of a chair directly next to the trampoline;
3. Place a chin-up bar in a doorway;
4. Place the trampoline under the bar of a swing set;
5. Place the trampoline under the armrest of the sofa;
6. Hold the headboard while bouncing/jumping on the bed;
7. Hold the crib rails while bouncing/jumping in the crib;
8. Place the sofa cushion on the floor under the armrest of the sofa;
9. Hold the back of the sofa while bouncing/jumping on the seat;
10. Use a "swinging bridge" at the playground and hold onto the railing.

Whatever he uses for hand support will need to be stable and he will need to be able to hold it effectively with his small hand size. You will need to vary the height of the support depending on what he is practicing. When he is bouncing with his feet flat, the support can be at chest to shoulder height. When he is practicing bouncing on toes and jumping, the support can be at shoulder to face height.

If you choose set-up #2 above, there are chairs with certain features that work best.

(fig. 14.5)

1. The "sled base" chair *(see figure 14.5)* is ideal because the base slides under the trampoline so your child can bounce/jump in the center of the trampoline rather than near the edge.
2. If you do not have a "sled base" chair, use a chair with an angled, rather than straight, back. With a straight back chair, your child would be standing on the edge of the trampoline, on the springs. If the back of the chair is angled, he will be standing on the trampoline surface.
3. Find a chair with a horizontal surface for your child to hold onto. If he tries to hold vertical bars instead, his hands will easily slide down them.
4. Use a heavy chair or sit on the chair to stabilize it and prevent it from sliding. If your child feels insecure and unstable because the chair moves, he will not challenge himself.

Try a variety of chairs to see what works best. Some examples are kitchen chairs, dining room chairs, metal folding chairs, patio/deck chairs, and chairs with wooden bases and removable cushions.

Practice jumping barefoot. Your child will be able to move his legs and feet best for bouncing and jumping if he is barefoot. When he is learning to jump on springy surfaces and the floor, make sure he is barefoot. When he knows how to jump on the floor and jump off, use flexible, rubber soled shoes. The shoes will give him a soft landing surface and reduce the force of impact when he lands.

Practice jumping for short periods of time or within your child's tolerance. Jumping requires a lot of strength and endurance. You will notice how strenuous it is for you as you practice doing several repetitions with your child. Look for signs of fatigue in your child and give him a break. Taking turns with a sister works well because he can bounce ten times and then take a break and let her have a turn. Your child will be able to practice longer if he does a series of bounces or jumps and takes a break in between each series.

When he has first learned to jump so that he can lift his feet off a surface, you may notice that you are not able to get him to repeat it. This is probably because he is too tired. You can try again later and look for it in the beginning practices when he is strong and most active.

Your child will build strength and endurance through practice. As his strength improves, he will be able to do more repetitions of bouncing and jumping. When he is able to do more repetitions, his endurance will also improve and he will be able to jump for longer periods of time before he fatigues.

temperament

If your child is an ***observer,*** you will need to introduce bouncing and jumping slowly and gradually. He will first need to adjust to standing on the springy surface. He will initially feel unstable and off balance because the surface will move. He will also need to adjust to the new movements of bouncing up and down. In the beginning, he will need to be convinced that this is fun!

You will need to set up the experience of bouncing and jumping so he feels safe and in control as much as possible. With each change in the routine, he will need time to adjust and practice until he feels comfortable. He will prefer small bounces for a couple of repetitions. He will need to build up his tolerance to bouncing by increasing the *distance* of the up/down motion, the *speed* of the bounces, and the number of *repetitions*. If you watch his responses and let him adjust gradually, he will be willing to practice. If you scare him, he may be reluctant to try it for awhile.

Practice bouncing and jumping when he shows you he is willing. Never force or impose jumping. Keep it fun and find ways to motivate him to try it. Have his brother jump and see if he will be motivated to take a turn. Look for other ways to motivate him if this does not work. For example, Lily became motivated when she practiced jumping with her baby doll. I sat on the trampoline with my feet on the floor and bounced while holding her baby doll on my back, with the doll's hands on my shoulders. After the baby doll jumped this way, Lily was willing to try bouncing with this support. We would take turns with Lily in charge. She would say "baby jump" and then "Lily jump." She would also tell me when she was "done."

Your child will prefer to hold on to your hands for support when he bounces or jumps. You will need to figure out when he is ready to progress to holding onto a surface rather than your hands. Later, he will prefer to hold onto the surface rather than jump without hand support. He will feel off balance when he does not have the hand support and will need to learn how to balance himself while jumping.

He will learn to jump on the floor by himself when he is ready. You will need to be patient waiting for him to be motivated to do it. He will also need to feel comfortable using the physical skills required for jumping, particularly the speed for lift off and maintaining his own balance. When he does jump, he will be very proud.

Jumping off will feel scary to him initially because of the downward motion. He will need time and practice to become familiar with this activity. You will need to begin with a 1-2 inch step and slowly increase the height of the step as tolerated.

If your child is **motor driven,** he will enjoy the feeling of bouncing and jumping. He will not need to be convinced that bouncing and jumping are fun. He will be ready to practice when he is placed on the springy surface. He will easily adjust to the surface and he will like the up/down motions.

You will need to supervise him so he is safe. He may let go or try some wild movements. For example, he may be standing and lift his legs up to bounce on his buttocks in sitting. You will need to keep him focused on the jumping activity he is practicing.

He will be motivated to practice bouncing and jumping. He will increase the number of times he bounces if you set it up as part of the routine. You can motivate him by counting, clapping, or simultaneously jumping on the floor when he is jumping and then he may do it for 5-20 repetitions. He will repeat the up/down rhythm as long as he is motivated. After he does a series of bounces or jumps, let him take a break and then repeat it again. He will love to take turns with his sibling or friend.

He will initially hold your thumbs for support but will easily change to holding onto a surface, like a chair or bar. He will want to bounce and jump independently and he will be in control if he is holding the surface by himself. He will experiment with how to pull up to help himself jump.

When he knows how to bounce and feels comfortable with the set-up, he will experiment with moving his legs more vigorously and increasing the speed of the bounces. He will try to lift his body up. He will see you jump, feel how you assist him with jumping, and he will try to do it by himself. Once he does it, he will work to repeat it again and again, until he can do it all the time. After he does it on the springy surface, he will want to try to do it on the floor. Both of you will be surprised when he does his first jump on the floor. He may do it when he is practicing, or, like Michael, he may do it when he is having a tantrum.

When he is ready to learn to jump off, he will not be scared. He will need your hand support to learn it and then will do it on his own. You will need to clear the area and supervise him so he is safe and does not bump into furniture.

activity #1   **Bouncing on a Springy Surface with Feet Flat**
Refer to the Steps and Guidelines sections of this chapter for examples of setups using springy surfaces and surfaces to hold.

1. Help your child stand on a springy surface.
2. Provide two-hand support, having him hold your fingers or thumbs or a surface such as a chair or bar. The hand support needs to be at chest to shoulder level. *(See figure 14.6.)*
    3. Encourage him to bounce up and down by:
        a. turning on music so he dances by bouncing up and down;
        b. using examples given earlier in the chapter in the section on "Bouncing with Feet Flat."
    4. Provide verbal and visual cues and use whatever motivators work. Clap for him and praise him after each set of bounces.
    5. When he is familiar with bouncing with support, thinks it is fun, and wants to do it, encourage him to bounce by himself. Begin with two to three repetitions and go to ten. Use the examples given earlier in the chapter in the section on "Bouncing with Feet Flat." To motivate him you can:
        a. stand on the floor and bounce in an exaggerated way while he is bouncing;
        b. have him take turns with his sibling and have his sibling bounce in an exaggerated way;
        c. bounce to lively music;
        d. make up a jump song and sing it while your child is bouncing.
    6. When your child can bounce by himself, using an up/down rhythm for ten or more repetitions, encourage him to jump harder and move the surface. Teach him what it feels like by:
        a. holding his lower legs and pushing them down to exaggerate the downward motion into the surface;
        b. standing on the surface with him and gradually bouncing harder to move the surface.
    7. Continue to practice until he can move the surface and bounce up and down for at least ten repetitions.

(fig. 14.6)

activity #2 | **Bouncing on a Springy Surface on Tiptoes**

Refer to the Steps and Guidelines sections of this chapter for examples of set-ups using springy surfaces and surfaces to hold.

1. Have your child stand on the springy surface with two-hand support.
2. Have him hold on to a surface at the level of his shoulders or face.
3. Encourage bouncing on his tiptoes by:
   a. holding his ankles and bouncing him on his toes while he stabilizes himself by holding onto the back of a chair;
   b. holding his armpits to assist with lifting him up;
   c. having his sibling do it in an exaggerated way and help your child focus on watching his feet and trying to imitate it;
   d. having him try to do it by himself by increasing the height of the surface he is holding onto.
4. Provide verbal and visual cues and use whatever motivators work. Clap for him and praise him after each set of bounces.
5. When he can bounce on his toes, encourage him to do it for a minimum of ten repetitions.
6. When you are practicing this activity, also practice standing on tiptoes on the floor during playtime. Encourage your child to reach up to food on the kitchen counter, reach up for a ball or bubbles, etc. Begin with hand support and work toward doing it without support. He will need to learn to rise up on his tiptoes and hold the position for a few seconds.

activity #3 | **Jumping Up and Down**

Refer to the Steps and Guidelines sections of the chapter for examples of set-ups using springy surfaces and surfaces to hold.

1. Have your child stand on a springy surface with two-hand support. Vary the height of the hand support from the level of his shoulders to his face to see if one works better for lifting himself up.
2. Encourage him to bounce up and down and try to lift his feet off the surface. Use the examples given earlier in the chapter in the section on "Jumping on a Springy Surface."
3. Provide verbal and visual cues and use whatever motivators work best. Clap for him and praise him especially when he lifts his feet up off the surface.
4. When he occasionally lifts his feet during a series of bounces, continue to practice, encouraging him to do it more.
5. Continue to practice until he can jump consistently.
6. When he can jump with two-hand support on a springy surface, begin practicing jumping on the floor with hand support.
   a. Have him hold your thumbs while you assist with lifting him.
   b. When he can jump holding your thumbs, have him hold onto a surface and do it.
7. When he jumps on the floor well with hand support, have him try to do it without hand support.
8. Continue to practice until he can jump on the floor without hand support consistently.

activity #4   Jumping Off

1. First, you will need to teach your child to jump forward. Follow these steps:

   a. Kneel or stand approximately 18-24 inches in front of your child, facing him.

   b. Have him hold your thumbs. Support his hands at shoulder level. (If needed, you can support them higher when you first try this activity; however, lower the support to shoulder level when he is ready.)

   c. Tell him to "jump to Mama/Daddy." When he begins to jump, move your thumbs forward toward you quickly so he feels you pull him forward as he is jumping.

   d. Practice several times so he becomes very familiar with the forward motion as he is jumping.

   e. When he is familiar with jumping forward, see if he can do it just holding your hands for balance.

   f. When he can jump forward using your hands for balance, see if he can do it without holding your hands. Set up a game such as having him jump over a line (masking tape).

2. When he can jump forward 6-9 inches and he is familiar with stepping down whatever height step you are using, begin practicing jumping off. Follow these steps:

   a. Place your child standing on a step 1-2 inches high.

   b. Kneel or stand 18-24 inches in front of your child, facing him.

   c. Have him hold your thumbs and support his hands at shoulder level.

   d. Tell him to "jump to Mama/Daddy." When he begins to jump, move your thumbs forward toward you quickly so he feels the forward motion. He will also feel the motion of moving downward to the floor.

   e. Practice several times until he is familiar.

   f. When he is familiar, see if he can jump off only using your hands for balance.

   g. When he can easily jump off holding your hands for balance, begin standing beside him and jump off together, holding only one of his hands.

   h. When he does that easily, see if he will do it without hand support. Make sure he learns to jump off with both feet together. You can try:

      1. Standing beside him and taking turns jumping off;

      2. Kneeling in front of him so you are at eye level to him and telling him to jump to you.

➤ Motor Milestone Checklist *on next page.* ➤

Motor Milestone Checklist

He bounces up and down on a springy surface with two-hand support, with hips and knees bending and feet flat:
- ❏ One to five repetitions
- ❏ Ten repetitions or more
- ❏ Moving the surface for ten repetitions

He bounces on his tiptoes on a springy surface with two-hand support:
- ❏ One to five repetitions
- ❏ Ten repetitions or more

- ❏ He jumps occasionally while bouncing on a springy surface with two-hand support
- ❏ He jumps consistently on a springy surface with two-hand support
- ❏ He jumps occasionally on the floor with two-hand support
- ❏ He jumps consistently on the floor with two-hand support
- ❏ He jumps on the floor without hand support
- ❏ He jumps forward 6-9 inches over a line without hand support
- ❏ He jumps off a 2-inch step without hand support
- ❏ He jumps off a 4-inch step without hand support
- ❏ He jumps off an 8-inch step without hand support

CHAPTER 15

Riding a Tricycle

Riding a tricycle is a complicated skill, and your child will be interested in it before she is actually able to do it. She will show an interest in it when she sees her siblings or friends riding their tricycles. She will be curious about what a tricycle is and will want to try it out. But she won't be ready to learn to ride until she can grapple with trying to make the tricycle move.

You can let her try riding a tricycle when she is interested, usually around the ages of 2½ to 3 years. She will need you to steer, push her forward, and support her feet on the pedals. She will not be able to do it by herself, and, at some point, this will probably bother her. To ride independently, you can teach her to scoot and steer a riding toy. She can start this even earlier, usually around the age of 2 years. You can alternate between letting her use the tricycle with your support and the riding toy by herself. Practicing with the riding toy and the tricycle will prepare her to ride the tricycle by herself. Children with Down syndrome usually learn to ride the tricycle by themselves for 15 feet between the ages of 4-6 years, with the average being 5 years.

To ride a tricycle, she will need to learn:
1. **to hold the handlebars and steer;**
2. **to keep her feet on the pedals;**
3. **to pedal by moving her hips, knees and feet in a smooth, continuous rhythm.**

You will teach her steering and pedaling separately. When she can do each skill, you can teach her to do them simultaneously in a coordinated way. The goal of this skill area will be to ride a tricycle using steering and pedaling for 15 feet. Once she can ride that far, she will know the basics for riding a tricycle, and, with practice, will increase the distance she rides and her speed.

Riding a tricycle will benefit your child in many ways, socially and physically. She will enjoy playing outside with other children. She will be proud and feel "big" to be riding her tricycle with the neighborhood kids. Her physical skills will also improve, as she learns to move her body in the following new ways:
1. To pedal, she will need to hold her knees up over the pedals rather than allow them to flop outward. Her knees and feet will need to be pointing straight ahead rather than turning outward.

Steps in: Learning to Ride a Tricycle

To achieve the goal of this skill area, your child will need to practice the following steps:
1. Climb on and off the riding toy or tricycle;
2. Scoot forward on a riding toy and steer;
3. Ride a tricycle with support to pedal and steer;
4. Steer and pedal a tricycle down an inclined surface;
5. Steer and pedal a tricycle on a level surface for 15 feet.

You want your child to have the experience of being independent on a riding toy first. When her legs are long enough to reach the pedals of a tricycle, you can begin practicing riding a tricycle with support. Your child will show you when she is interested in learning to steer and pedal.

2. She will bend and straighten her hips and knees, with each leg doing a separate movement. Each leg will need to be strong to keep the rhythm going.
3. She will move her ankles up and down and push with her feet.
4. She will develop strength and coordination using both sides of her body rather than relying on her preferred side.
5. She will learn to use her arms, legs, and trunk together in a coordinated way to simultaneously pedal and steer.

climbing on and off

You will need to teach your child how to climb on and off the riding toy or tricycle. If you teach her how to do it from the beginning, she will do it by herself rather than rely on you to put her on or take her off. She will learn quickly and be motivated to do it because she will want to be independent and in control.

When she is climbing on or off, you will need to hold the riding toy or tricycle to prevent it from sliding or moving. To climb on, her initial position will be critical to her success. She should stand next to the seat, with her body facing the handlebars. She will hold onto the handlebars with both hands and then lift the leg closest to the seat over the seat. *(See figure 15.1.)* She will probably bend her hip and knee to lift her leg in front of her body. You can help her lift her leg over if she needs your support. Once her legs are positioned on each side of the seat, she can sit down. To climb off, she will stand up, hold onto the handlebars, and lift the leg she chooses over the seat.

With practice, your child will climb on and off by herself and will only need you to keep the riding toy or tricycle stable. Later, depending on how easily the tricycle moves on the surface it is on, she will learn to climb on and off without you holding it.

(fig. 15.1)

scooting forward on a riding toy and steering

You should shop around and test the different riding toys available. You need to check out the following features:

1. *Seat width:* it is better if it is narrow so your child learns to scoot her legs with her thighs closer together rather than wide apart.
2. *Height of the seat:* your child's feet should be flat on the floor with her hips and knees bent approximately 45 degrees.
3. *Handlebars:* buy a toy with handlebars so your child will have the opportunity to learn to steer when she is ready.
4. *Rear wheels:* look at how close they are to the seat and how wide they are positioned. Test the riding toy to see if your child's feet will hit the rear wheels when she is pushing off with her feet. If her feet bump into the wheels when she is pushing off, she will be frustrated and will not use the riding toy.

The riding toy has to fit your child properly so she can be successful using it. Try a variety of styles to see which one works best for your child. Some of the models you

(fig. 15.2)

may wish to try are: Little Tikes: Mini Cycle, Soft Pony, and Toddler Tractor; Playskool: First Ride Trike; and V-Tech: Little Smart Tutor Scooter. The latest style combines a riding toy with a tricycle; for example, the Fisher Price Push 'n Pedal Trike.

Your child will probably first learn to push herself backwards. She will be happy she is moving and will continue to straighten her knees and push off with her feet to move backwards. *(See figure 15.2.)*

You can help her move herself forward by moving her legs for her. Hold her lower legs and bend her knees, pushing her feet against the ground to move forward. Then see if she will try to do it herself. You may need to provide a motivator to encourage her to try to move forward. She will scoot forward by moving both legs together or moving one foot at a time. Begin with short distances and increase the distance when she is ready, until she rides it spontaneously by herself.

In addition to learning how to move her legs, she will also need to learn how to position her trunk and buttocks to use her legs effectively. If she is sitting on the riding toy with her trunk and buttocks leaning back, it will be much harder to do the leg motions required to move herself forward. If she sits with her trunk and buttocks leaning forward, it will be easier to do the leg motions. You can help her lean her trunk and buttocks forward by putting your hand against her lower back and pressing it forward.

After she learns to use her legs to scoot forward, you can practice steering. You can begin by letting her bump into obstacles and then assisting her. Say "turn" and put your hands over hers and turn the handlebars. Let her scoot along and wait until she bumps into another obstacle. Help her again and repeat this until she begins to turn the handlebars by herself when she bumps into obstacles. The next step will be to say "turn" before she bumps into the obstacle. She will learn how to steer and how to plan ahead to turn before she gets stuck.

(fig. 15.3)   *(fig. 15.4)*

When she can steer and scoot forward on a riding toy, you can try using the car, van, truck, and coupe models. It will take her time to learn how to use them because they will be heavier to push. She will also tend to lean her trunk and buttocks back in the seat and will not be able to use her legs to scoot forward. She will need to lean forward toward the steering wheel to effectively use her legs to move forward. She also may not be in a hurry to ride in the car and may prefer to play by turning the steering wheel, beeping the horn, opening and closing the door, and talking on the car phone.

riding a tricycle with support to pedal and steer

When your child shows an interest in a tricycle and her legs are long enough for her feet to easily reach the pedals, you can begin practicing riding a tricycle with support. The initial set-up and fit of the tricycle is critical. You need to use the tricycle that fits her the best. Look for these features:

1. *Handlebars:* these should be positioned close to her trunk or angled toward her trunk as she sits on the seat of the tricycle. Since her arm length is probably shorter than average, you want to use a tricycle that has a short distance from the back of the seat to the handlebars. If the handlebars are too far to reach, it will be harder for her steer.

2. *Pedals:* the pedals need to be positioned close enough to the seat so your child can easily rest her feet on them as they move within a complete revolution. To check that her feet reach the pedals, place one pedal in the farthest position from the seat. Make sure your child's leg is long enough to fit this length with her foot flat on the pedal.

3. *Seat:* make sure the seat has a back support at least 4-5 inches high. A bucket seat works best since it will also support her trunk. You could also use a contoured seat that rises up behind her buttocks (4-5 inches). Without this support, her buttocks will slide back on the seat as she tries to push with her legs and feet, and she will not be able to effectively move forward. With this support, she will move forward every time she pushes with her legs and feet.

(fig. 15.5)

4. *Base:* the base of the tricycle needs to be wide so it is stable and does not tip over easily. Measure the width between the outside edges of the rear wheels. The wider it is, the more stable it is.

See the photos of the tricycles to the left *(figs. 15.3, 15.4, and 15.5).* They work well for 3-year-olds and have the special features described above [Rand trike, Push 'n Pedal trike, and One Step Ahead trike].

In addition to needing these special features, your child also needs her feet stabilized on the pedals. It will be too difficult for her to try to keep her feet on the pedals in the beginning. She may be able to place her feet on the pedals but they will slip off easily when the pedals are moving. For example, Chantell was able to put her feet on the pedals and even maintain them while turning the handlebars. She was unable, however, to push the pedals to move herself forward, and, when I pushed her, she could not keep her feet on the pedals. She was able to *rest* her feet on the pedals but was not able to *push* the pedals with her feet. Later, when she is able to push the pedals with her feet, she will be able to keep her feet on the pedals.

With her feet secured to the pedals and her buttocks stabilized on the seat, your child will feel the leg and foot movements needed to ride the tricycle as you push her. You can secure your child's feet to the pedals with masking tape or you can make or purchase footpedal attachments. *(See figure 15.6.)* You can order footpedal attachments through Equipment Shop, P.O. Box 33, Bedford, MA 01730; 617-275-7681. Masking tape is simple and fast to put on and rip off. The footpedal attachments are sturdy and conveniently attached. You can see which will work best for you and your child.

(fig. 15.6)

Be very careful when your child's feet are secured on the pedals. If she tips over, she will not be able to put her foot out to catch herself. You need to stand by her and closely supervise her to keep her from tipping over or to catch her if she begins to tip over.

Once your child is set up with the right tricycle and her feet are supported on the pedals, your job will be to make riding a tricycle fun. You will push her and take her for many rides. While she is learning to ride the tricycle with support, she will go through periods of liking it and periods of not being interested at all. Follow her lead and practice when she wants to. If she wants to stop, try again another time. It may help to motivate her if her brother rides his bicycle or tricycle at the same time. Practice with the goal of having fun and gradually increase the time she will ride the tricycle with support.

She will need a lot of practice to learn to use the leg and foot motions needed to pedal the tricycle. You will first give her the experience by pushing her on the tricycle and steering it for her. To push her, stand behind her and hold the seat, inconspicuously. She will not want you to hold the handlebars and will push your hand away. Only touch the handlebar briefly to steer when needed. She will need time to become familiar with the leg motions since she has never used them before in other skills. While you are pushing her, she can also get used to the other aspects of riding a tricycle. For example, Yehuda explored the handlebars, looked down at his feet, watched the sidewalk go by, and looked sideways at the grass and flowers while he was being pushed. Once he was familiar with these aspects, he paid less attention to them and was able to focus more on his feet and pedaling.

When your child is familiar with the leg motions, tolerates them and likes riding the tricycle, try letting her ride down a 1-2 degree inclined driveway or sidewalk. Help her initiate moving forward and encourage her to pedal to continue moving down the inclined surface. You will need to assist her if she stops. She will stop moving if she stops pedaling. Gravity will make it easier for her to pedal and she will be motivated to do it because she will feel successful. She will want to be independent so she may like doing it this way rather than have you push her all the time. You will need to steer for her since she will be focusing on pedaling.

While you are pushing her on the tricycle, she can practice steering if she shows an interest. She may already know how to steer from using a riding toy. Or, you can teach her as discussed in the section "Scooting Forward on a Riding Toy and Steering." If she is not interested, you can steer for her and have her focus on pedaling.

steering and pedaling a tricycle down an inclined surface

When your child is familiar with moving down an inclined surface, you can lessen your support. Encourage her to do the pedaling first, and when she can do that, teach her to steer.

To pedal, your child will need to:
1. **Bend and straighten her hips and knees, pushing one leg forward at a time;**
2. **Move her feet to push the pedals around in a circular motion.**

Figuring out how to move her legs and feet to move the tricycle forward is something she will need to grapple with. She will need to continue having her feet secured to the pedals so she can focus on pushing with her feet rather than wrestling with trying to keep her feet on the pedals.

It will be hard to communicate to your child what she needs to do to learn to pedal by herself. If you say "push your legs" and you push down on her knee, she may imitate you and use her hand to push her knee. If you say "move your feet," she may move them but not enough. If you say "go," she may rock her trunk forward and back, trying to move the tricycle forward. These cues will not teach her the full motions necessary to pedal. You will need to experiment with what to say and do to help your child understand how to pedal. For example, when Yehuda was riding down the incline, his mother said "go, feet, go." He would watch his feet and would try to keep moving them to ride. When he stopped, he would try to move his feet to go again. By saying "go, feet, go," he focused on the *action*, which was to *go*, and on his *feet*, which are what he needed to move. He understood what he needed to do and would keep moving his feet as his mother repeated the words.

When your child is at the top of the inclined surface she will need to move her legs and feet to start moving forward. Once she is in motion, it will be easier to stay in motion. If she stops, she will need to initiate moving forward again. Your job will be to encourage her to keep moving down the incline until she reaches the bottom or where the surface becomes level. When she reaches the end of the incline, you will push her back to the top so she can practice riding down again. This will give her a break in between practices and you can make it fun by going fast.

steering and pedaling a tricycle on level surfaces

When your child tries to pedal on level surfaces or keeps pedaling after the inclined surface becomes level, you can begin practicing pedaling on level surfaces. She will be ready to grapple with how to move herself forward. You will let her do what she can, helping her if she gets stuck. She will want to move forward and will be motivated to keep trying if she can keep herself moving. If she moves slowly and laboriously on level surfaces, alternate between using inclined and level surfaces or use the lower end of the inclined surface to give her momentum to ride where it becomes level. *(See figure 15.7.)* As you practice, try to keep a balance between challenging her to do it by herself and having her succeed in moving forward.

When she is stuck, one knee will probably be almost straight while the other knee will be bent. She will stay stuck because she will continue to push harder with the leg that is almost straight, rather than with her other leg. You will notice that

(fig. 15.7)

this "stuck" position repeats itself often. The leg she is pushing harder with is typically her stronger leg. She will continue to get stuck in this position until she strengthens her other leg so each leg pushes evenly to maintain the continuous, circular motion. You can help her by teaching her to push better with the leg whose knee is bent. She will need to learn to move her legs together in a coordinated way to pedal effectively.

Begin practicing with a distance of 3-5 feet, and then increase the distance when she is ready. When she can pedal on level surfaces for 15 feet, she will know how to pedal and can work on increasing the distance to 100 feet or more. When she feels comfortable pedaling, she will spontaneously improve her speed and endurance.

When she is focusing on pedaling, you will need to steer for her. She may even know how to steer but will need you to do it for her so she can keep her attention on pedaling. For example, when Jawanda was learning to pedal on level surfaces, she wanted to look at her legs and feet. If she concentrated on them, she could pedal and move forward. If she looked up to steer, her leg motion stopped and it was hard for her to get started again. Since she was so focused on pedaling, she could not pay attention to steering and would bump into obstacles. Later, when she can pedal well, she will not need to look at her feet and she will be able to look ahead and steer. She will be ready to practice steering and pedaling simultaneously.

When your child is practicing steering and pedaling and is doing well, you can experiment with not securing her feet to the pedals. Now that she has learned to push with her legs and feet to pedal, she will be able to keep her feet on the pedals without support. It will be easier to keep her feet on the pedals when she is riding in the forward direction and be harder when she is turning. With practice, she will easily learn to keep her feet on the pedals whether she is moving straight or turning.

activity guidelines

Choose the typical tricycle style rather than the "Big Wheels" style. *(See figure 15.8.)* With the typical tricycle, your child will be sitting up straight and pushing downward with her legs. With this positioning, gravity will assist the motions and she will primarily use her leg and foot muscles to pedal. With the "Big Wheels" style, she will lean back in sitting and push her legs more horizontally to pedal. This position will also require her to use her stomach muscles to hold her legs upward as she is pedaling outward. Since the stomach muscles tend to be weak in children with Down syndrome, the "Big Wheels" style will be harder to learn.

(fig. 15.8)

Use a tricycle that is small for her rather than large. With a small tricycle, it will be easier for her to push with her legs and keep her feet on the pedals. She will also feel more stable and in control. If you buy a tricycle that is large so she can grow into it, it may be difficult for her feet to rest on the pedals comfortably, particularly when the pedal is in the furthest position from the seat. If she needs to use her toes to touch the pedals, it will be very difficult to keep her feet on the pedals and make it harder to pedal.

When she is learning to ride a tricycle, limit the accessories. If the tricycle has streamers, a horn, or fancy decorations around the handlebars, your child will want to play with them rather than focus on learning to ride the tricycle. She will be distracted by the accessories and want to explore them. It may be hard to divert her attention to pedaling and steering. It is best if the tricycle is plain at first, and, later, you can add the accessories.

Teach her pedaling and steering separately. Focus on one skill at a time. If you try to do both, you will overwhelm her. You will be giving her too many instructions to handle. You will be saying "go, feet, go," "turn," "push," etc., and riding a tricycle will not be fun. Generally, she will focus on pedaling first while you steer. When she shows an interest in steering or if she has learned pedaling, you can practice steering.

Use motivators and practice when she wants to. The best motivators are siblings or neighborhood friends riding their tricycles. Your child will especially want to ride when other kids are doing it. For example, Allison was very motivated to learn to ride a trike when she started attending a daycare where the children routinely rode trikes and riding toys in the gym. She observed the "big kids" flying by on their trikes and kept plugging away until she too could pedal a trike forward. Your child will also practice when it is just the two of you if it feels fun to her. Whenever you practice, do it *when* she is interested and for *as long as* she wants to, even if it is brief. If you impose riding on her, she will resist and may not want to do it again for awhile.

Provide verbal, visual, and tactile cues. She will learn to do each activity through feeling it, seeing others doing it, or watching herself do it, and if you give her simple and direct verbal cues. For example, she will learn to pedal by feeling the motions when someone pushes her, by watching others or watching her feet, and by trying to pedal by herself when you say "go, feet, go." When you are teaching her each activity, experiment and find the verbal, visual, and tactile cues that work best for your child. These cues will help her understand each activity so that she can try to do it by herself. Examples of using these cues are included in the Steps section of this chapter.

Use a smooth surface and large open space. Your child will be able to pedal more easily and further on a smooth surface like vinyl flooring, tile, or concrete. If the surface is rough or uneven, it will be harder to pedal. For example, if the sidewalk is cracked or the surface has small pebbles, she will get stuck often.

In a large, open space, she will not bump into furniture or other obstacles. If there are obstacles in the environment, they will distract her and she will need to learn to maneuver around them. When she is free to ride everywhere, less steering is needed and she can choose to ride or stop without having to stop because of environmental obstacles. For example, when she rides on the sidewalk, she will have a limited width to move within and you will need to steer often to keep her from riding off the sidewalk into the grass. If she rides on the driveway or in a gym, she will need less assistance and be able to ride on her own.

Practice riding a tricycle with shoes. Since she will initially have her feet secured to the pedals, it will be easier to secure the shoes to the pedals and it will be more comfortable if she wears shoes. Later, when she rides without her feet secured to the pedals, the rubber soles of her shoes will help her keep her feet on the pedals.

When she changes from a tricycle to a bicycle with training wheels, she will need time to adjust to the new set-up. Even though she will be able to ride a tricycle, she will not immediately be able to ride a bicycle with training wheels. She will feel the following differences:

1. The pedals will be directly under her seat (rather than in front of the seat);
2. The seat will be smaller and less supportive and it will be positioned higher;
3. The bicycle will have brakes.

She will need to modify her pedaling and learn to use brakes. With practice, she will feel stable on the bicycle and be able to pedal and steer. When she is comfortable riding the bicycle, you can teach her to use the brakes.

temperament

Your child will show you when she is interested in practicing and learning to ride a tricycle. Learning to ride a tricycle will depend on her *motivation* more than her temperament. When she is motivated, she will be persistent in learning how to do it, whether she is an observer or motor driven. She may become motivated because she is around other children who ride a lot or she may just like doing it. She will want to do it by herself and will let you know by pushing your hand away when you push, steer, or intervene. She will want to be independent, riding her tricycle with the other kids.

If your child is an *observer,* she will generally be patient and tolerant when sitting on the riding toy, riding the tricycle with support, and riding down an inclined surface. Once she learns to scoot with her legs, she will want to use scooting whether she is on the riding toy or tricycle. At that point, you will need to alternate letting her scoot by herself and supporting her feet so she can learn pedaling. When she learns to ride the tricycle, she will ride at an average, safe speed so she can feel in control.

If your child is *motor driven,* she will tend to be impatient and impulsive when she is learning to scoot on the riding toy and to pedal the tricycle. She will want to move fast, so if she cannot make the riding toy move, she will climb off.

When she can scoot with her legs, you will need to alternate letting her scoot and supporting her feet so she can learn pedaling. When she is riding the tricycle with support, she may not like having her feet secured to the pedals. You will want to practice this for short periods, as tolerated, and when she is finished, quickly free her feet. She will suddenly decide she wants to get off the tricycle and you will need to respond quickly. She may tolerate this activity longer if you move quickly and make it fun when you push her. She will like riding down the inclined surface, if she can keep moving. When she learns to ride the tricycle, she will ride at a fast speed, so you will need to make sure she can steer safely and effectively.

activity #1   **Scooting and Steering a Riding Toy**
1. Hold the riding toy and encourage her to climb on. Have her stand beside the seat, facing the handlebars, with both hands on the handlebars. Assist her if needed in lifting her foot over the seat.
2. Encourage her to move forward for 3-5 feet to a motivator. Say "go" or take turns with a sibling or friend. If she is unable to move forward, help her using these methods:
   a. Hold her lower legs and move them together using the scooting motion (bend her knees and push off with her feet against the ground).
   b. Place your hand across her lower back and push it forward to lean her trunk and buttocks forward.
   c. Use a mildly inclined surface (1-2 degrees).
3. When she moves forward with or without your help, praise her and clap for her.
4. When she can move forward for 5 feet, increase the distance until she is able to scoot by herself.
5. When she can scoot with her legs, begin to teach her steering. (Prior to this, you steer for her.) Let her bump into obstacles. Then put your hands over hers, say "turn," and turn the handlebars. Repeat this until she starts turning by herself.
6. Continue to practice until she can scoot and steer the riding toy all by herself.
7. If she wants to get off the riding toy, hold it still and encourage her to climb off. Assist her if needed in lifting her leg over the seat.

activity #2   **Riding a Tricycle**
Select the appropriate tricycle as discussed on pages 210-11.
1. Hold the tricycle and have your child climb on. Assist if needed.
2. Secure her feet to the pedals using masking tape or footpedal attachments.
3. Have her hold the handlebars.
4. Hold the back of the seat of the tricycle and push her (unless the tricycle comes with a push handle). Hold the handlebar briefly to steer as needed. Take her for a ride as long as tolerated.
5. When she is familiar with it and likes it, set her up on a small incline (1-2 degrees) and let her ride down it. Say "go, feet, go." Assist her as needed with moving forward and steering. When she reaches the

bottom of the incline, push her back to the top and let her ride down again. Repeat as tolerated.

6. Continue to practice riding down the incline until she can consistently use her legs and feet to pedal the distance. When she is able to pedal or shows an interest in steering, teach her how to steer. Let her bump into obstacles and then put your hands over hers, say "turn," and turn the handlebars. Repeat this until she starts turning by herself.

7. When she can pedal down inclines consistently, encourage her to pedal on level surfaces. Use motivators and encourage her to move forward 2-3 feet, assisting her as needed to pedal and steer. Clap for her and praise her when she moves forward. Increase the distance when she is ready.

8. When she can pedal on level surfaces, encourage her to practice pedaling and steering simultaneously. When she can do this, stop using tape or footpedal attachments and have her hold her feet on the pedals herself.

9. Continue to practice riding a tricycle using pedaling and steering until she can do it automatically, maintaining a continuous rate of speed for at least 500 feet.

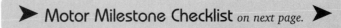

➤ Motor Milestone Checklist *on next page.* ➤

Motor Milestone Checklist

She climbs on a riding toy/tricycle:
- ❏ while you hold it
- ❏ without support

She climbs off a riding toy/tricycle:
- ❏ while you hold it
- ❏ without support

- ❏ She scoots backwards on a riding toy for 10 feet
- ❏ She scoots forward on a riding toy for 15 feet
- ❏ She steers while scooting forward on a riding toy for 15 feet
- ❏ She scoots forward in a car, van, truck, or coupe model
- ❏ She enjoys being pushed on the tricycle with full support for 100 feet
- ❏ She rides the tricycle down a small incline (1-2 degrees) with intermittent support to assist with pedaling and steering
- ❏ She rides the tricycle down a small incline, pedaling by herself and needing assistance to steer
- ❏ She rides the tricycle down a small incline, pedaling and steering by herself
- ❏ She rides the tricycle for 5-10 feet on level surfaces, needing assistance to steer
- ❏ She rides the tricycle for 15 feet on level surfaces, pedaling and steering by herself

CHAPTER 16

What's Next?

Congratulations. You have come a long way. You and your child have mastered the basic gross motor skills. Your child has greatly increased his strength and has challenged muscle areas that were previously weak and made them much stronger. He has improved his balance, which has improved his walking pattern and his foot positioning. You have seen great improvements in his endurance and in his overall coordination. He is now able to hold his own on the playground and can join in the games of the neighborhood kids.

These are not small accomplishments, and you should be proud of what you and your child have achieved through persistence, practice, and hard work.

THE VALUE OF PHYSICAL ACTIVITY

The benefits of regular physical exercise for everyone are well documented. It is also well documented that we tend to neglect exercise because of the multiple other demands of our lives. Because your child has now mastered the basic skills of gross motor development, your attention will necessarily and appropriately be drawn to other areas, such as speech and language development and school performance. Still, physical exercise can be an area of strength and success for your child. It is an area where he has already learned to succeed. Because children with Down syndrome often prefer lower levels of physical activity, a regular program of exercise can be even more important for them than it is for you or me.

Most children with Down syndrome are no longer receiving formal physical therapy at this age. They may have yearly evaluations for recommendations for physical education programs or to monitor their posture. But ensuring that your child gets the right amounts and types of exercises will largely be up to you, the parent.

The physical benefits of regular exercise are the most obvious. A program of regular physical exercise will keep your child physically fit and help him control his weight. It will continue to improve his strength, balance, coordination, and endurance. His exercise program should be aerobic—that is, it should challenge his respiratory and cardiovascular fitness. It should have him breathing hard and working up a sweat.

There are also mental benefits to regular exercise. People who engage in regular strenuous physical activity tend to be mentally more alert. They are better able to handle mental challenges and tire less easily.

You may also find that there are important social benefits to physical exercise programs. This is an arena where it is easy and natural to make friends. You may also find that group sports offer great ways to learn how to interact with groups and how to be a team player. They also enlarge his world so that he learns to be active and independent in the community, going to the YMCA or participating in dance classes.

Finally, there are important emotional benefits. Your child will be proud of what he can do. His confidence will continue to increase and he will develop more and more trust in his abilities and what he is able to do. And when he is confident, he will be willing to challenge himself more. I have also found that physical activity is very effective in changing a child's mood. Often a child who is sedentary, obstinate, frustrated, or tired will become energized and exhilarated by vigorous physical activity.

THE GOAL NOW

The goal now is for physical exercise to become an integral and enjoyable part of your child's day to day life. You could continue to practice specific gross motor skills like skipping or walking across a 2-inch balance beam, but these are likely to seem boring. He is much more likely to be successful and to stick with it if he chooses an area that interests *him*.

You want to let him choose activities that he really likes. The goal will be for him to learn to do it and to have fun. The activity that he chooses may change from year to year. Some examples of possible activities are: running, swimming, dancing, walking, roller skating, ice skating, horseback riding, hiking, karate, skiing, bicycling, and some organized sports activities. (When looking at organized sports, make certain that the rules do not make the game too complex for your child to follow and that it is safe for him to participate. Sometimes, specially modified forms of the sport may be more appropriate.)

setting your child up for success

Pick an activity based on your child's interests. What does he like to do? What kinds of activities does the family like to engage in? It needs to be something that your child can do easily and regularly. The opportunities need to be easily accessible at home or nearby in the community.

A program can be structured in a wide variety of settings. For instance, your child can learn to play soccer in the back yard with you or a sibling as the coach. He can participate in a physical education program at school. He can go to community recreational programs. For example, programs are available through the local Department of Parks and Recreation, the YMCA, private health clubs, and church groups. You can also find exercise and physical fitness programs in the Yellow Pages.

You will want to observe the programs and choose instructors who are committed to having your child succeed.

Whatever sports or exercise program your child decides to do, you can teach him using the same steps that you have used to teach each of the skills in the book. Break the learning process into the following steps:

1. Think of the component parts of the motions needed. You can do this by asking the instructor to break the motions down into parts or by doing the activity yourself in slow motion.
2. Teach your child each part separately and practice it until he knows it. To teach him, use verbal, visual, and tactile cues. When you practice, do it the same way until it becomes established.
3. When he has mastered each of the parts separately, combine them. Support him through the sequencing of the parts until he can put them together on his own.
4. Use motivators to make it fun. Some examples are: doing it to music, doing it with him, or challenging him with races. Always praise him for each accomplishment.
5. Once he has mastered the basic skill, work on speed, distance, endurance, and performing in other more challenging settings.

If your child is unable to do a particular activity, a good technique for identifying what's missing or why it doesn't work is for you to imitate what he is doing. You

can then help him make the needed changes. You may also find that physical limitations are preventing him from succeeding, for instance shortness of arms or legs. If so, you may need to modify the equipment or find some other strategy that allows him to succeed.

Finally, help your child learn to enjoy his physical self. Throughout his life it will be one of his strengths. Most of all, have fun and don't be afraid to try new things. Henry David Thoreau said of mankind:

"Man's capacities have never been measured, nor are we to judge of what he can do by any precedents, so little has been tried."

It is even more true of children with Down syndrome.

Gross Motor Milestone Statistics

Over the past 10 years I have kept track of when 154 children with Down syndrome have achieved 45 specific motor milestones. This appendix presents that data. The goal is to give you a better idea of what constitutes "normal" development for a child with Down syndrome. The appendix is divided into two parts. The first provides a definition for each skill, and the second presents the actual data.

DEFINITIONS

This section will spell out the qualitative criteria for each of the motor milestones. There are specific tests that each child must meet in order for a motor milestone to be counted as actually having been mastered. Some of these criteria are the same for all of the milestones, and some of them are specific to a particular milestone. For instructions on how to help your child achieve a particular milestone, you should refer to the appropriate chapter. In order for your child to receive credit for having achieved a milestone, he must meet the following criteria:

- ◆ Your child must do it by himself, without assistance;
- ◆ Your child can be encouraged and motivated, but not assisted;
- ◆ Your child must perform the skill in a controlled manner, not by accident;
- ◆ Your child must be able to repeat the skill.

motor skills

1. **Rolls from back to stomach**—This skill needs to be performed on a firm surface, like a carpeted floor, not a bed.

2. **Rolls from stomach to back**—This skill needs to be performed on a firm surface in a controlled manner.

3. **Hand to foot play**—Placed on his back, he kicks his legs up and holds his feet for 5 seconds.

4. **Sits**—On a firm surface, he sits and maintains balance for 5 minutes without propping.

5. **Pivots in stomach-lying 360 degrees**—He follows a toy until he has moved in a full circle.

6. **Assumes quadruped**—From stomach-lying, he pushes up onto hands and knees.

7. **Moves from sitting to stomach-lying by moving to the side**—From sitting, he leans to the side, props on hands, and moves down to the floor without bumping his face.

8. **Moves from sitting to quadruped by moving to the side**—From sitting, he props his hands to one side and then lifts buttocks up to move to quadruped.

9. **Moves from stomach-lying to sitting by moving to the side**—From stomach-lying, he moves to side-lying on his elbow and then pushes up on his hands to sitting.

10. **Moves from quadruped to sitting**—From quadruped, he leans his hips to the side and down to the floor and then pushes up to sitting with his hands.

11. **Pulls to kneel from sitting using a surface with an edge**—From sitting, he uses a surface with an edge to pull to kneel with both feet pointing behind his body.

12. **Pulls to kneel from quadruped using a surface with an edge**—From quadruped, he places one hand on the edge and then the other and he moves his knees forward reciprocally until his knees are under his hips.

13. **Belly crawls**—He moves forward on his belly using any method for a distance of 5 feet.

14. **Creeps in quadruped**—He moves forward for 10 feet without moving out of quadruped.

15. **Bear walking**—He moves forward for 10 feet without moving out of the plantigrade position.

16. **Pulls to stand from sitting on the floor**—From sitting, he places his hands on a surface with an edge, pulls to kneel, and then pulls to stand.

17. **Pulls to stand from quadruped**—From quadruped, he places his hands on a surface with an edge, pulls to kneel, and then pulls to stand.

18. **Pulls to stand through half kneel**—From sitting or quadruped, he pulls to kneel, moves to half kneel, and then pulls to stand.

19. **Moves from standing to sitting on the floor with knees bent**—He bends his hips and knees to lower himself to sitting on the floor.

20. **Cruises in one direction**—He steps sideways with balance for 8 consecutive steps.

21. **Steps 10 feet with two-hand support**—He steps forward 10 feet holding your thumbs at his shoulder level or lower.

22. **Stands without support for 10 seconds**

23. **Takes 2 independent steps**—Standing alone or with support behind him, he takes 2 lunging steps to a person or the sofa.

24. **Walks 10 feet with a push toy**—He pushes a toy with control on a carpeted surface for 10 feet. The push toy should not be weighted for stability.

25. **Walks 10 feet with one-hand support**—He walks forward for 10 feet holding your thumb with one hand at his shoulder level or lower.

26. **Walks 15 feet without support**—He walks forward 15 feet taking consecutive steps.

27. **Climbs up a flight of stairs**—He climbs up a flight of at least six stairs with supervision but without assistance.

28. **Climbs down a flight of stairs**—He climbs safely down a flight of at least six stairs with supervision but without assistance.

29. **Climbs onto the sofa with the seat cushion removed**

30. **Climbs off the sofa with the seat cushion in place**—From sitting on the sofa with his back against the backrest, he rolls to his stomach and slides off until his feet touch the floor.

31. **Moves from plantigrade to standing**

32. **Walks (fast walk) 100 feet in less than 25 seconds**

33. **Runs 100 feet in less than 15 seconds**

34. **Walks up a 4-inch curb without hand support**—He steps up a 4-inch curb without support and maintains balance.

35. **Walks down a 4-inch curb without hand support**—He steps down a 4-inch curb without support and maintains balance.

36. **Walks up an 8-inch curb without hand support**—He steps up an 8-inch curb without support and maintains balance.

37. **Walks down an 8-inch curb without hand support**—He steps down an 8-inch curb without support and maintains balance.

38. **Walks up stairs marking time holding the rail**—Facing forward, holding the rail with one hand and the other hand at his side, he steps up with one foot and then brings the other foot to the same stair.

39. **Walks down stairs marking time holding the rail**—Same as #38, except going down the stairs.

40. **Walks up stairs holding the rail alternating feet**—Facing forward, holding the rail with one hand and the other hand at his side, he steps up with one foot and then brings the other foot past the first foot to the next stair.

41. **Walks down stairs holding the rail alternating feet**—Same as #40.

42. **Walks across an 8-foot long, 7-inch wide balance beam without hand support**—He walks across the length without stepping off.

43. **Walks across an 8-foot long, 4-inch wide balance beam without hand support**—Same as #42.

44. **Jumps**—Without hand support, he jumps lifting both feet off the floor.

45. **Rides a tricycle 15 feet**—He pedals and steers tricycle for 15 feet. You may use a seat that supports his back and you may secure his feet to the pedals.

GROSS MOTOR MILESTONE DATA

This data was gathered by observing the gross motor development of a total of 154 children with Down syndrome. This is a small sample to begin with. Additionally, not every child has completed each of the 45 milestones to date. I also only included data when I could personally confirm when the skill had been achieved. This makes the sample for each individual skill only a fraction of the total. For instance, of the 154 children in the sample, there is reliable data for when they rolled from their backs to their stomachs for only 63.

Because the sample size is small, care must be taken about drawing conclusions from it. It is my experience, however, that the data does provide a reasonably accurate picture of when a child with Down syndrome can be expected to master these gross motor skills. Muscle tone is by far the most important factor affecting the age at which skills are achieved. The lower a child's tone, the longer acquisition will be delayed.

The left hand column of the chart specifies the skill. The second column, "n," is the number of children for whom there is data for that particular skill. The third column is the average age in months when the skill was achieved. The fourth column is the standard deviation in months. The standard deviation helps you to understand the normal distribution of when children achieve a particular skill. 68% of the children in a sample will achieve a particular skill within plus or minus one standard deviation from the average, and 95% will achieve it within plus or minus two standard deviations. Let's use Milestone 22 as an example.

MOTOR MILESTONE	*n*	Avg	STD
22. Stands without support for 10 seconds	46	21	5

We have data on 46 children in the sample. The average age when children achieved this milestone was 21 months, and the standard deviation was 5 months. According to the rule: 68% of the children achieved the milestone +/- one standard deviation, which means that 68% of the children stood without support for 10 seconds between 16 and 26 months of age (21—the average age—minus 5 is 16; 21 plus 5 is 26). 95% achieved the skill between 11 and 31 months (21 minus 10—2 standard deviations—is 11; 21 plus 10 is 31).

MOTOR MILESTONE	*n*	Avg	STD
1. Rolls from back to stomach	63	7	2
2. Rolls from stomach to back	58	6	2
3. Hand to foot play	59	7	2
4. Sits	87	11	4
5. Pivots in stomach-lying 360 degrees	72	10	3
6. Assumes quadruped	73	14	6
7. Moves from sitting to stomach-lying by moving to the side	70	13	5
8. Moves from sitting to quadruped by moving to the side	47	16	7
9. Moves from stomach-lying to sitting by moving to the side	22	17	7
10. Moves from quadruped to sitting	73	16	7
11. Pulls to kneel from sitting using a surface with an edge	47	15	4
12. Pulls to kneel from quadruped using a surface with an edge	60	16	5
13. Belly crawls	71	14	5
14. Creeps in quadruped	67	17	7
15. Bear walking	14	19	4
16. Pulls to stand from sitting on the floor	39	15	3
17. Pulls to stand from quadruped	64	17	6

MOTOR MILESTONE	*n*	Avg	STD
18. Pulls to stand through half kneel	68	17	6
19. Moves from standing to sitting on the floor with knees bent	52	17	7
20. Cruises in one direction	67	18	6
21. Steps 10 feet with two-hand support	66	19	6
22. Stands without support for 10 seconds	46	21	5
23. Takes 2 independent steps	60	23	8
24. Walks 10 feet with a push toy	53	22	8
25. Walks 10 feet with one-hand support	57	23	8
26. Walks 15 feet without hand support	74	26	9
27. Climbs up a flight of stairs	56	20	8
28. Climbs down a flight of stairs	37	25	10
29. Climbs onto the sofa with the seat cushion removed	59	20	7
30. Climbs off the sofa with the seat cushion in place	49	22	7
31. Moves from plantigrade to standing	70	24	9
32. Walks (fast walk) 100 feet in less than 25 seconds	38	37	12
33. Runs 100 feet in less than 15 seconds	20	52	11
34. Walks up a 4-inch curb without hand support	46	36	12
35. Walks down a 4-inch curb without hand support	46	35	12
36. Walks up an 8-inch curb without hand support	33	49	13
37. Walks down an 8-inch curb without hand support	38	47	12
38. Walks up stairs marking time holding the rail	57	39	9
39. Walks down stairs marking time holding the rail	50	40	10
40. Walks up stairs holding the rail alternating feet	18	56	10
41. Walks down stairs holding the rail alternating feet	5	81	21
42. Walks across an 8-foot-long, 7-inch-wide balance beam without hand support	40	38	9
43. Walks across an 8-foot-long, 4-inch-wide balance beam without hand support	8	64	25
44. Jumps	31	47	12
45. Rides a tricycle 15 feet	16	61	11

Index

Resources

organizations

The Arc of the United States
500 E. Border St., Ste. 300
Arlington, TX 76010
(817) 261-6003; (817) 277-0553 (TDD)
E-mail: thearc@metronet.com
http//TheArc.org/welcome.html

    The Arc (formerly the Association for Retarded Citizens) works to improve the lives of all children and adults with mental retardation and their families. The ARC provides information and referral about mental retardation, the Arc's programs, and local chapters. It advocates for inclusion of individuals with mental retardation in community life; fosters research and education regarding prevention of mental retardation. The ARC has an extensive catalog of publications.

Association for Children with Down Syndrome, Inc.
2616 Martin Ave.
Bellmore, NY 11710
(516) 221-4700; (516) 221-4311 (fax)
E-mail: info@acds.org
http://www.acds.org

    The ACDS publishes and distributes a variety of videos, books, and manuals, including a Music and Dance curriculum for infants and young children with Down syndrome and a guide to Down Syndrome Developmental Milestones. Locally, the ACDS provides educational, therapeutic, behavioral, and health-related services to persons with Down syndrome and their families.

Canadian Association for Community Living
Kinsmen Building, York University
4700 Keele St.
North York, Ontario M3J 1P3
Canada
(416) 661-9611; (416) 661-5701 (fax)
http://indie/ca/cacl/index.htm/

    The CACL focuses on developing a welcoming, supportive community for all Canadians by working to ensure that people with mental handicaps become active members of their communities. The CACL publishes a newsletter and other publications; advocates for people with mental handicaps and their families; and has a network of local chapters across Canada.

Canadian Down Syndrome Society
811 Fourteenth Street, N.W.
Calgary, Alberta T2N 2A4
Canada
(403) 270-8500; 403-270-8291 (fax)
(800) 883-5608 (in Canada)

The CDSS strives to enhance the quality of life for people with Down syndrome, to increase public awareness of Down syndrome, to provide information and resources about Down syndrome, and to build a communication network among all people with interests relevant to Down syndrome. There are local chapters across Canada. The national society has an information clearinghouse and publishes a newsletter and a "Resource Catalog" containing publications on Down syndrome from a variety of sources.

National Association for Down Syndrome
P.O. Box 4542
Oak Brook, IL 60522-4542
(708) 325-9112
http://www.nads.org/

This membership organization promotes the growth and development of individuals with Down syndrome and encourages research into Down syndrome. It focuses its parent support work mostly in the Chicago area. It also publishes and distributes a newsletter, brochures, and videos.

National Down Syndrome Congress
1605 Chantilly Dr., Suite 250
Atlanta, GA 30324
800-232-NDSC
E-mail: ndsc@charities.usa.com
http://members.carol.net/ndsc/

The NDSC is a membership organization that works to enhance all aspects of life for persons with Down syndrome. It acts as a clearinghouse for information on Down syndrome, sponsors an annual convention, and advocates for individuals with Down syndrome and their families. Publications include pamphlets and a newsletter for members.

National Down Syndrome Society
666 Broadway, Ste. 800
New York, NY 10012-2317
(212) 460-9330; 212-979-2872 fax
800-221-4602 (Information and Referral)
http://www.ndss.org/

The NDSS strives to ensure that all people with Down syndrome are given the opportunity to reach their full potential, through education, research, and advocacy. The society supports research, sponsors symposiums and conferences, and provides free information and referral services. It develops and distributes educational materials for parents and professionals and publishes a newsletter.

National Information Center for Children and Youth with Disabilities (NICHCY)
P.O. Box 1492
Washington, DC 20013-1492
(800) 695-0285; (202) 884-8441 (fax)
E-mail: nichcy@aed.org
http://www.aed.org/nichcy

NICHCY is a federally funded clearinghouse that provides information on disabilities and disability-related issues, with an emphasis on children and young people birth to age 22. The center provides personal responses to questions on disability issues; makes referrals to other organizations and agencies; performs database searches; and offers many low-cost publications, especially on educational issues.

Special Olympics
1325 G St., NW, Ste. 500
Washington, DC 20005
(202) 628-3630; (202) 824-0200 (fax)

Special Olympics is an international program of physical fitness, sports training, and athletic competition for children and adults with mental disabilities.

internet sites

Disability Solutions (online newsletter)
http://www.teleport.com/~dsolns

Down Syndrome: WWW Page
http://www.nas.com/downsyn

Down Syndrome Association of New South Wales (Australia)
http://www.span.com.au/downsynd_nsw/index.html

Down Syndrome Association of the United Kingdom
http://www.helpnet.org.uk/hlpn08a.html

Down Syndrome Canadian Resources
http://www.io.org/~dsamt/Canadian.html

Down Syndrome Listserv/Newsgroup
To subscribe, send E-mail to: listserv@listserv.nodak.edu and type subscribe down-syn <your name> in the body of the message

Down Syndrome Quarterly (online journal)
http://www.denison.edu/dsq/

Down Syndrome Society of Southern Australia
http://www.span.com.au/span/downsyn.htm

European Down Syndrome Association
http://www.nas.com/downsyn/europe.html

Family Empowerment Network
http://www.downsyndrome.com/

What's Up with Downs?
http://www2.pcix.com/~kehler/What'sUp.html

Sarah Duffen Centre's DownsNet Home Page (United Kingdom)
http://www.downsnet.org/

❖ notes ❖

❖ notes ❖

❖ notes ❖

❖ notes ❖

❖ notes ❖

about the author

Patricia C. Winders is a physical therapist who specializes in the gross motor development of children with Down syndrome. Currently, she works with children and adults with Down syndrome at the Kennedy Krieger Institute in Baltimore, Maryland. Her work also includes speaking about motor skills at national and local conferences and serving on the Professional Advisory Committee of the National Down Syndrome Congress.
To contact her with questions or comments, write to her at:

Patricia Winders
P.O. Box 433
North East, MD 21901
e-mail: wind3829@dpnet.net